IMAGES
of America

AROUND SKANEATELES LAKE

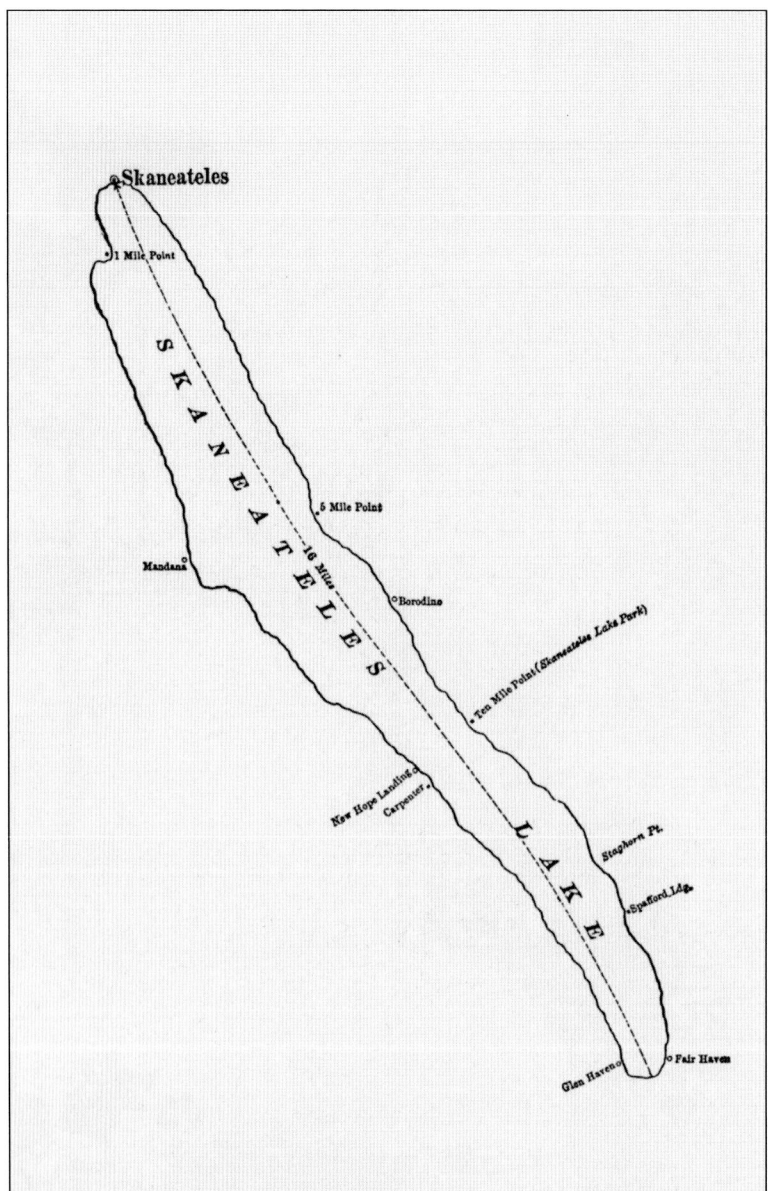

The map was revised from a late-19th-century railroad map showing railroad stops around the lake. The map has been simplified to highlight key towns and points mentioned throughout the book. (Courtesy of the Skaneateles Historical Society.)

ON THE COVER: This late-19th-century photograph depicts an individual in a small sailboat in front of the Willowbank boathouse located in the village along the shores of Skaneateles Lake. Cornelius Tyler Longstreet gifted Willowbank as a country house to his daughter Cornelia upon her marriage to Charles Henry Poor II in 1871. The boathouse is still in existence today. (Courtesy of the Skaneateles Historical Society).

IMAGES
of America

AROUND SKANEATELES LAKE

Julie Clark DiBagio and C.E. Malmgren

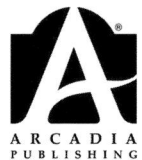

Copyright © 2025 by Julie Clark DiBagio and C.E. Malmgren
ISBN 978-1-4671-6138-1

Published by Arcadia Publishing
Charleston, South Carolina

Printed in the United States of America

Library of Congress Control Number: 2025935419

For all general information, please contact Arcadia Publishing:
Telephone 843-853-2070
Fax 843-853-0044
E-mail sales@arcadiapublishing.com

Visit us on the Internet at www.arcadiapublishing.com

Contents

Acknowledgments		6
Introduction		7
1.	Harnessing Skaneateles Lake	9
2.	Skaneateles Boats	17
3.	The North Shore	35
4.	The West Shore	59
5.	The East Shore	81
6.	The South Shore	113
Bibliography		126
About the Skaneateles Historical Society		127

Acknowledgments

A journey of a thousand miles begins with one step. This journey began four years ago with a quest to find a footprint of a boathouse. A new property owner on the lake was interested in knowing if there was any indication of a larger boathouse that existed before the present one on the property. In our naïveté, we thought that finding this information would be a fairly easy task. To the contrary, after combing maps, deeds, and wills, much to our chagrin, we came up empty-handed. We had learned that little was known about historic boathouses. Our curiosity was hooked. The project quickly moved beyond boathouses. It became necessary to include boats, the people who used them, and of course, the iconic lake on which they sailed.

Along the way, many people generously shared their knowledge and provided assistance, making the journey an interesting one: Geralyn Huba, director of the Skaneateles Historical Museum (2019-2024) made all museum resources available, and her enthusiasm for the project never wavered; Kihm Winship, the author who not only finds the historical facts but also the story behind them; Laurie Winship, who works in research and is never too busy to help find information or to explain the working of the computer as many times as necessary; Bob Eggelston, a local architect who works with new homes and the restoration of older buildings; Tyde Richards, Kihm Winship, Bruce Kenan, Norman Shepard and others who have generously shared their personal postcards and images with the Skaneateles Historical Society; Dave Miller, the boat historian whose information about the lake and its boat history is unmatched; Scott Hauver, current president of the Spafford Historical Society; Sally Holben, who has worked on other local literary projects fully supported this one; Andy Ramsgard, who explained the riparian nature of boathouses; Bill Stinson, of the Stinson family, which ran the mailboat on the lake for many years; Barb Patrick, a native of Skaneateles who loves the area history; Janet Aaron, Skaneateles, a town supervisor (2018-2023), who was never too busy to answer a question; the Honorable Charles T. Major, town justice, who has lived and written about Skaneateles history most of his life; Ron Beavers, who had the patience to read and research property deeds and wills in the Onondaga County clerk's office; Stephen and Ellen Wikstrom, avid sailors; Peggy Robinson Manring, Rob Howard, and Claire Robinson Howard of the Robinson musical family; Charles W. Jeremy Jr., president of the Glen Haven Historical Society; Alexandra Perry, executive director of the Barrow Art Gallery; and Frank Moses, executive director of the Skaneateles Lake Association.

Unless otherwise noted, all images appear courtesy of the Skaneateles Historical Society.

Introduction

Skaneateles Lake, flowing 16 miles south to north, is one of eleven lakes in the Finger Lakes Region of Central New York. The lake has long been considered a premier destination because of its pristine water that stretches across three counties from the village of Skaneateles in the north to Glen Haven in the south. The lake is sometimes referred to as the "Roof Garden of the Lakes" because it sits higher than the other Finger Lakes at an elevation of 863 feet. It has an average width of .75 miles with a maximum width of 1.5 miles and a maximum depth of 315 feet.

Skaneateles Lake is fed by spring tributaries and a narrow watershed that limits polluted runoff. The lake is oligotrophic, meaning it is low in nutrients, which helps keep algae and pollutants low. It's the purest of all the Finger Lakes and is used to provide unfiltered water to local municipalities and to the City of Syracuse, located 20 miles away. The Finger Lakes, which resemble long fingers, were carved out as glaciers receded about 10,000 years ago. The Haudenosaunee, a confederation of six Native American nations (formerly known as the Iroquois Confederacy) occupied much of the region prior to European settlement. They believed these lakes were the handprint of the Great Spirit. It is believed that the name Skaneateles comes from the Haudenosaunee word for "long waters."

The Onondagas, one of the six nations of the Haudenosaunee Confederation, navigated Skaneateles Lake by canoe, using the lake and heavily forested area around the lake for fishing and hunting prior to European settlement. Early European settlers who came to the region built rafts to transport animals, goods, and people to their settlements on the lake. After the American Revolution, the population around Skaneateles began to grow, and the lake was harnessed to power local industries. Later, the area became a draw for recreation and tourism. The beauty and purity of the lake attracted the wealthy, who built lavish summer homes and boathouses for family enjoyment. As early as the 1830s, Skaneateles Lake and small communities along its shores became popular destinations for boating, recreation, and even restorative health because of its pristine water.

During the second half of the 19th century, there was a proliferation of elegant mansions and summer homes along the lake, built by wealthy businesspeople and tourists who came to the area to enjoy the benefits of lakeside living. Many of these lakefront homes included boathouses to store their locally-built boats and to serve as guest houses and summer retreats. The history of boathouses along Skaneateles Lake is somewhat difficult to trace through the late 19th and early 20th centuries. Permits were not required, and boathouses were not listed as property in deeds or wills. Maps were often inaccurate because boathouses were riparian in nature (situated along the banks of the lake) and were, therefore, under a different set of regulations than land not located along the lake. The best source of boathouse information from that time period is often found in old photo albums and local newspaper accounts.

Around Skaneateles Lake features vintage images highlighting some of the lakeshore's unique cultural and geographic features as well as showcasing an assortment of lakefront properties, boathouses, and boats of the late 19th and early 20th centuries. In the pages that follow, chapter one begins with a focus on how the lake itself was harnessed as a source of water and waterpower. Chapter two highlights some of the late-19th- and early-20th-century boats found on Skaneateles Lake and references two local boat manufacturers of the same era. Chapters three through six take the reader on a journey around the lake by region: the North Shore, the West Shore, the East Shore, and the South Shore.

Chapter three, The North Shore, encompasses the village of Skaneateles, and as a result, the majority of boathouses will be found in this section. In addition, there will be mention of other features along the village shoreline, such as the lake outlet, local parks, businesses, and some of the wealthy businessmen of the time period. Chapter four, The West Shore, will focus on the boathouses and other important features and communities along the west shore of the lake (running from the village of Skaneateles in the north down to Glen Haven at the south end of the lake). In particular, the northern section of the west shore (just west of the village of Skaneateles) will be highlighted. This area, known as the Gold Coast, referred to the elegant homes built by the wealthy in the late 19th century. Other communities and features located south of the Gold Coast along the west shore will also be included in this chapter. Chapter five, The East Shore, will focus on the boathouses and other important features and communities along the east shore of the lake (running from the village of Skaneateles in the north down to Fair Haven at the south end of the lake). Finally, chapter six will focus on important features at the south end of the lake; in particular, the Glen Haven area, which became well known for its 19th-century health resort, will be emphasized. The *Glen Haven Hotel and Water Cure* brought the lake's summer residents and travelers from near and far by steamboats from the north end of the lake.

One

HARNESSING SKANEATELES LAKE

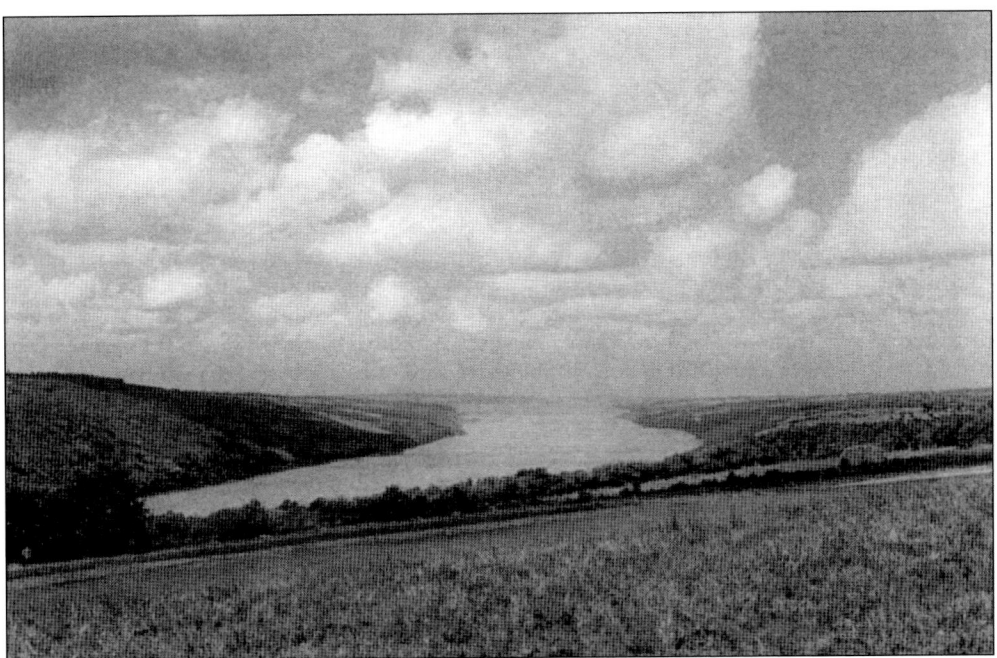

In the 19th century, the beauty of Skaneateles Lake was not the only draw to the area. The cleanliness of the lake and its potential for water power were under the governance of New York State and the City of Syracuse. Col. Edwin Sherman Jenney, testifying in 1889 on a water bill hearing in Albany, New York, had this to say: "I live on this lake. I say that God may be able to make something more beautiful than Skaneateles Lake but I don't believe He ever did so. The people of Skaneateles village use the water and I wish the Syracuse people could have all they want of it."

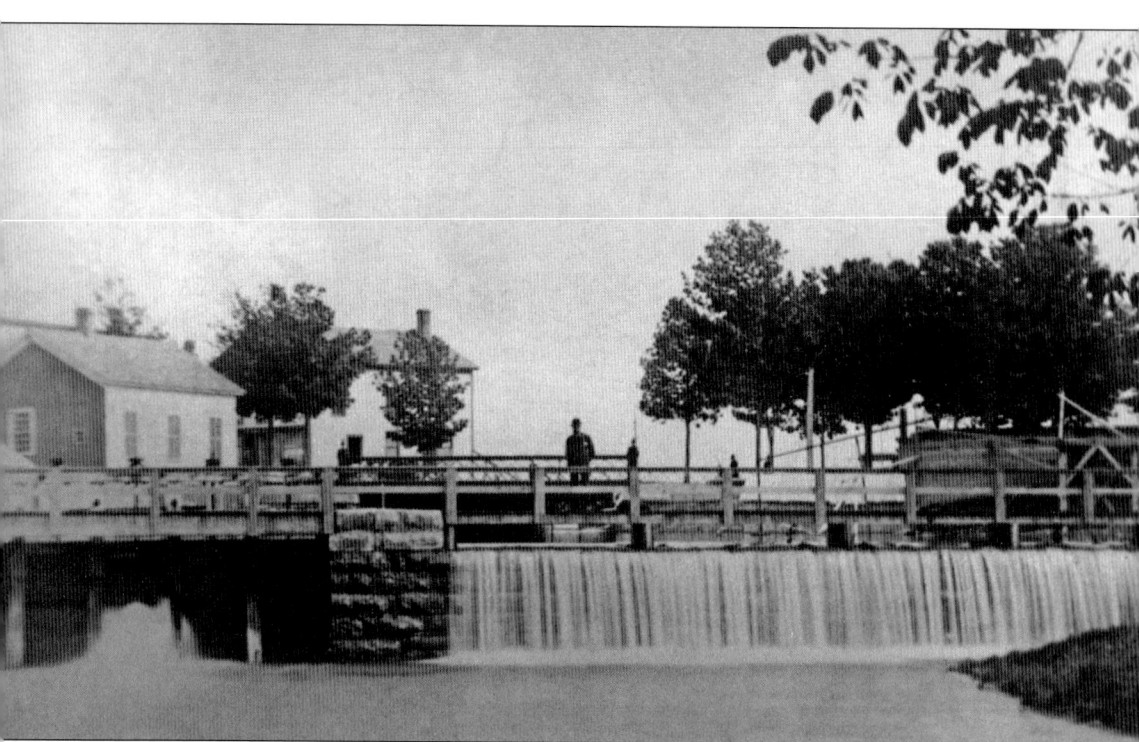

The first dam to redirect and harness lake water was made of logs in 1797. It was located on the west side of Jordan Street in the village of Skaneateles. The purpose of the dam was to create a millpond that would provide water power for a nearby grist mill. The dam resulted in raising the lake level three to four feet. This, in turn, flooded the swamp at the foot of the lake, washing away the shoreline and leaving driftwood and tree snags. In 1800, a bridge was built across the dam to accommodate the construction of the road being built at the time.

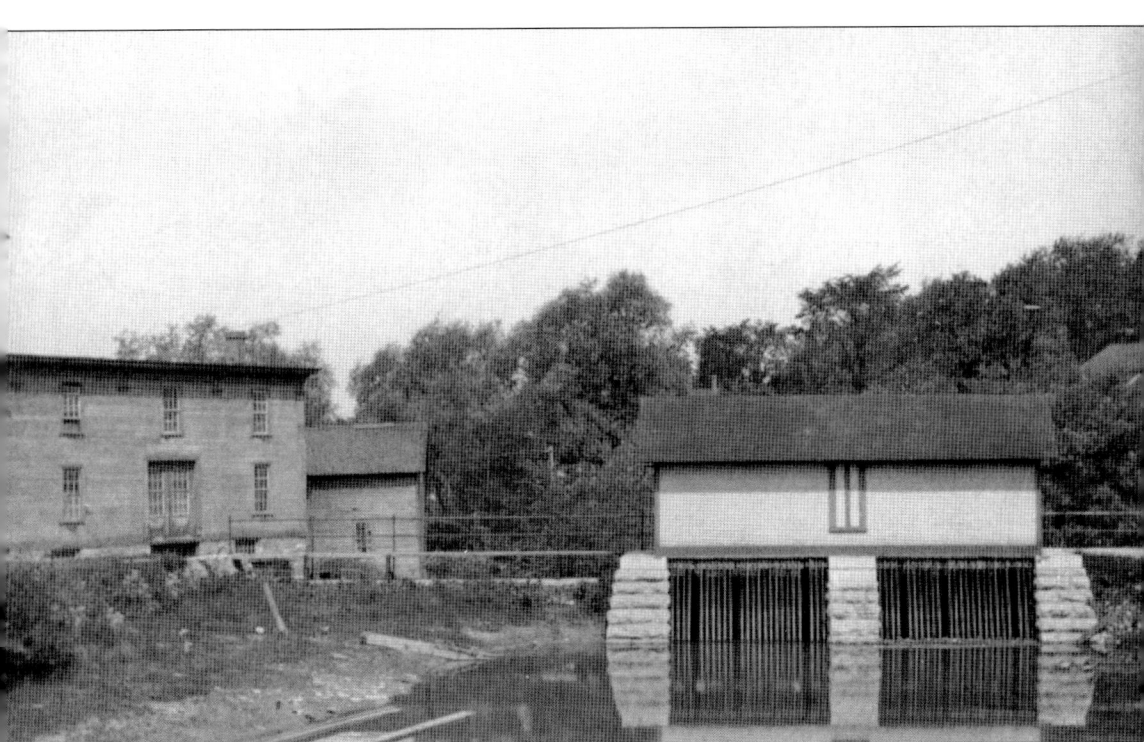

As early as 1841, New York State sought to harness the lake in order to divert water to the Erie Canal. The canal, which opened in 1825, was located about 20 miles north of Skaneateles. A dam was built to control the lake water flow. That same year, a canal commissioner and two engineers came to the village to force the gates of the dam to release water. Outraged by efforts to redirect water to the Erie Canal, a prominent citizen of Skaneateles, Deacon Hall, greeted the commissioner at the village line with a cannon. According to Leslie's History of Skaneateles and Vicinity, Deacon Hall was heard to say, "They will find thunder and blood in Skaneateles if they try." In 1843, the state appropriated water from the lake to be used for the Erie Canal despite Hall's objections.

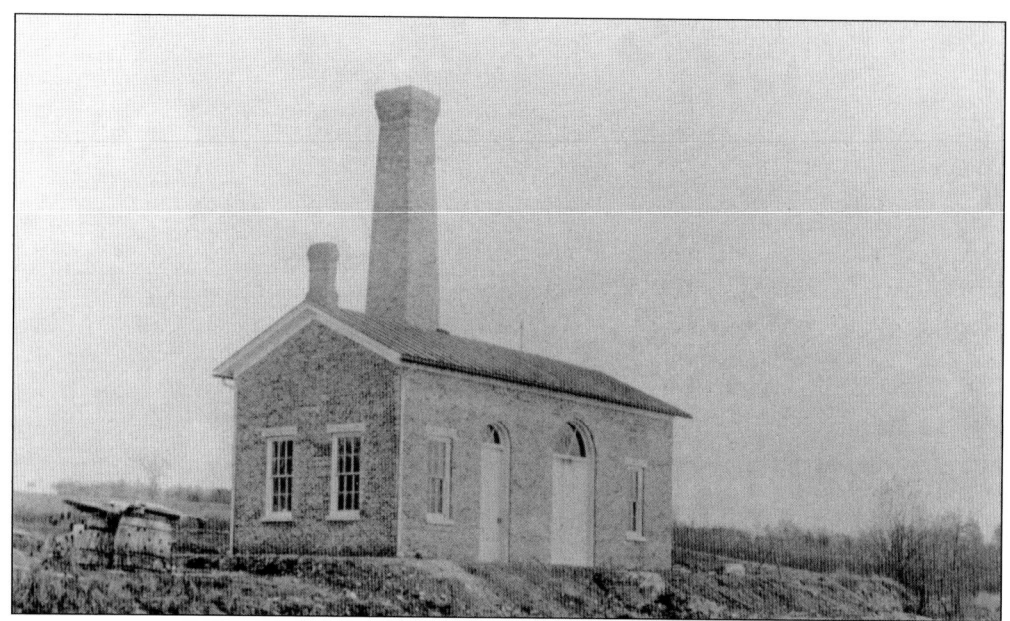

In 1887, George Barrow and other prominent citizens formed the Skaneateles Water Works Company to provide water for fire hydrants and village homes. The company's location was in a pumphouse at what was then East Lake Road. Following legal difficulties, a municipal water system was established, offering lower prices. Residents could choose between the private and the municipal companies.

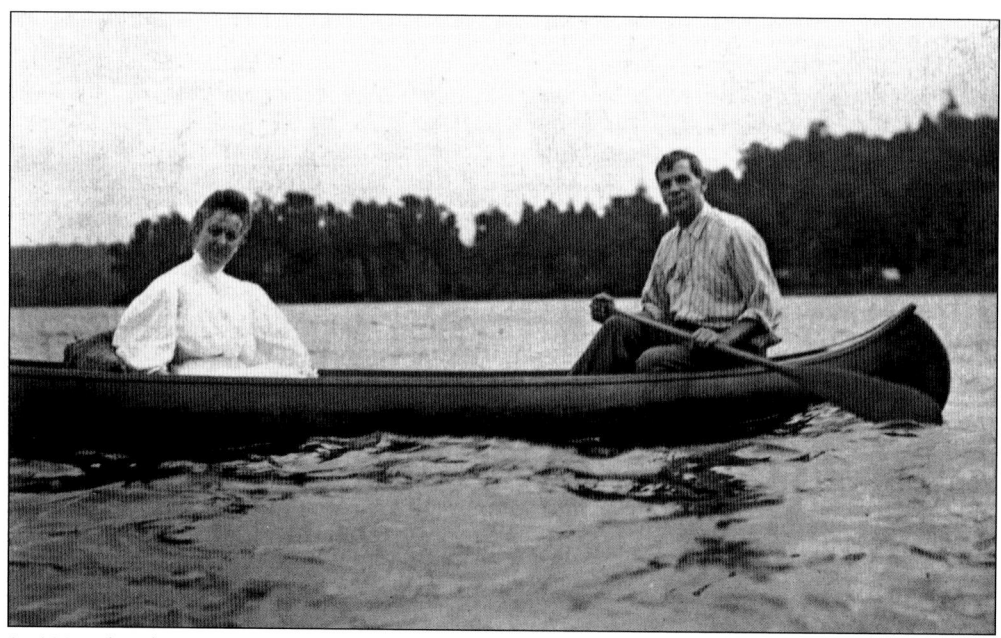

In 1927, the Skaneateles Water Works was operating at a loss. The land and pumphouse were sold to furniture maker Gustav Stickley, who used it as a summer home. In this photograph, Gustav and his wife, Eda Ann Simmons, are enjoying a canoe ride on the lake.

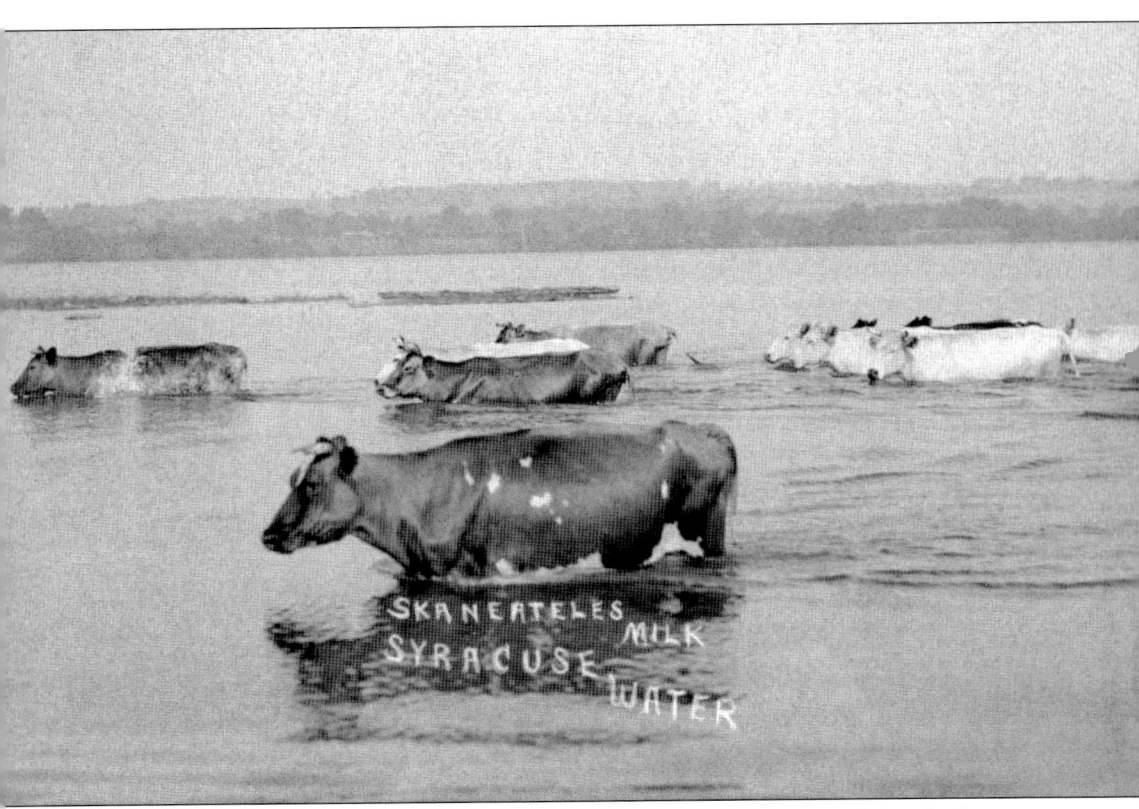

Since 1870, the City of Syracuse had been interested in obtaining water from the lake. The Syracuse water supply for the city's growing population was inadequate and disease-infested. Skaneateles Lake had the highest elevation of the Finger Lakes and could provide clean water through a gravity feed to the city. There was opposition on both sides. The owners of the mills along Skaneateles Creek feared the loss of water power for their businesses. The residents of Syracuse did not relish drinking water from a source where farm animals swam. The postcard was a tongue-in-cheek reminder as to the source of the drinking water.

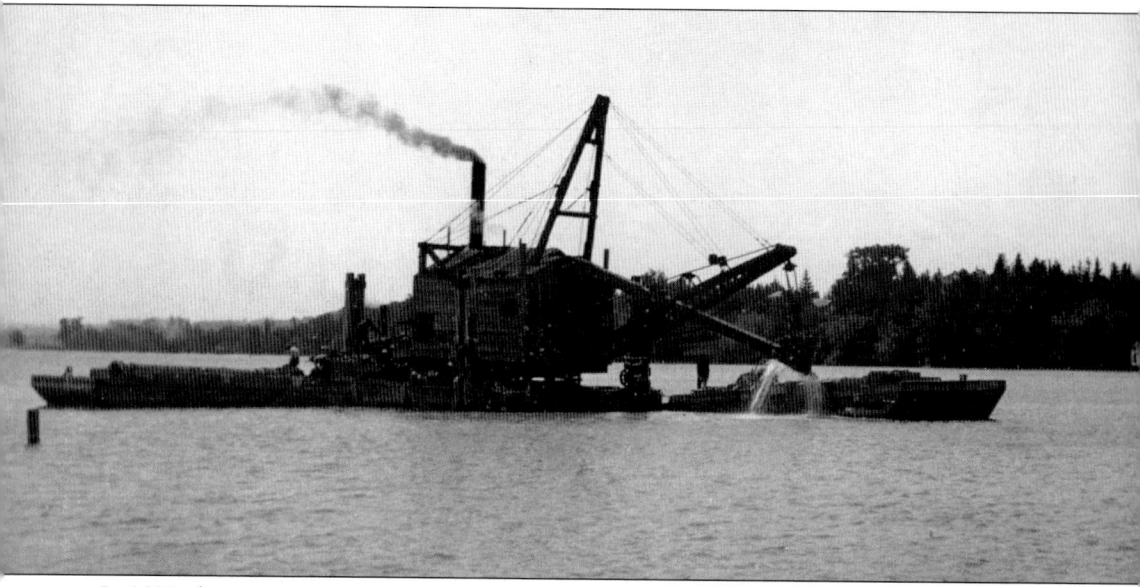

In 1899, the state empowered Syracuse with the right to acquire land, water easements, and property necessary to build a system of waterworks that would transport water to the city. In 1890, amended laws had given the state superior rights of claim to the water. As seen in the photograph, dredging and drilling to install a 30-inch pipeline began. In 1894, the people of Syracuse started using water from the lake. For many years, the action taken by the state was known as the "Water Steal."

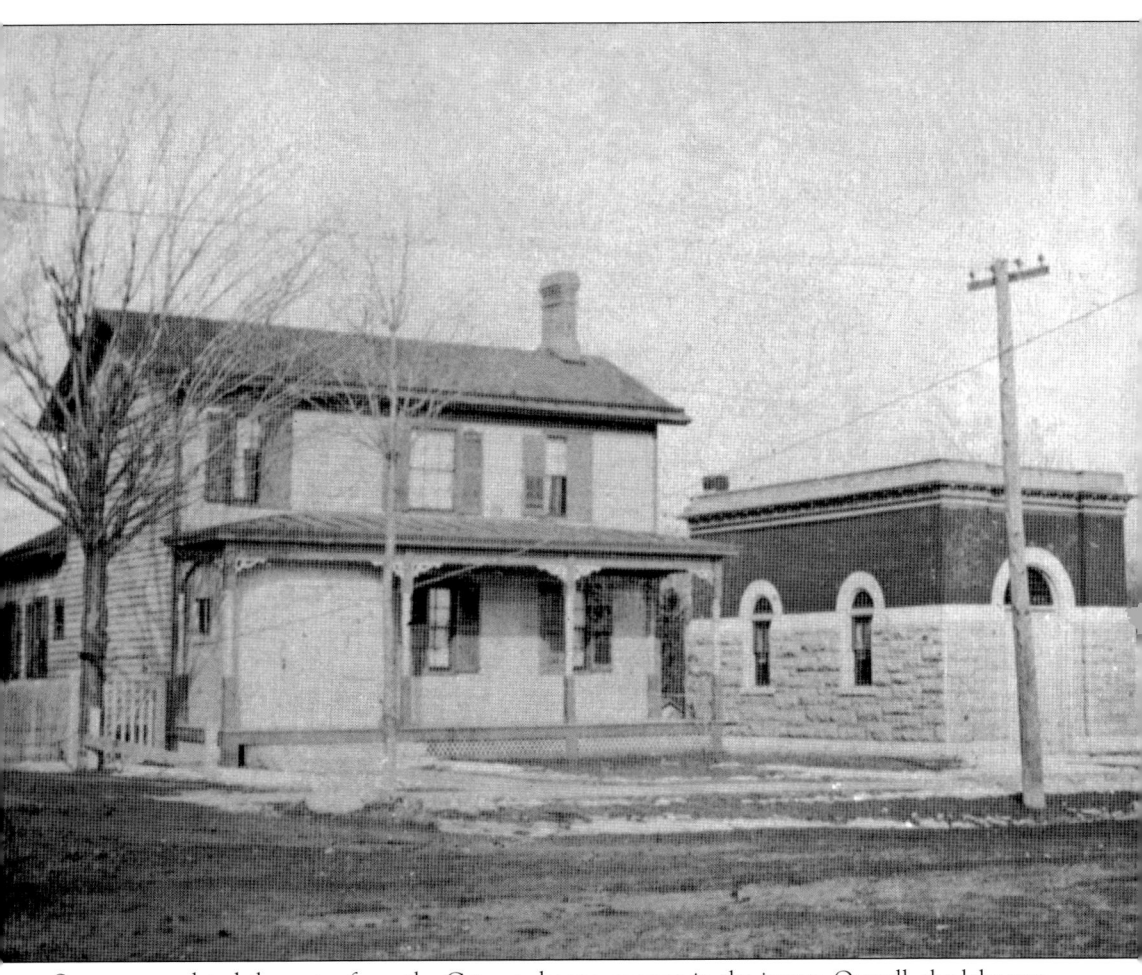

Syracuse regulated the water from the Gateway house, as seen in the image. Overall, the lake was seven feet higher than it had been in previous years. Both New York State and the City of Syracuse had interests in the lake and its shoreline.

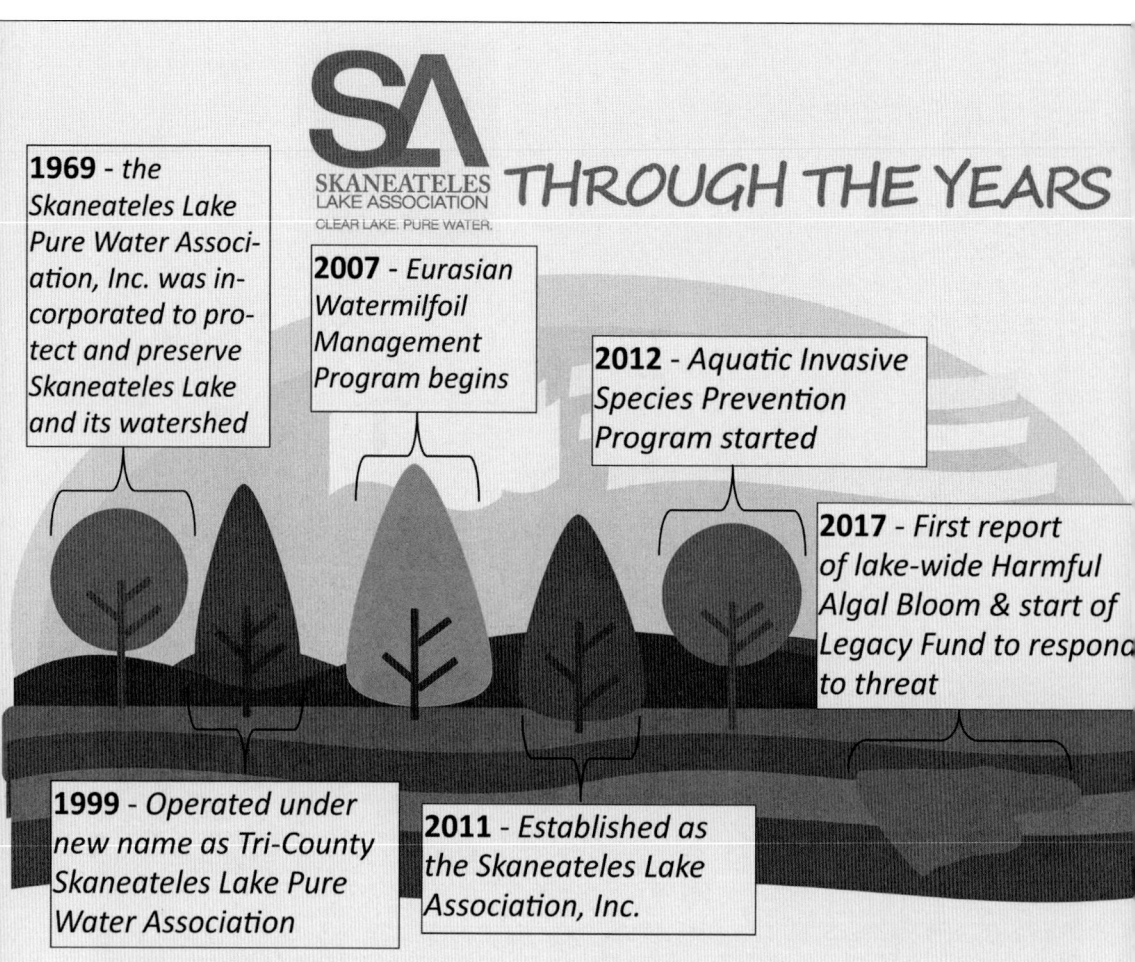

Skaneateles Lake maintained its reputation as one of the world's cleanest lakes until the mid-1960s. In 1968, citizens were concerned that the lake was polluted. An article in the *Skaneateles Press* on September 12, 1968, reported that there were instances of raw sewage in the lake and that the coliform count was considered critical in terms of pollution. At that time, the village and town had no authority regarding health matters, which had been taken over by a newly created New York State Department of Health. At a town board discussion, it was determined that the city, county, and state health departments were negligent in maintaining the purity of the lake water. As a result of private and public meetings, a nonprofit group concerned with saving Skaneateles Lake was formed. Today, the Skaneateles Lake Association is dedicated to the mission of promoting environmentally and aesthetically sound regional management of the Skaneateles Lake and its watershed.

Two
SKANEATELES BOATS

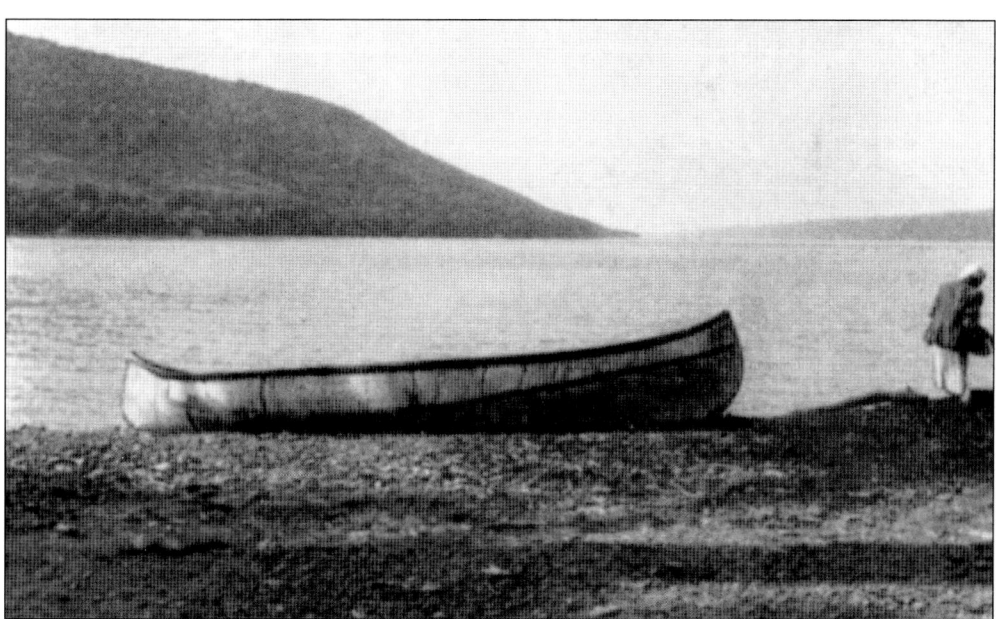

For over 1,000 years, the first sailing craft on Skaneateles Lake were the canoes of the Haudenosaunee Native Americans. The canoes were made of light wood and covered with birch bark or dug out from logs, capable of carrying up to 30 people. During the 19th century, population and business growth dictated the need for modern sailing vessels. The boat industry flourished, providing steamboats, gas-powered wooden boats, and modern sailing crafts.

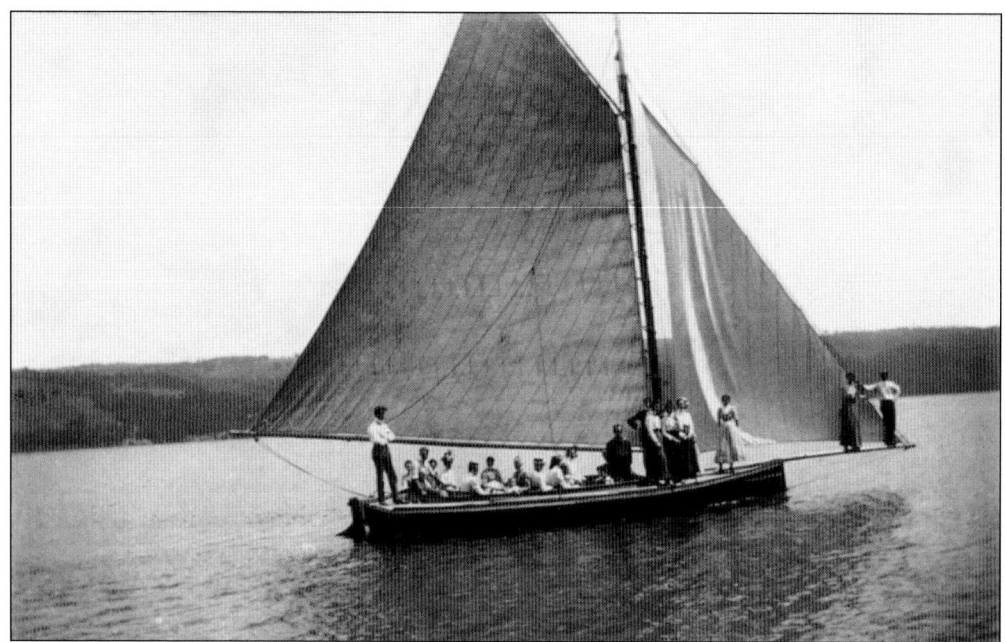
Recreational boats remained rudimentary until the early 1800s. The first sailing yacht was built in 1811 for Col. J.V. Vredenburgh by a New York City magnate.

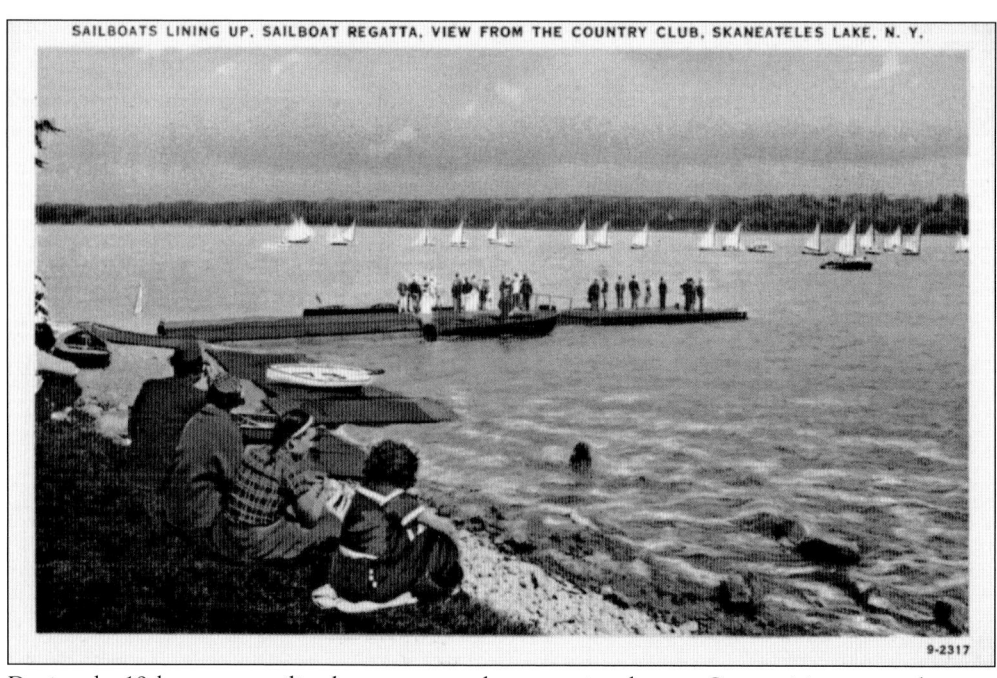
During the 19th century, sailing became a popular recreational sport. Competitive regattas became a favorite pastime of the wealthy.

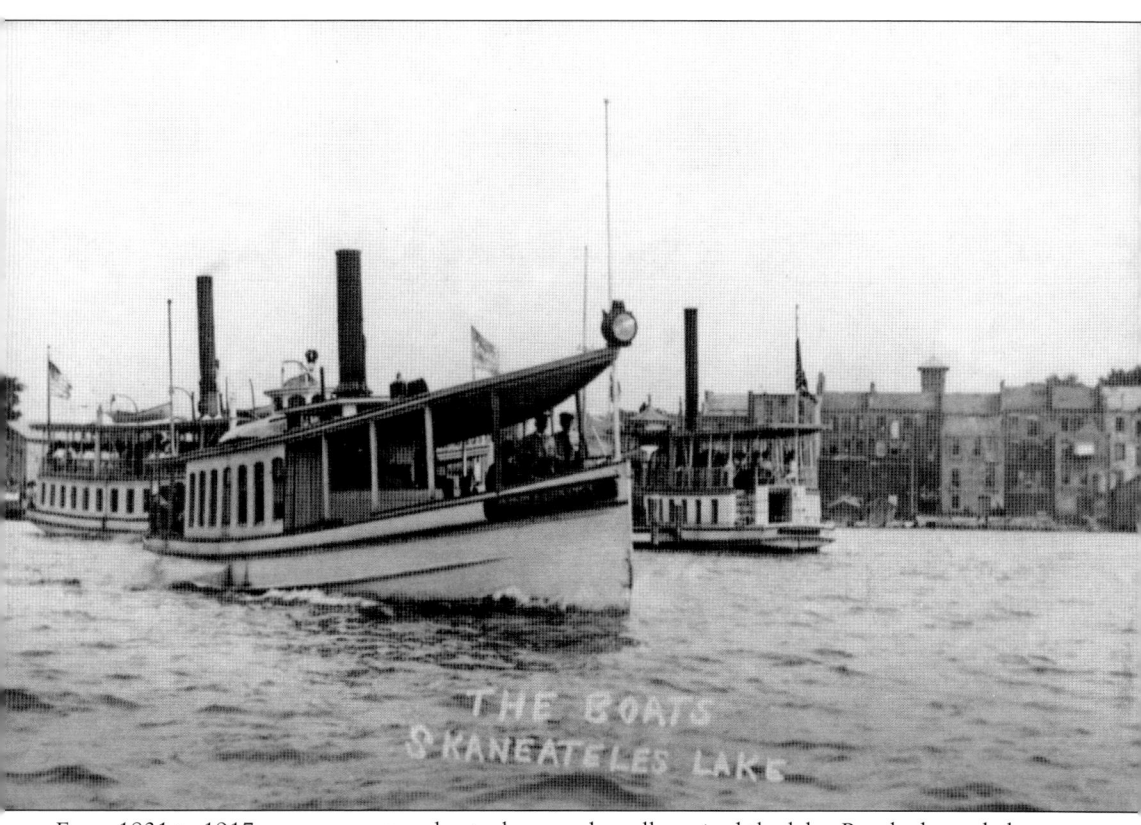

From 1831 to 1917, numerous steamboats, large and small, cruised the lake. People depended on them for transportation, mail delivery, freight, and getting products to market. The *Independent* was the first steamship to traverse the lake in 1831. The most well-known were the *Glen Haven* (1876–1897), the *Ossahinta* (1887–1909), and the *City of Syracuse* (1900–1917). During the winter months, the boats were dry-docked on land or moored in the outlet at the steamboat wharf.

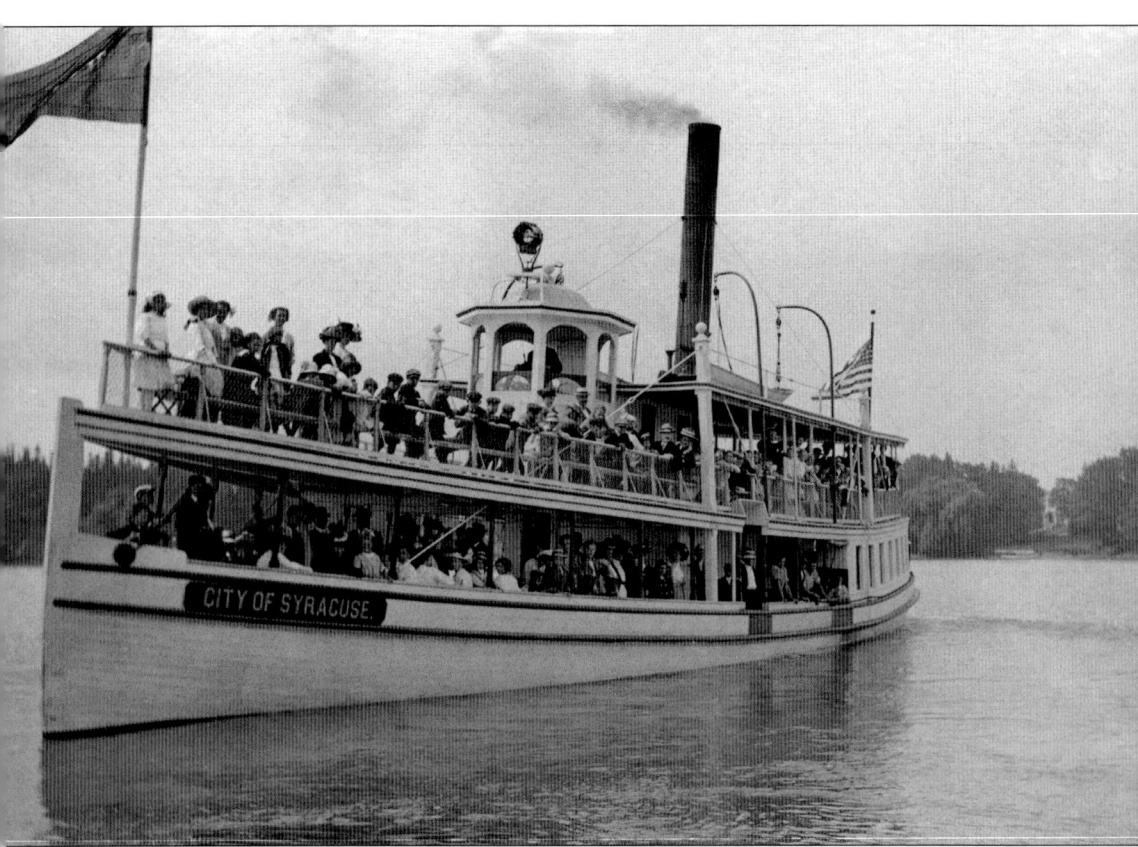

In 1891, Clifford Beebe, owner of the Syracuse Electric Railway, was commissioned to build a steamboat. It was the largest steamboat on the lake, accommodating 600 passengers, and appropriately named the *City of Syracuse*. The boat operated in conjunction with the rail schedule. A round-trip ticket was purchased in Syracuse and included the rail ride to Skaneateles and a boat ride to a destination on the lake. The steamboat era ended in 1917 as automobiles became the preferred mode of transportation. Also, Syracuse wished to maintain clean drinking water for the city's residents. In 1917, the *City of Syracuse* was moored at the end of the old steamboat wharf, where it sat for three years, both the boat and the wharf falling into disrepair. Eventually, the pilot house was saved and turned into a gazebo. The remaining boat was torpedoed and sunk. The skeletal remains can be viewed today on the lake floor at the end of the pier.

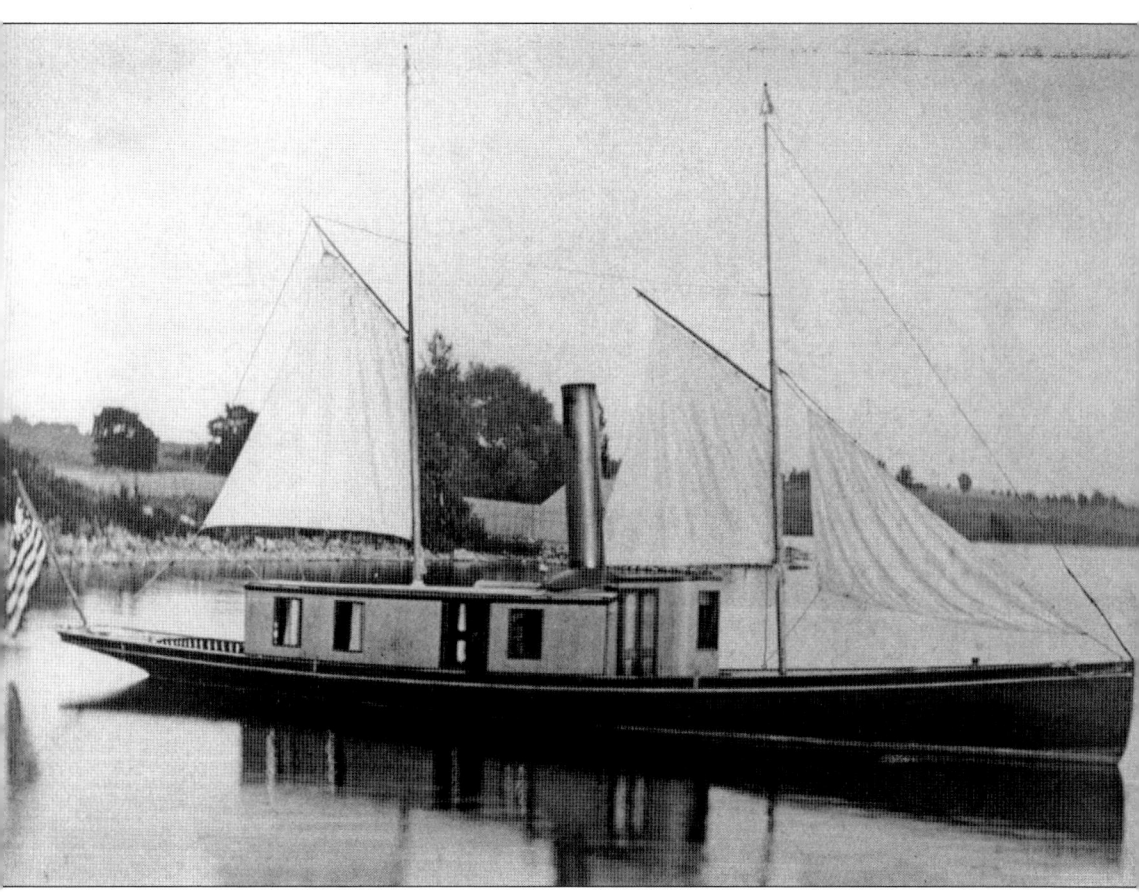

Steamboats began mail delivery on the lake in the early 19th century. Mail delivery by boat was the only way to reach cottages. Early autos could not traverse the steep cliffs around the lake. After the steamboats quit working in 1917, mail contracts were issued to private boat-line owners. The steamboat *Lotus* was built in 1876 in New York City and bought by Fred Roosevelt, a Skaneatelesean. Leslie Barber purchased the *Lotus* in 1906. Following some modifications, the *Lotus* carried mail and passengers on the lake from 1922 to 1927.

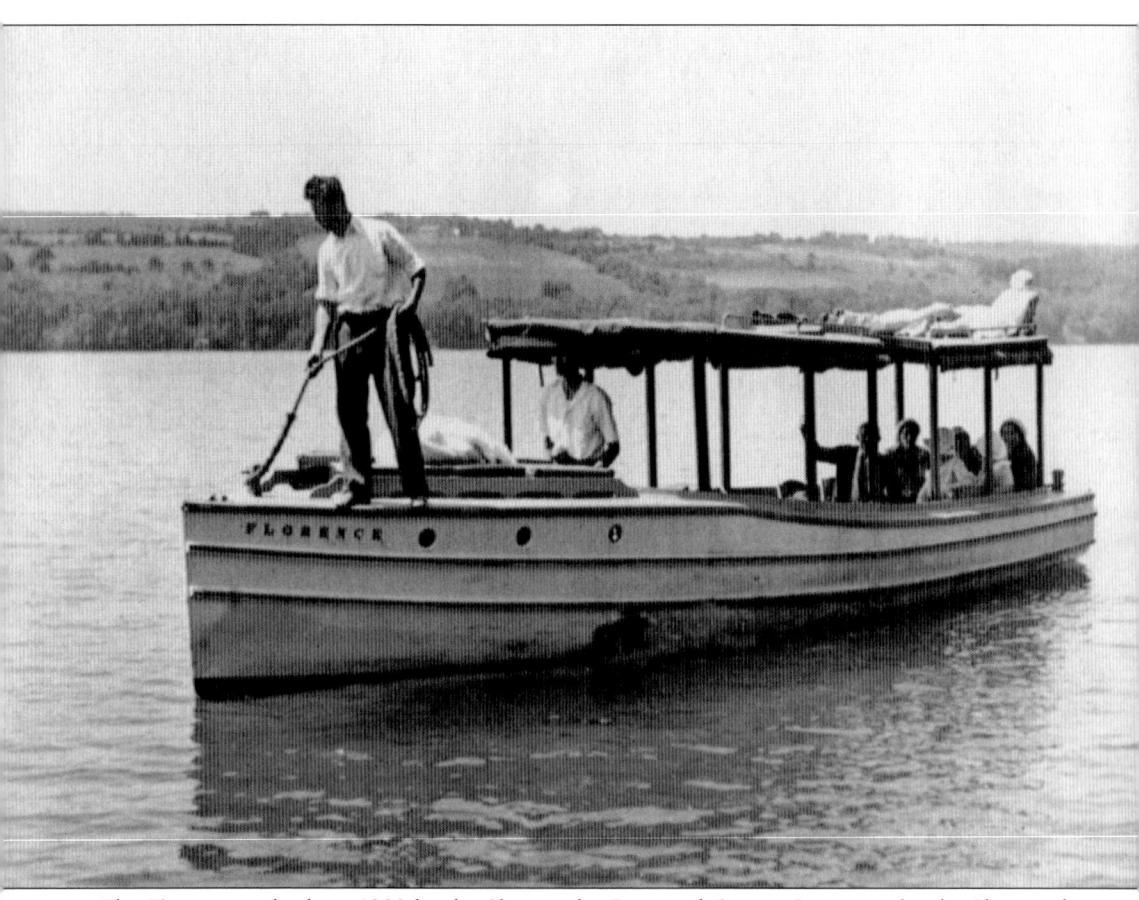

The *Florence* was built in 1922 by the Skaneateles Boat and Canoe Company for the Skaneateles Navigation Company, a nonprofit organization comprised of summer cottage owners. She carried mail, groceries, and passengers to camps up and down the lake. The trip of 40 stops took six hours, leaving at 10:00 a.m. and returning to the wharf in Skaneateles at about 4:00 p.m. *Florence* was in use through the 1920s and 1930s, sinking in the outlet in 1943. However, her story had not ended. The Stinson boat line began operations in 1939. The *Florence* had been replaced by the *Spray*. In 1941, gasoline rationing was a threat to the viability of the boat service on the lake. Bob, Bill, and Don Stinson from the Stinson family went off to war. Mail delivery ceased on the lake. In 1943, Allie Hoffman of Hoffman's Pharmacy bought the derelict *Florence* and outfitted her to run as a steam launch, delivering mail in the summers of 1944 and 1945. It was a well-deserved run after her long service.

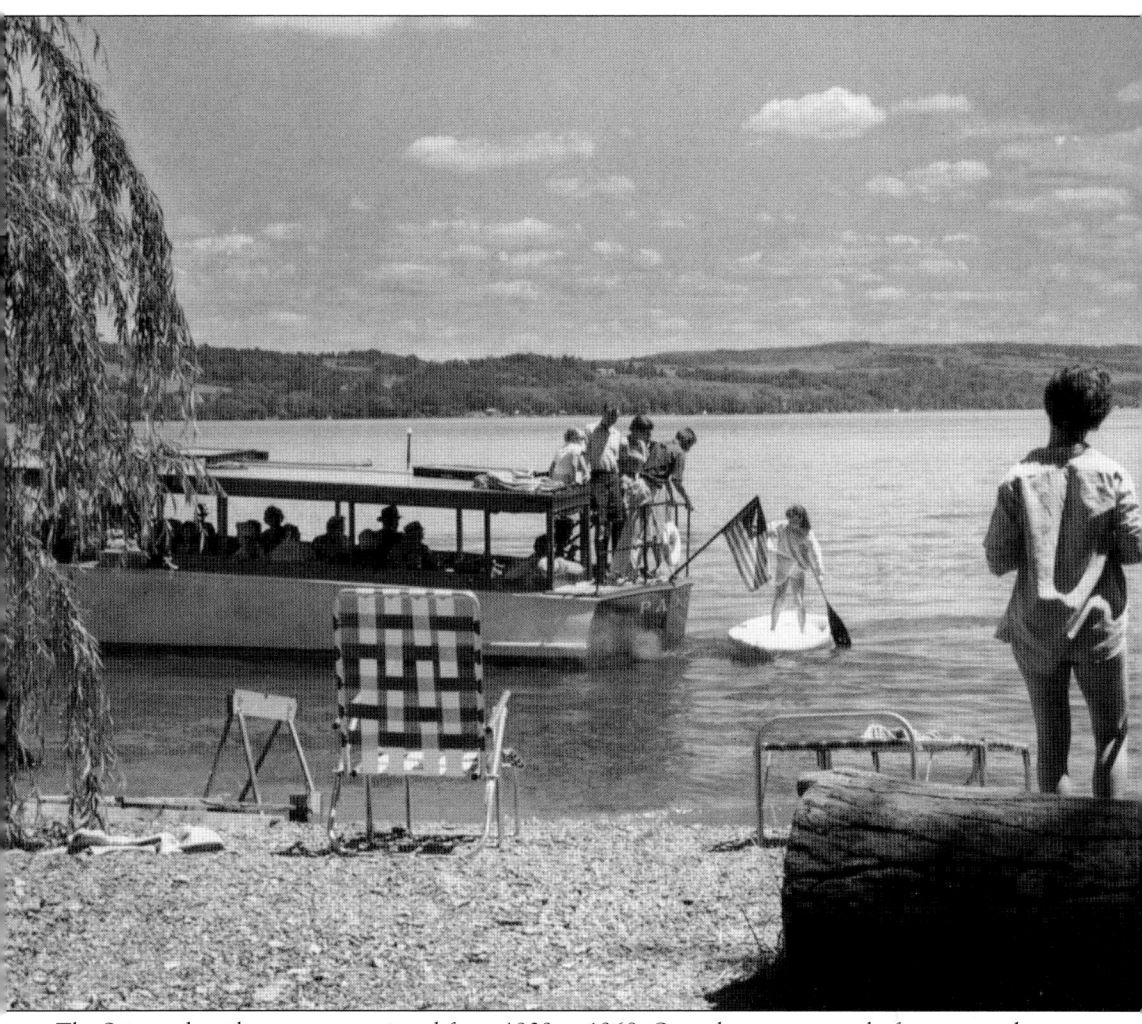

The Stinson boat line was operational from 1939 to 1968. Over the years, a total of seven wooden boats delivered mail and provided tours during the summer. The *Pat II* was in service with the Stinson boat line from 1956 to 1968. The 39-foot mahogany and cedar launch was built in 1927 in the Thousand Islands and served on the St. Lawrence River until 1956. *Pat II*, which carried 28 passengers, delivered mail on the lake for 35 years with a crew of two. The captain drove the boat and narrated a tour for the passengers while maneuvering the boat close to the shore for pickup and delivery of mail to customers waiting on a dock or raft or in a boat. The captain's crew of one climbed on the roof and dropped to the bow of the boat, often with a small net attached to a pole to reach the mail. The *Pat II* continued to deliver mail until 1991. She eventually found a home in the Finger Lakes Boating Museum, where she has been fully restored. (Photo courtesy of Bill Stinson).

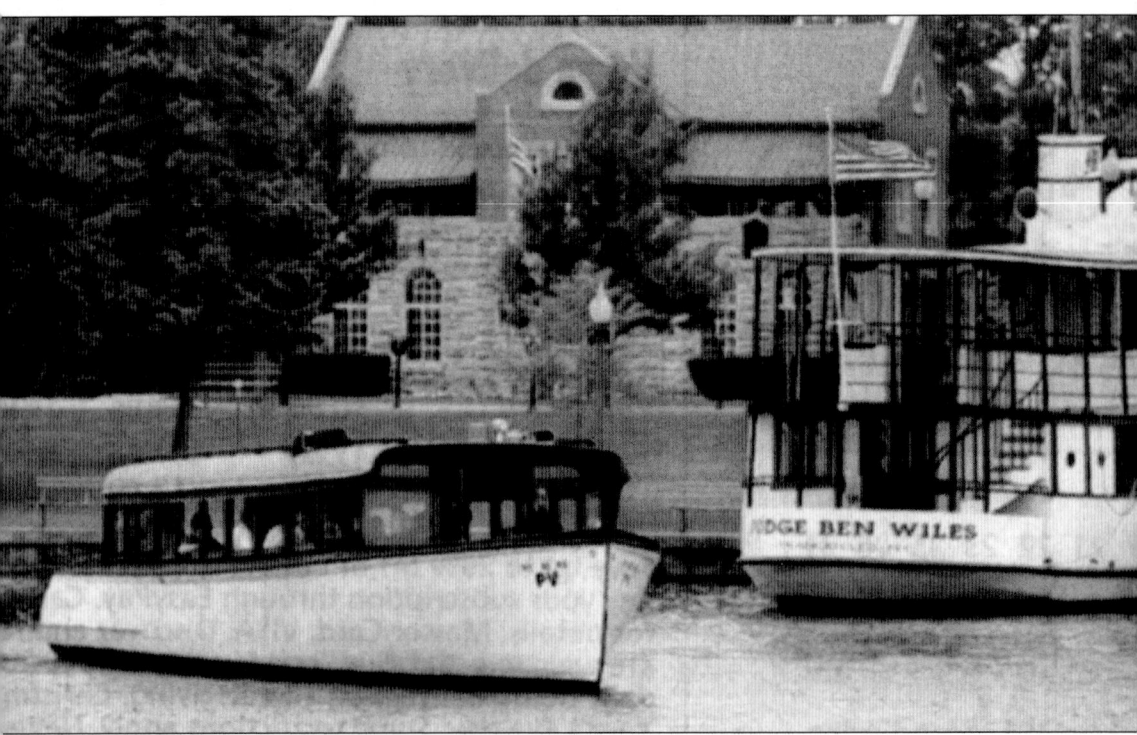

The Stinson boat line was purchased by the Mid-Lakes Navigation Company in 1968. Following the retirement of the *Pat II* in 1991, the *Barbara S. Wiles* (smallest boat seen in the photograph) was purchased from a tour company in Lake George. She continued to deliver mail until the summer of 2024, when she was taken out of service to assess her future viability and safety.

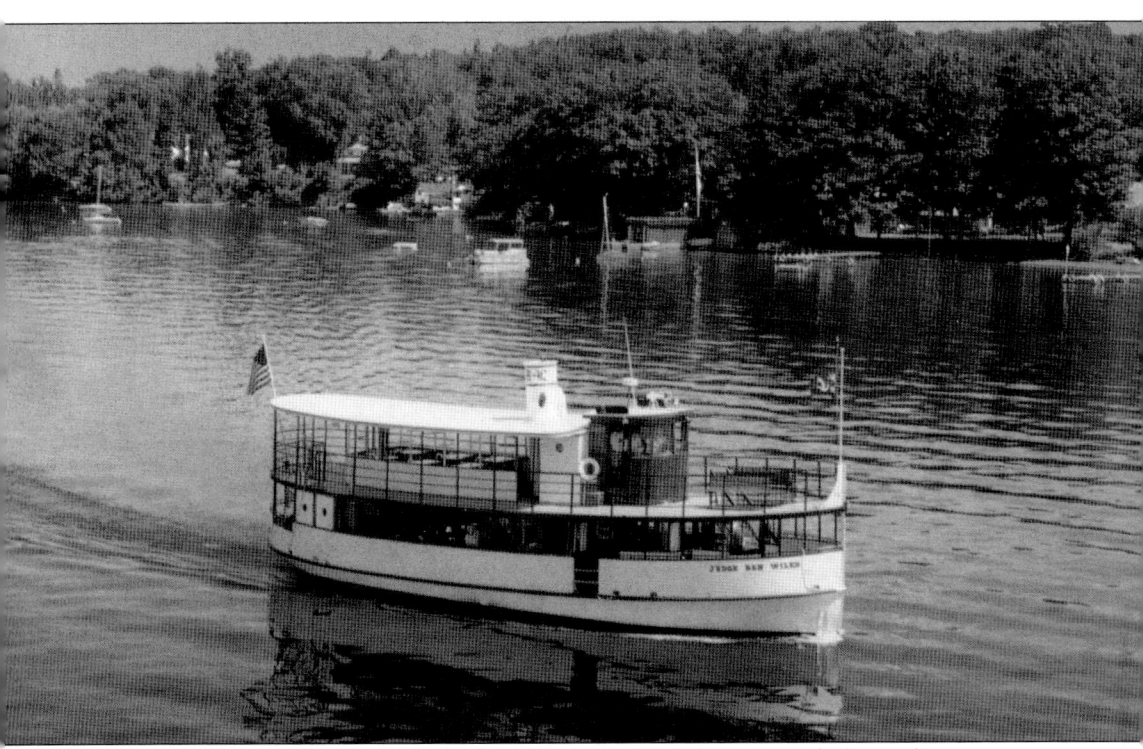

During the summer tourist season, *Judge Ben Wiles* provides daily tours, including a dinner cruise. All Mid-Lakes boats are stored in a barn in Borodino during the winter months.

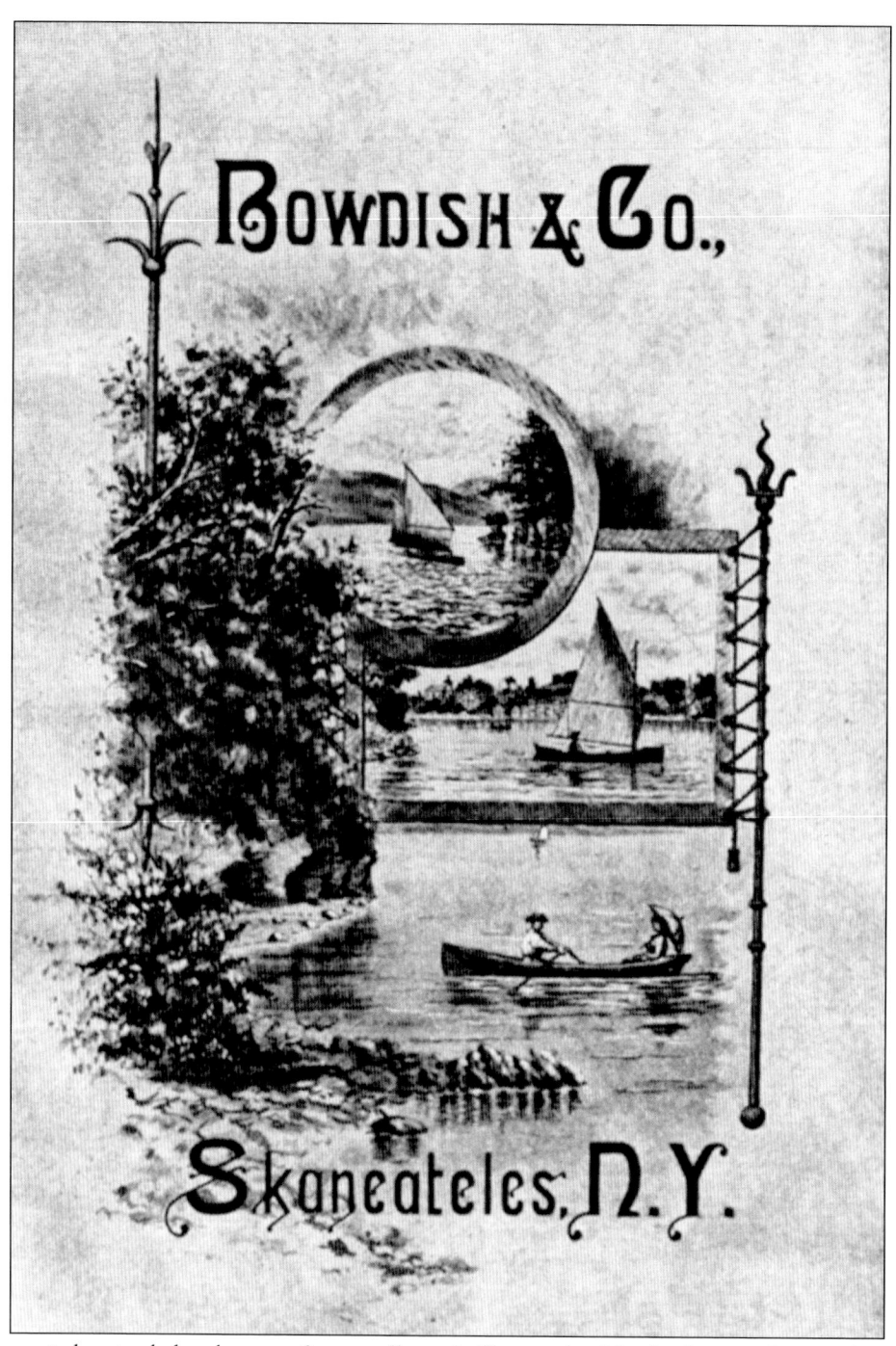

Interest in boating led to the manufacture of boats in Skaneateles. The first large-scale manufacturer was the Bowdish and Company, established in the 1880s by Nelson Samuel Bowdish and his son Edward from Cooperstown, New York. Sailboats, canoes, rowboats, and small steamboats were initially manufactured on the second and third floors of the Kelly building on Jordan Street and later in a new building at Railroad and Austin Streets. The boats were renowned for their design and quality of manufacture in the yachting world.

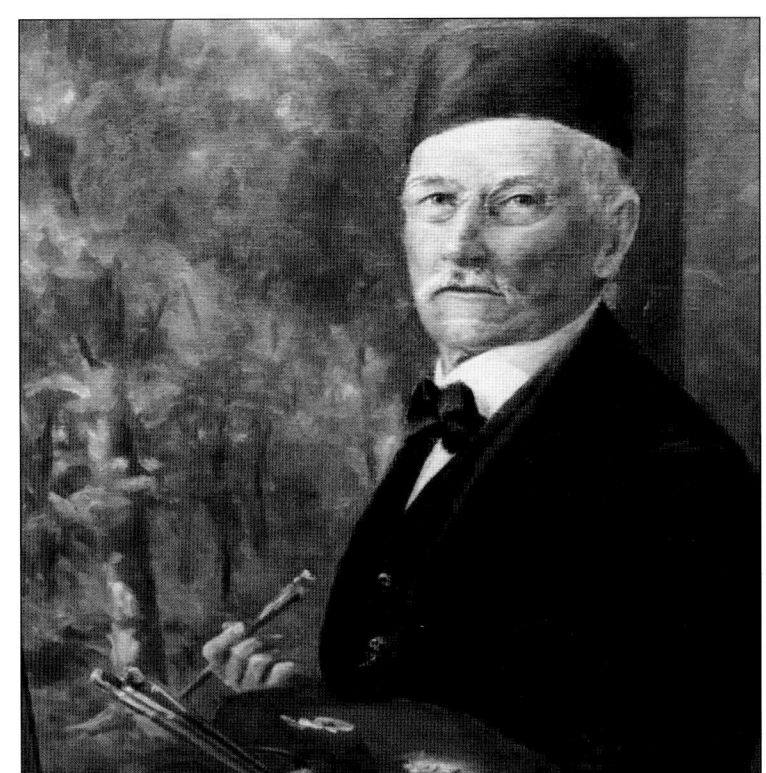

In addition to boat building, Nelson and Edward Bowdish were also well-known landscape artists who worked with oil on canvas. The portraits of both men were done by Edward.

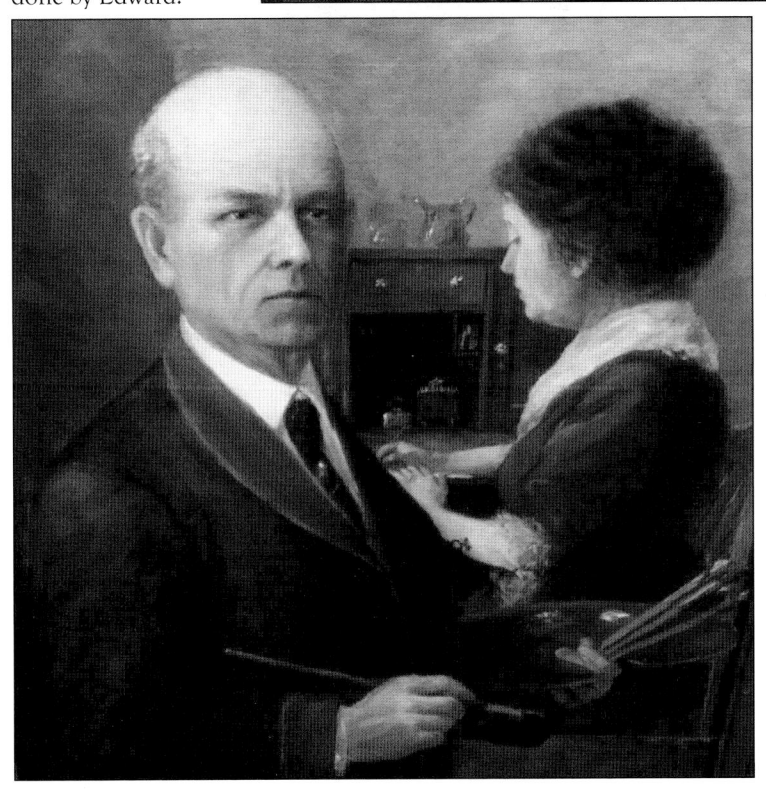

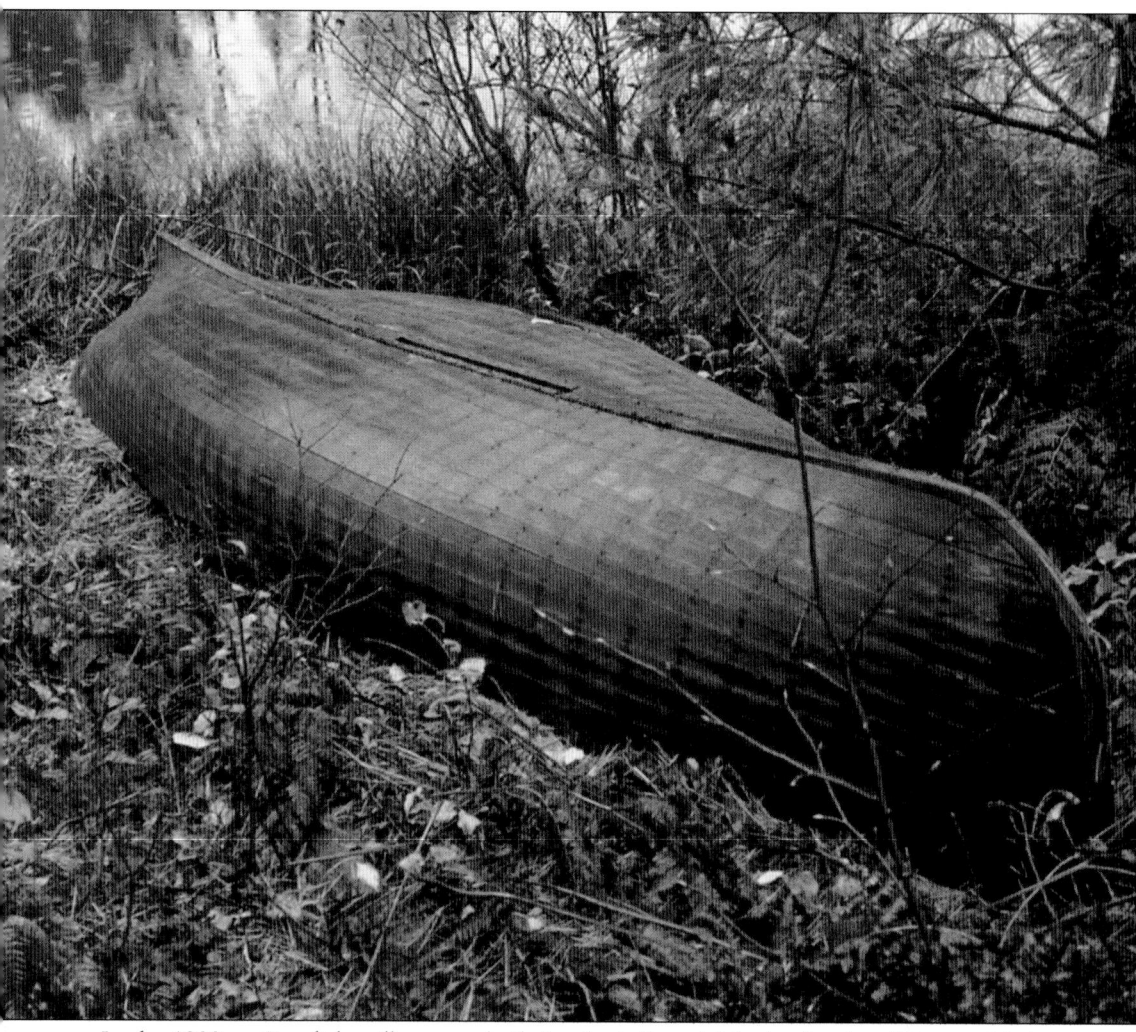

In the 1800s, a Bowdish sailboat was built for the influential Lodge family of Detroit, Michigan. It was found, neglected, in Michigan's Upper Peninsula by Mary Braamse Edgar. She fell in love with the boat and its hourglass stern. Together with Dr. John Parlin, who was interested in boat restoration, they began a long process of rescuing the boat from its dilapidated state in Michigan.

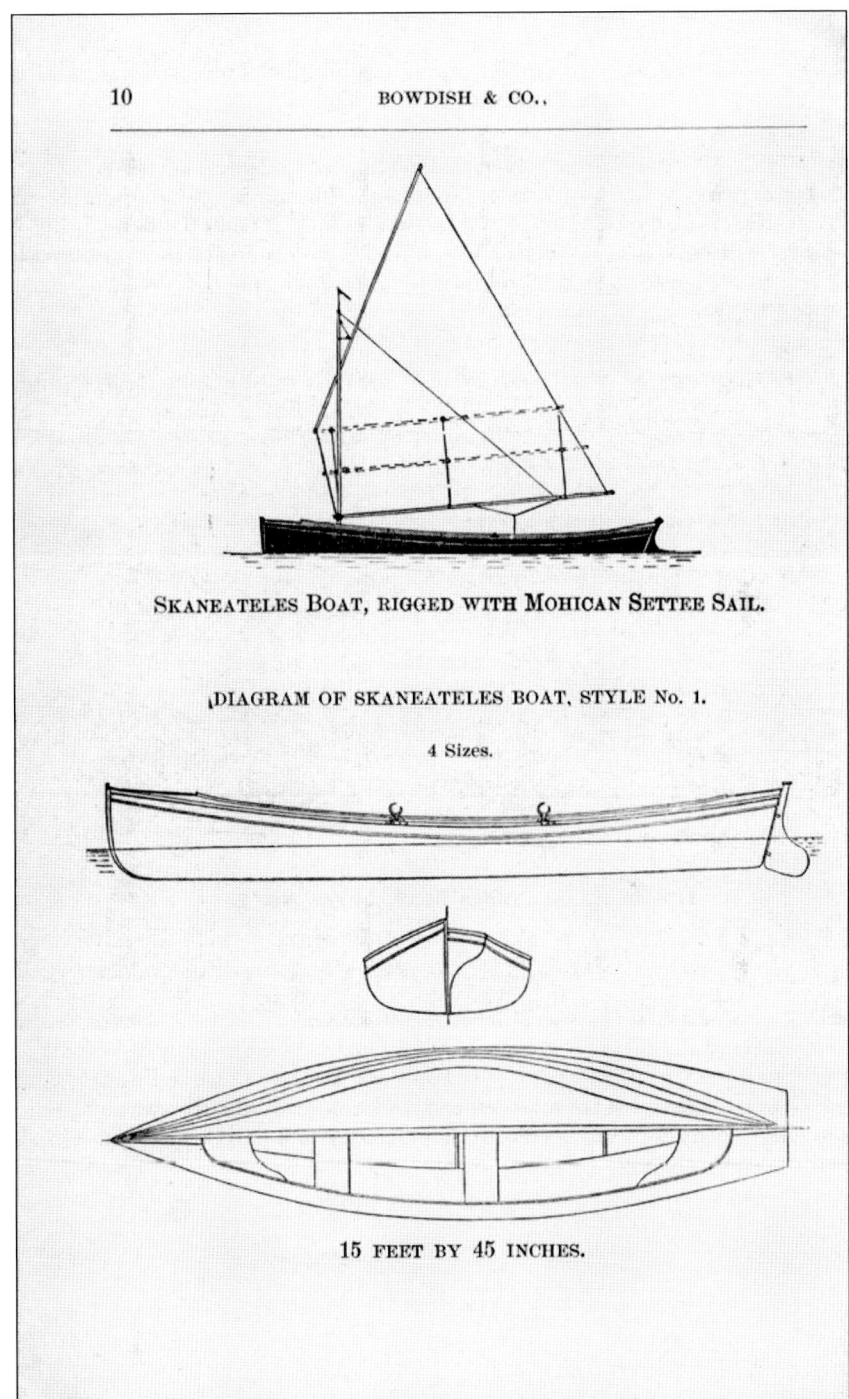

The diagram from the Bowdish catalog of 1887 is the model diagram for the restored sailboat. The boat was "hogged," sagging in the middle from snow pile-up over many winters, which broke many of its ribs. The trim pieces were missing or rotted, but every effort was made to use original wood species, correct hardware, and fasteners to bring it back to its original condition. The painstaking process took 11 years.

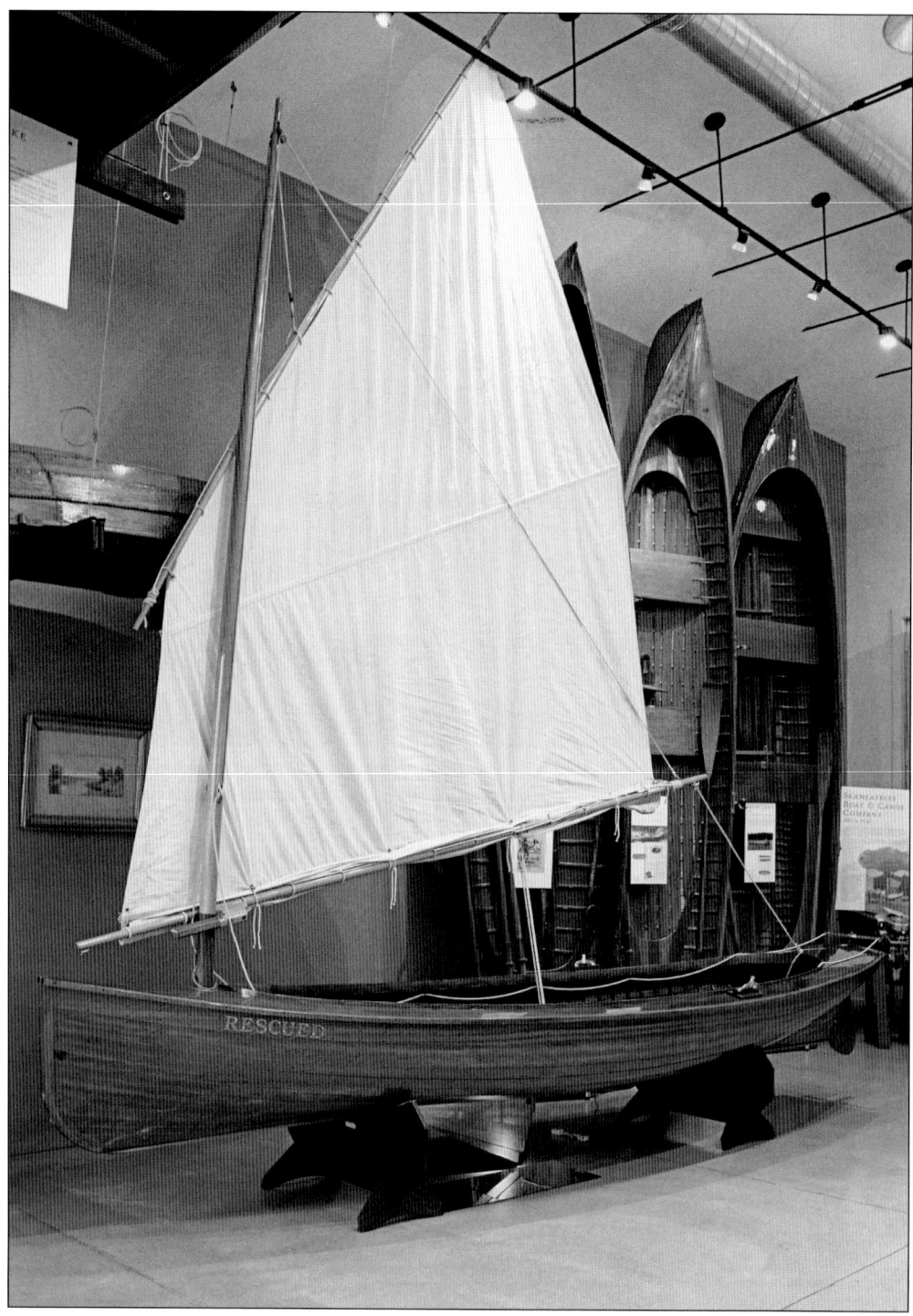

In 2020, the restored boat was named Rescued by Dr. Parlin, who gifted her to the Skaneateles Historical Society Museum. Almost 150 years later, she is home, now on display in the boat wing of the Skaneateles Historical Society Museum. (Photo courtesy of C.E. Malmgren.)

| SEDGWICK SMITH | GEORGE SMITH |
| PRESIDENT | SUPT. OF CONSTRUCTION |

SKANEATELES
Boat and Canoe Company

ESTABLISHED 1893

BUILDERS OF

"Boats That Will Last"

SKANEATELES, NEW YORK

TELEPHONE SKANEATELES 115

Our shop is located on Jordan Street in the village of Skaneateles, (at the north end of Skaneateles Lake) 18 miles from Syracuse and 7 miles from Auburn. We can be reached from either city by railroad or trolley, and from all directions by state roads.

In 1839, two former Bowdish employees, George Smith and James Ruth, established the Skaneateles Boat and Canoe Company at 14 West Genesee Street. In 1901, the operation was moved to an old wooden foundry building on Jordan Street. The company's reputation for fine manufacture of small boats was worldwide. Sir Thomas Lipton of the Lipton Tea Company and a renowned yachtsman, ordered 100 boats for his boating party, bringing $75,000 ($1 million today) to the lakeside industry in 1920. This image is from the 1893 Skaneateles Boat and Canoe Company catalog.

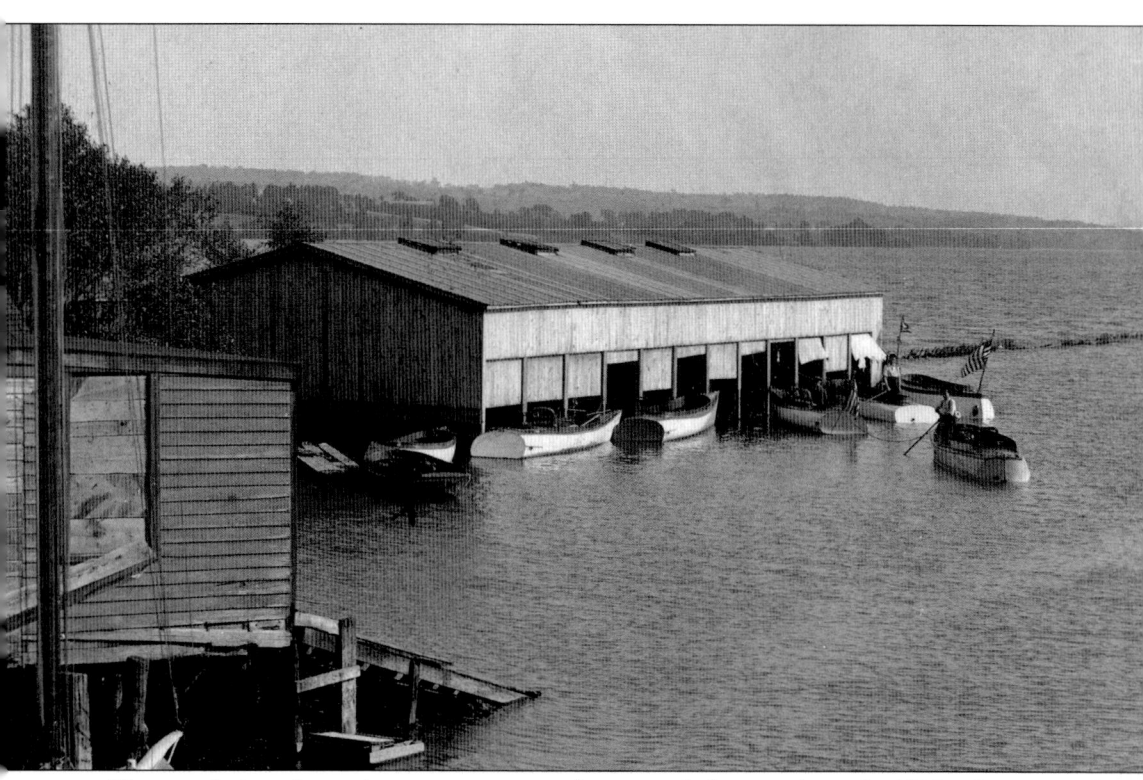

The popularity of steamboat transportation began to decline in the early 1900s. Gas-powered automobiles were taking over land transportation. The Skaneateles Boat Company recognized that gas-powered boats could be as economical on water and began their manufacture in 1905. These boats were known as the modified Dolphins. The boats were easy to maintain, eventually replacing steamboat transport around the lake. Many of these boats were housed in boat liveries, as seen in the photograph.

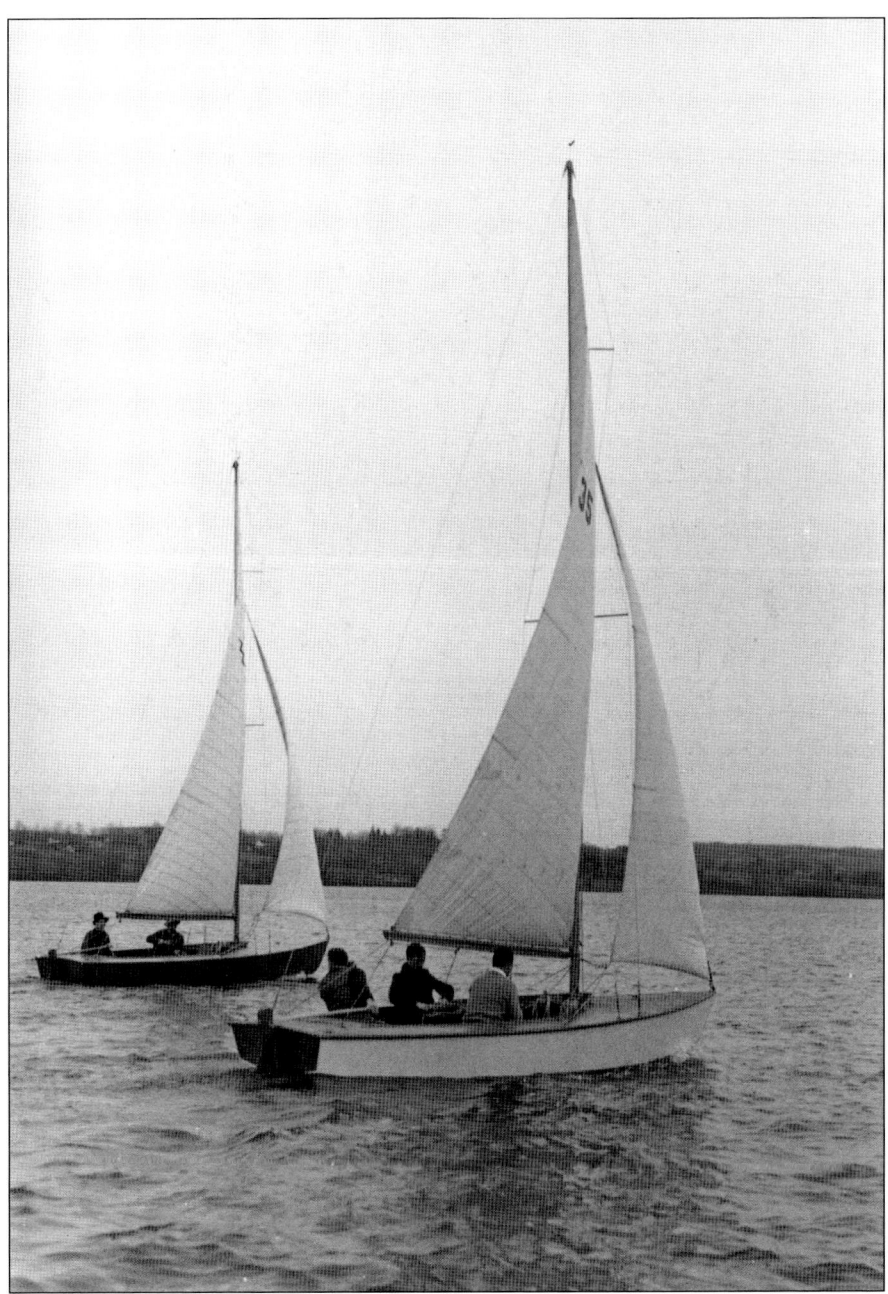

In 1930, a fire destroyed the boat company on Jordan Street. A cement building was built on the site. George Barnes, Arthur Emmerick, and Wescott Barber purchased the Skaneateles Boat and Canoe Company. The business was reorganized under Skaneateles Boats Incorporated in 1932. George Smith was retained as a master craftsman. The Comet sailboat was a big success for the Skaneateles Boat Company but only seated two to three sailors. The Barnes brothers contacted Sparkman and Stephens, noted yacht designers from New York City, to design a day sailing boat suitable for families and racing. The Lightning was the result, launched in 1938. It became the most successful one-design sailboat under 19 feet in sailing history. Anniversary Lightning regattas are held every 10 years on Skaneateles Lake.

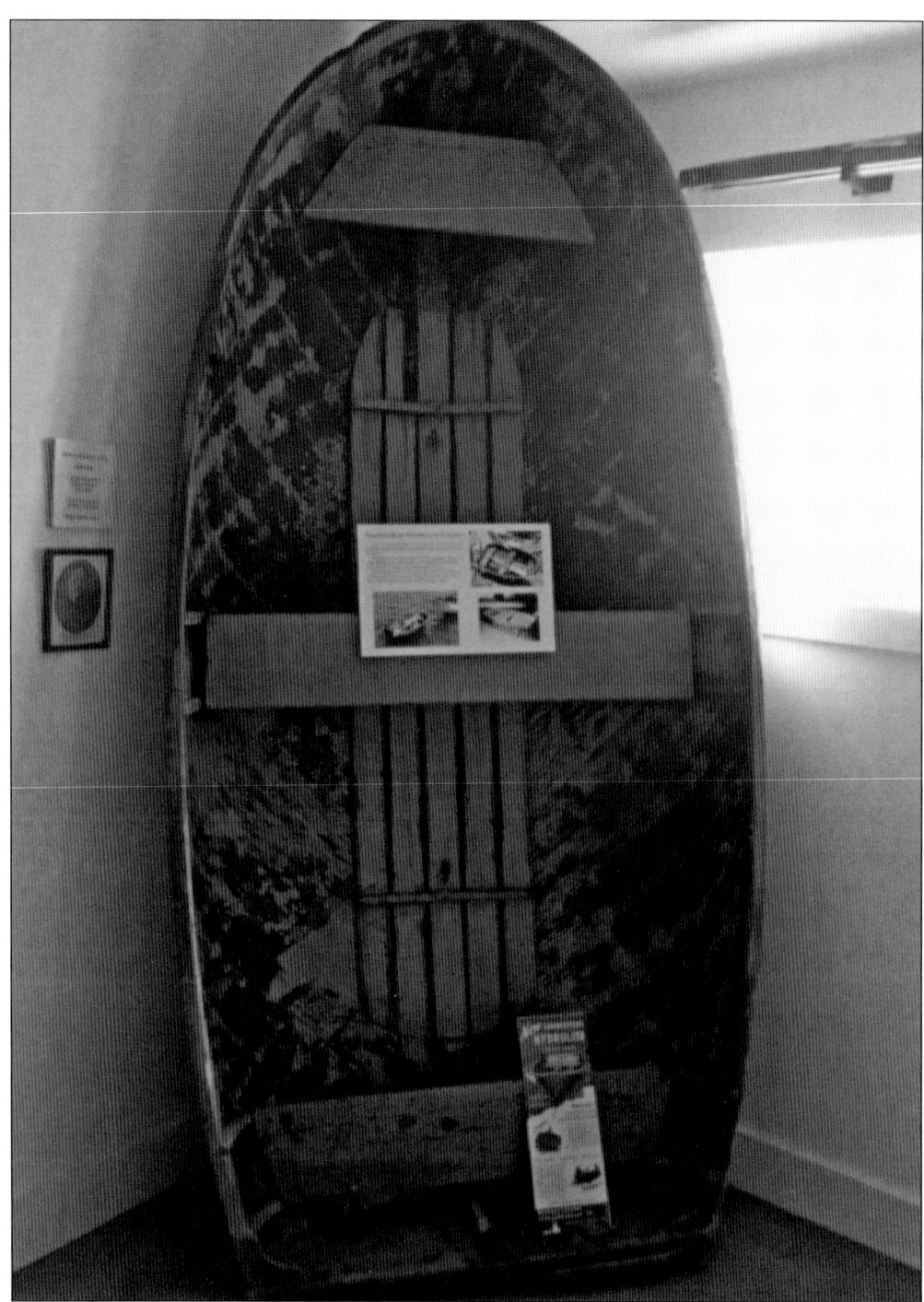

George Barnes and Olin Spencer collaborated on a lightweight boat tender (dinghy) made from glued-up strips of mahogany that were baked in an autoclave. The one-person Skaneateles Hydrolite Dinghy was used by the US Navy during World War II. Skaneateles Boats Incorporated moved to Willow Glen just north of the village. In 1957, wood boat production ceased as fiberglass came into use. George Barnes died in 1961.

Three

THE NORTH SHORE

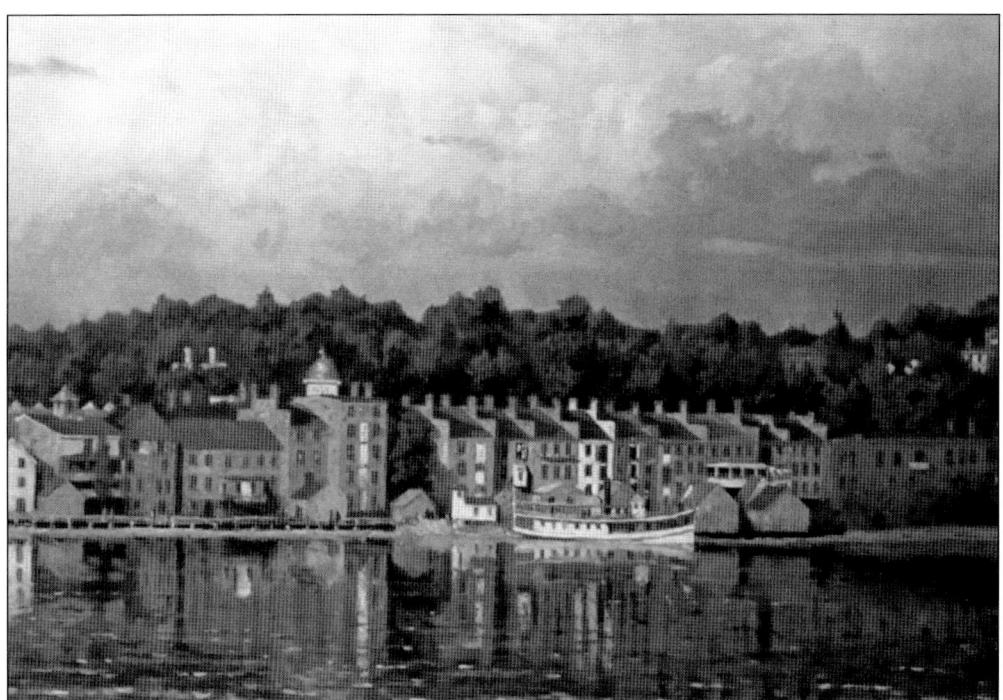

The 19th century was a period of expansion along the north shore at the foot of Skaneateles Lake. The swamp and heavily forested area that existed on the north shore became suitable for building as the outlet was cleared and became a waterway that supported boat transportation. Village businesses grew along the north shore. The village was incorporated in 1833. John Dodgson Barrow (1824-1906), a prominent Skaneateles citizen, was a prolific artist known for his oil on canvas landscapes, influenced by the Hudson River School of artists. One of his most famous landscapes is the "Back of the Village" along the north shore in the 1800s. The painting is part of the Barrow collection in the John Barrow Art Gallery in the Skaneateles village. (Image courtes of The Barrow Gallery, Skaneateles.)

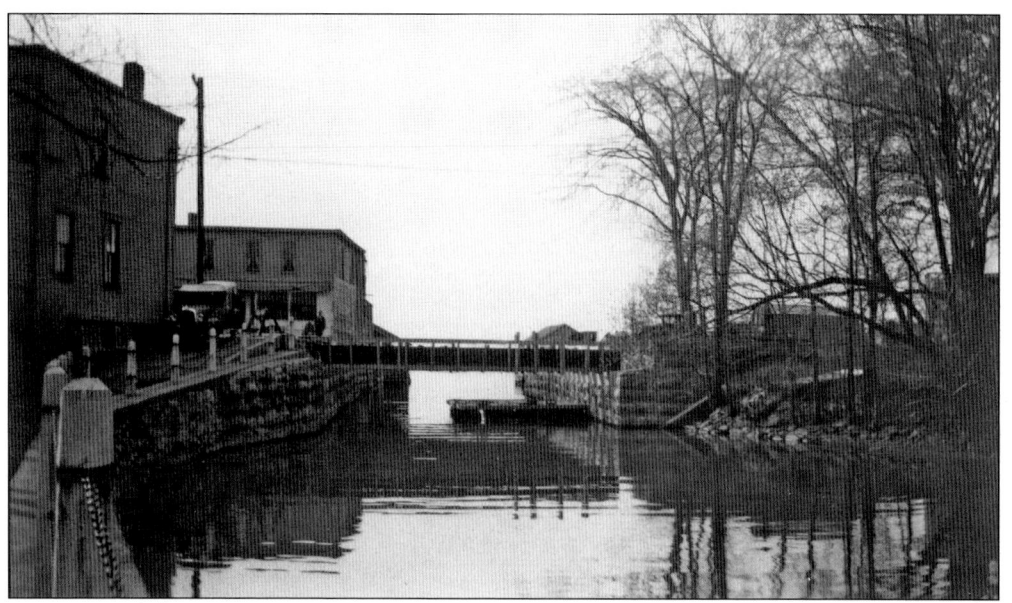

The outlet, originally a heavily forested swamp, was gradually cleared as trees were removed to be used for building materials, and the lake levels rose. In the 1800s, the outlet at the west end of the north shore was transformed from a small stream to a waterway providing a connection between Skaneateles Creek and the lake. Boat liveries, a steamboat wharf, and a pier were built.

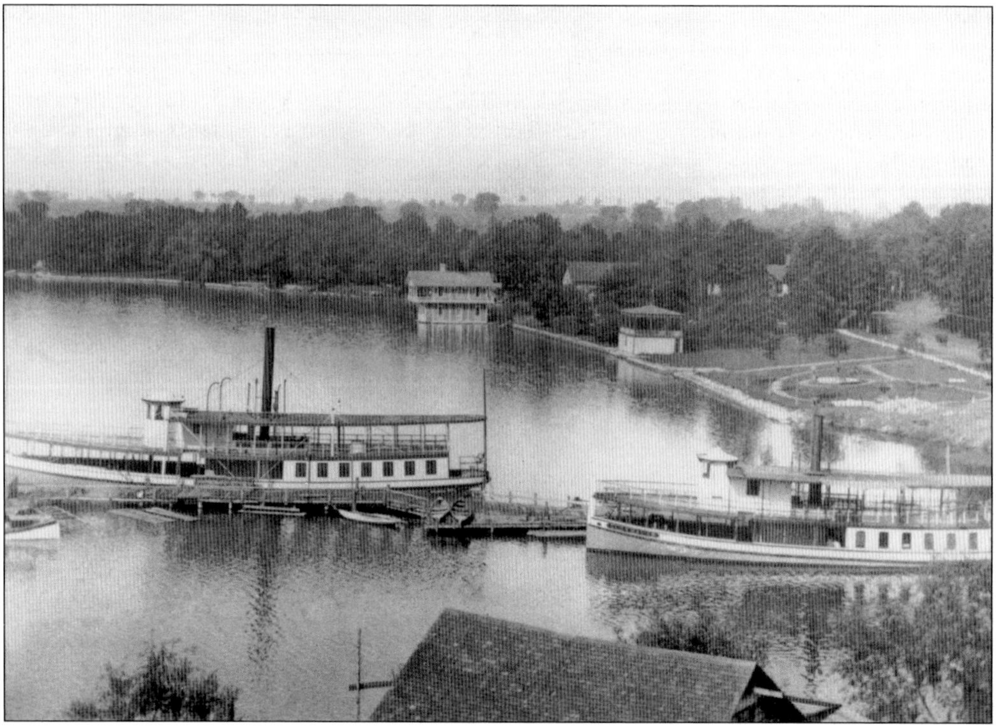

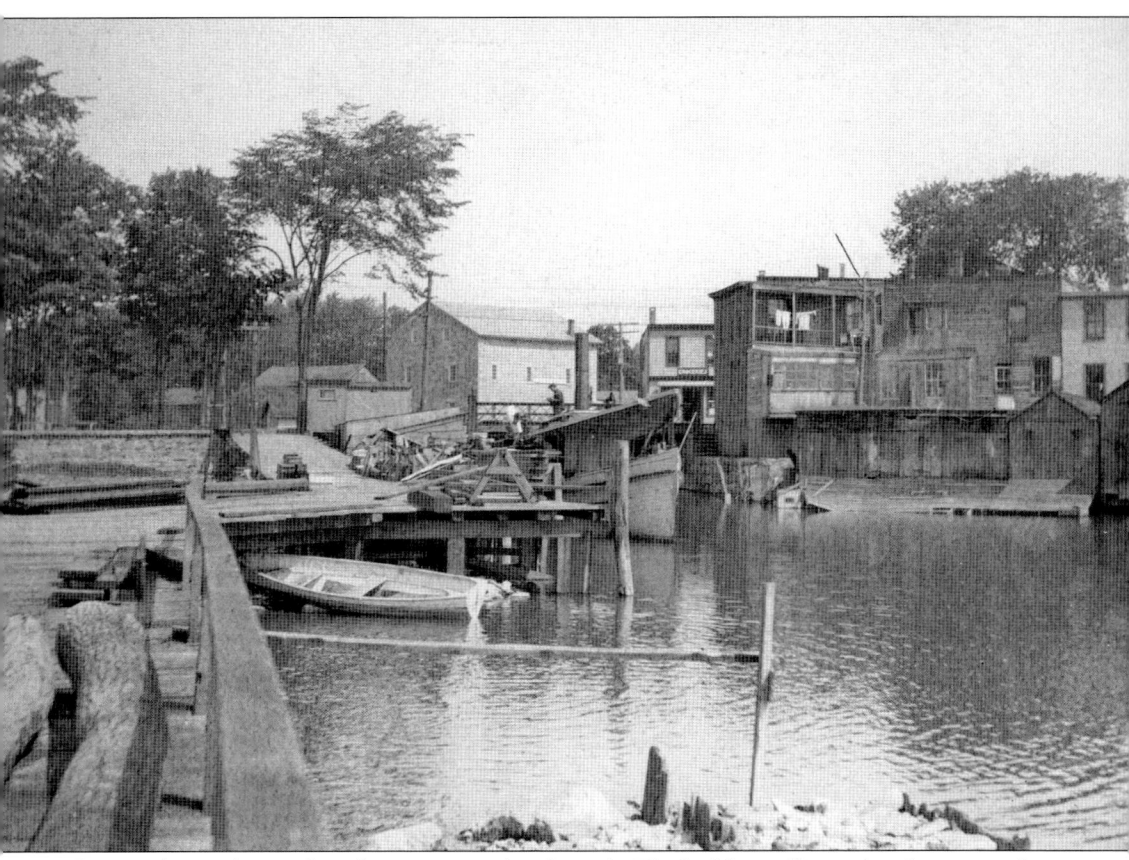

Following the Civil War, the village continued to flourish. The building of boats, boathouses, and liveries became profitable. Liveries were long wooden structures with boat slips that were owned or rented. These were the early commercial boathouses behind the village buildings, adjacent to the outlet. They were unsightly, as were the shanties also being built. Before 1900, permits to build had not been required. In the early 1900s, the locals began to complain about the appearance along the outlet. The state complained that they were infringing on state-owned property. In 1909, the state authorities called a halt to the construction of buildings on state-owned property in the village. The *Skaneateles Democrat* reported in May 1909, "To permit the outlet being lined with boathouses of promiscuous architecture, while of benefit to the few who own them, would offend the senses of the vast majority of our citizens out of all proportion to the value of these buildings. And yet we all recognize the absolute necessity of their existence, the question narrows down to the least offensive."

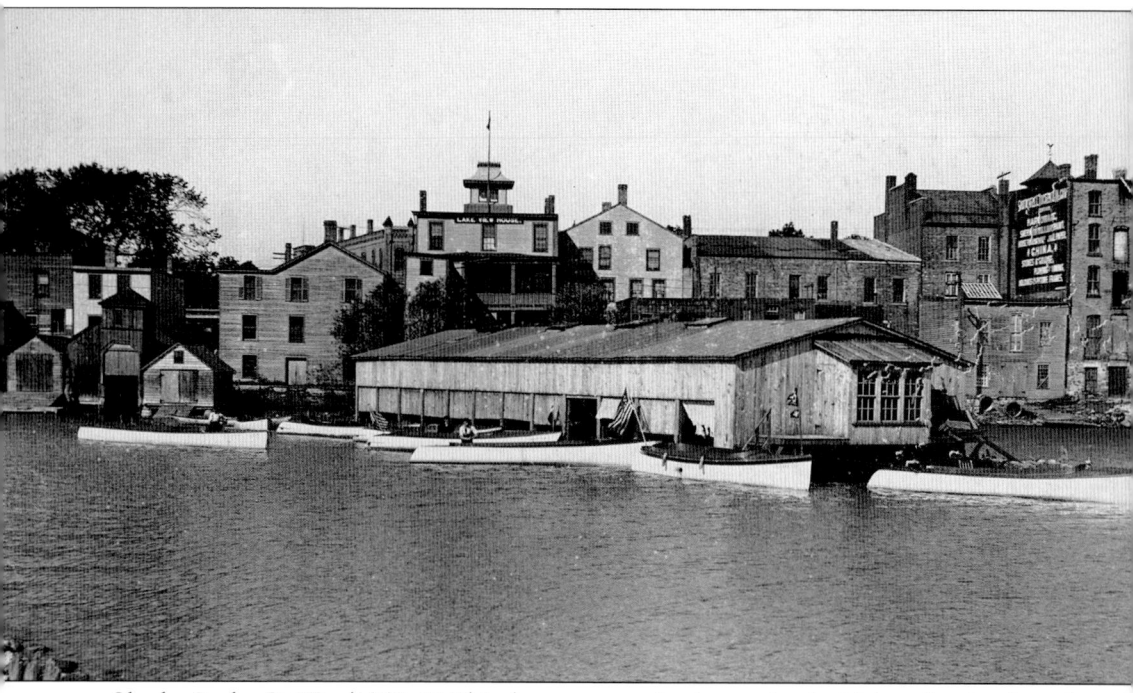

Charles Pardee DeWitt (1868–1943) is the man most closely associated with boat liveries along the outlet. He was active in politics, serving as trustee and mayor of Skaneateles. He was the owner and proprietor of what was probably the first livery boathouse. In 1909, he requested permission to rebuild it. Permission was granted with the understanding that no more state property would be preempted by Dewitt and that no one else would be allowed to build on state property without the sanction of the superintendent of public works. Shortly after this, Dewitt retired from the livery business and went to manage the Skaneateles Kraut Company, where he worked for years.

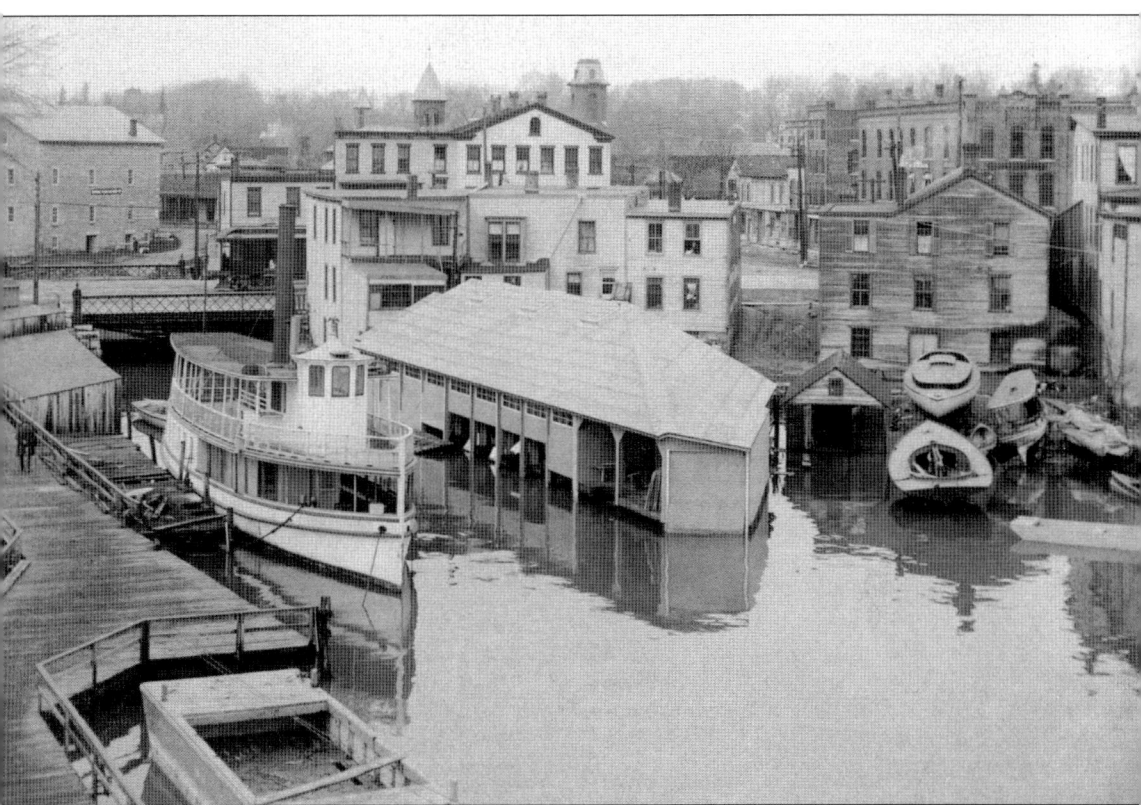

In 1907, the *Skaneateles Democrat* reported, "Vice Commodore William H. Olmstead of the Skaneateles Yacht Club has purchased a plot of land bordering the outlet in the rear of the Hall Block and in company with other Syracusans owning motorboats on the lake, will build a boathouse with twelve or fifteen slips for the accommodation of their crafts. The boathouse will be of tasteful design with a veranda facing the lake and the environments, so far as possible, to be beautiful with a lawn and gravel walk." Construction began in November 1907 and, as seen in the image, delivered what was promised, with the exception of the lawn and gravel walk.

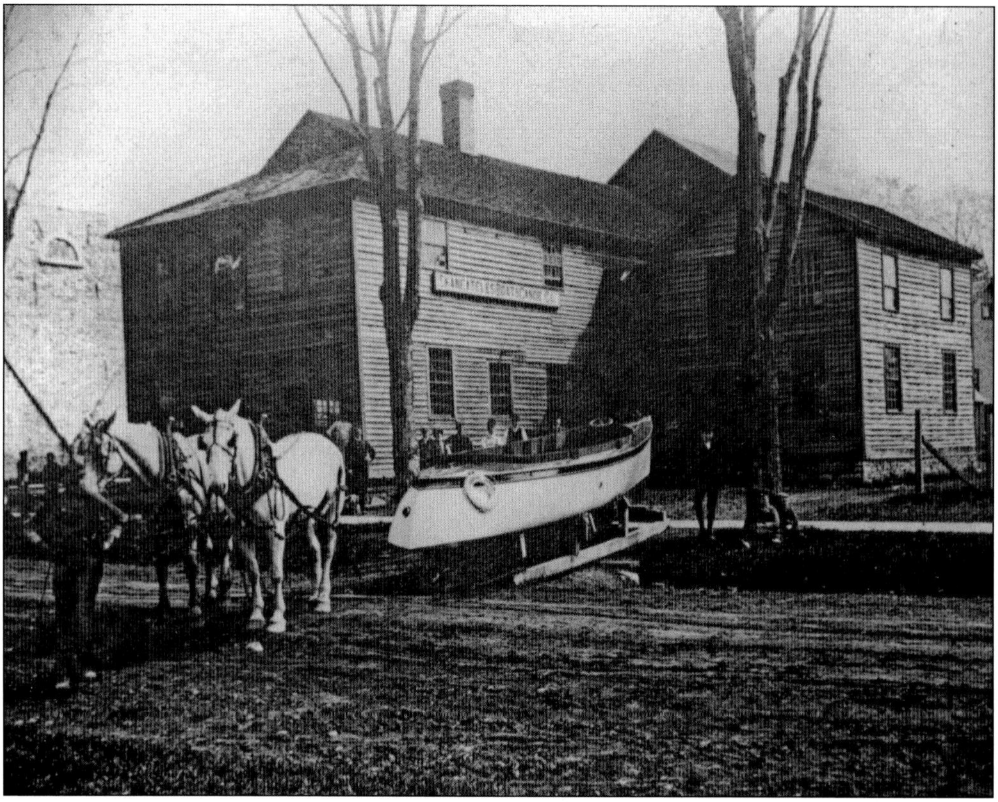

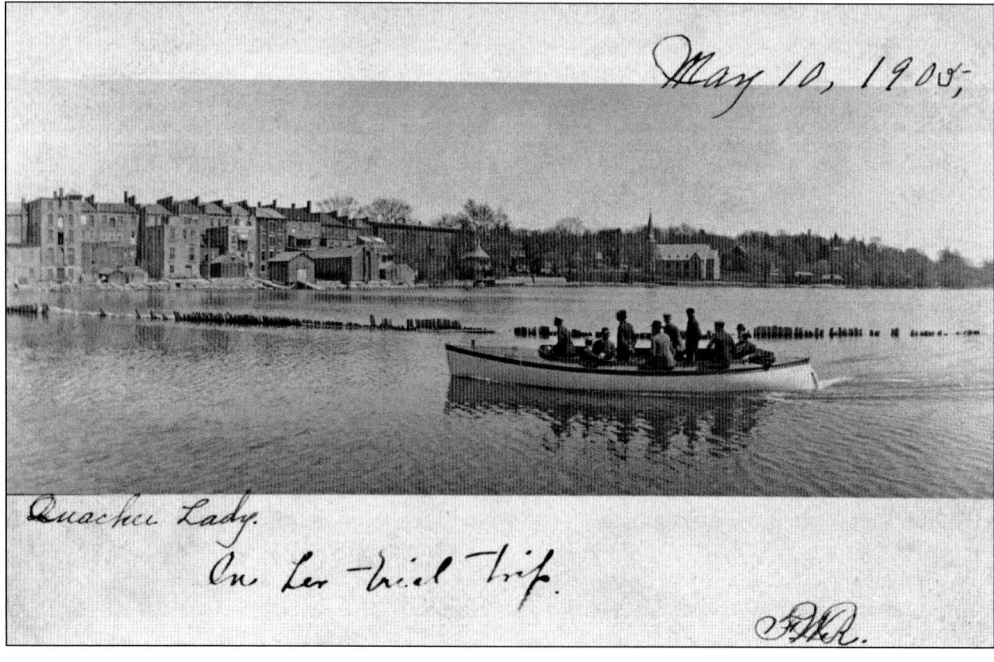

The *Quaker Lady*, a 28-foot gas-powered boat, was built by the Syracuse Boat and Canoe Company for Vice Commodore Olmstead. In the photographs, she is seen leaving the boat company in preparation for her trial voyage on the lake and a new home in the livery.

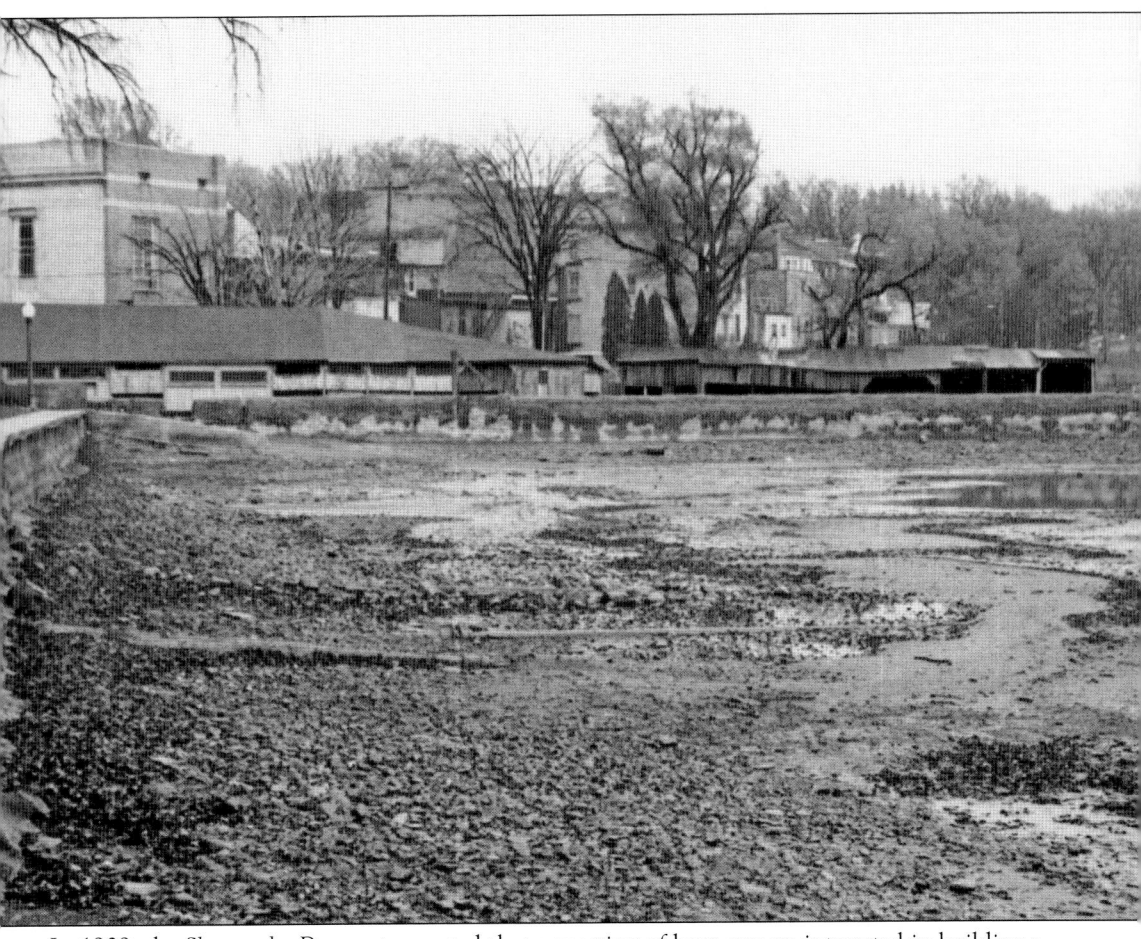

In 1909, the *Skaneateles Democrat* reported that a meeting of boat owners interested in building a boat livery next to the Dewitt boat livery was held, and a committee was appointed to secure bids and proceed with construction. The new livery will contain 17 slips. The architecture will conform to the lines of the Dewitt Livery structure. Many years later, in 1989, the two liveries remained standing when the lake was dredged to repair the pier, as seen in the photograph.

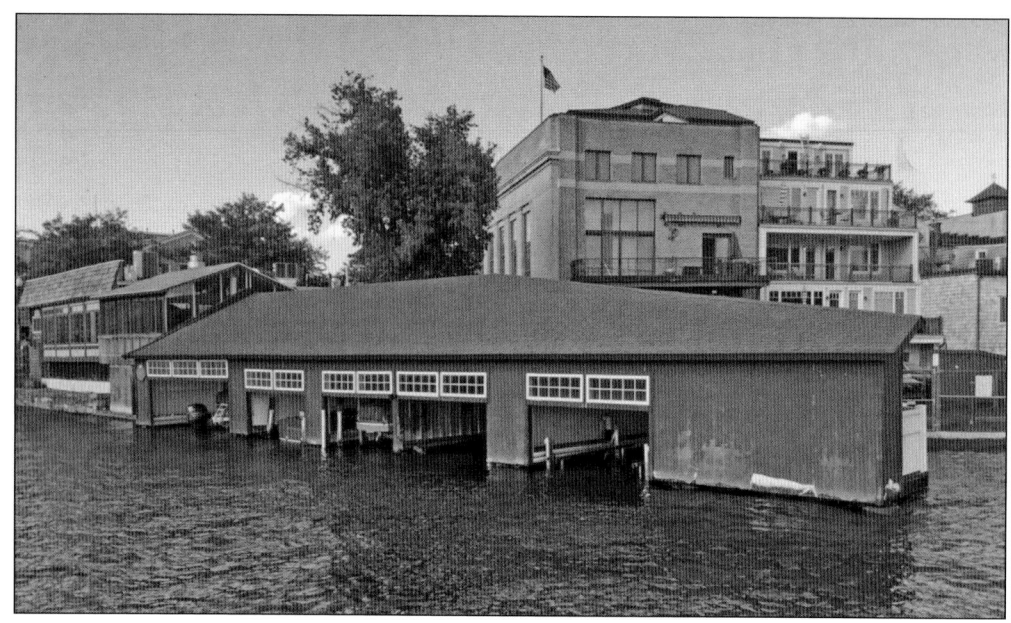

The boathouses that once existed on the shoreline behind the village businesses are gone. The boat liveries with slips have always been privately owned. At times, they have been subdivided. The slips are used by the owners or rented to others. Maintenance is the responsibility of the owners. In 2006, the Skaneateles Landmark Historical Preservation Committee voted to reconstruct one of the two remaining liveries on the outlet. Today, two well-tended liveries remain on the outlet.

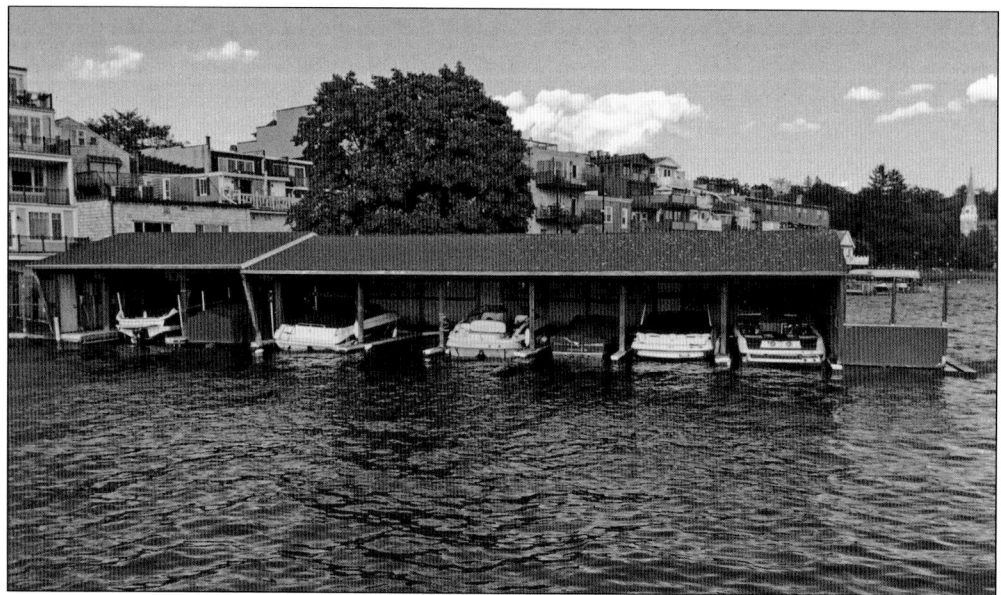

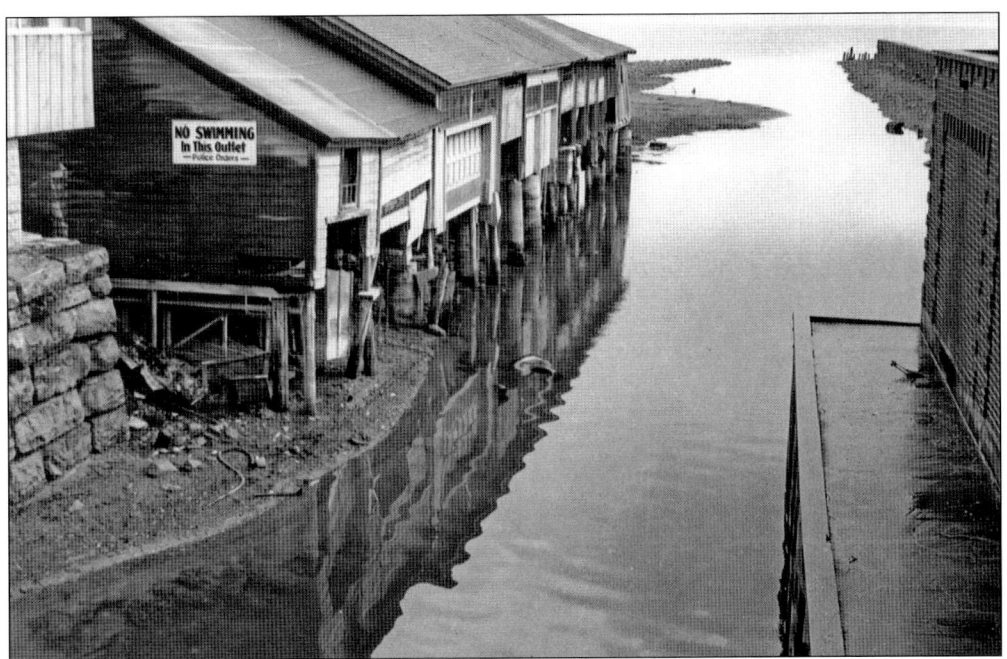

In 1920, the steamboats had stopped running. The outlet became a favorite swimming hole. On a hot summer day, a "no swimming" sign was not a deterrent to a rooftop climb and a plunge into the deep, cool water of the outlet.

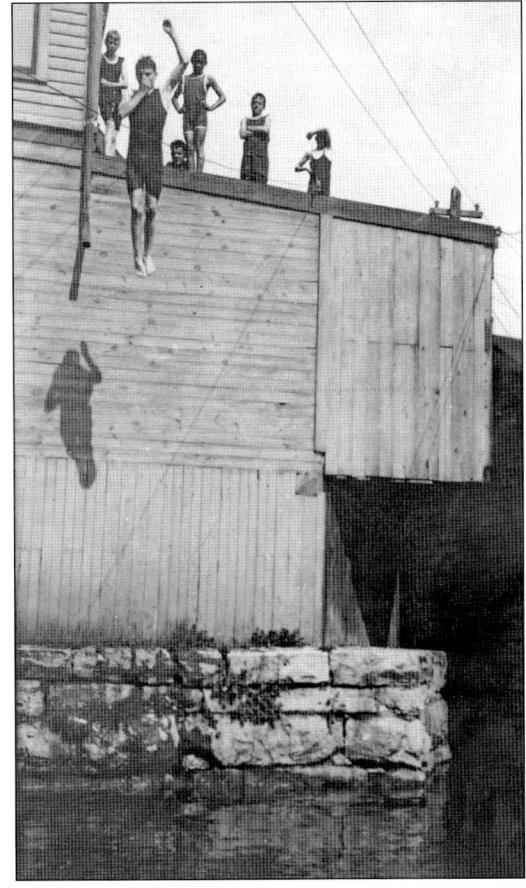

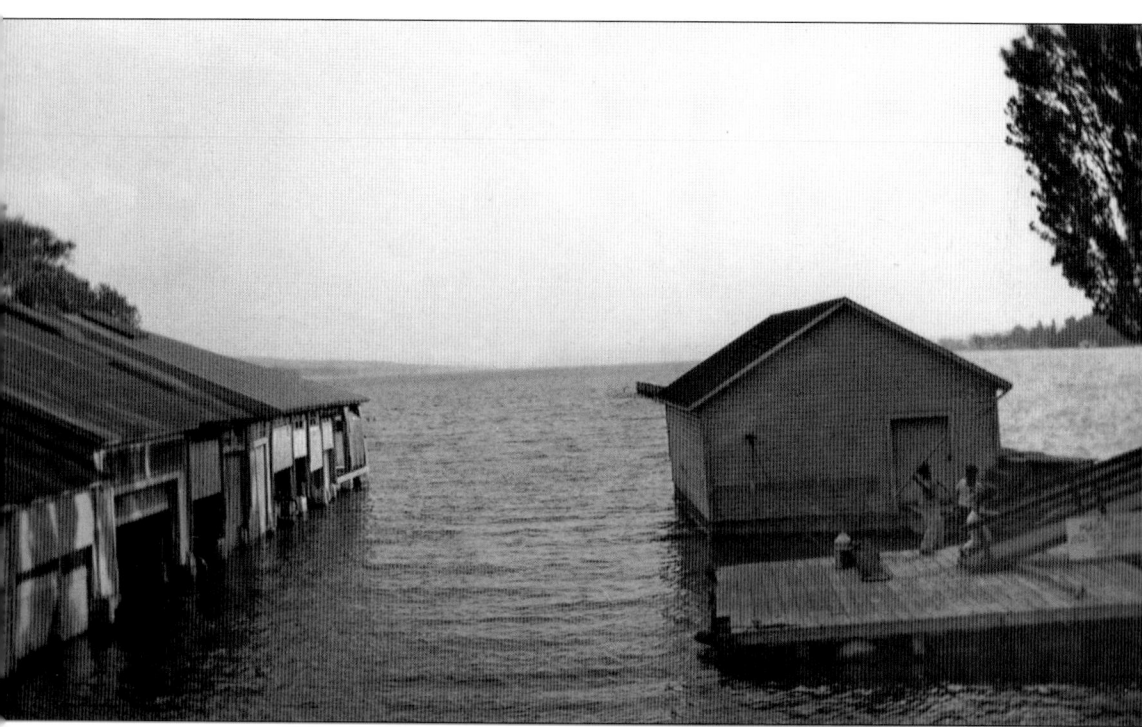

The age of the old boathouse adjacent to the seawall in the photograph is uncertain. In the early 1900s, it was owned by the village and served as a drop-off point for mail to be delivered by boat to residents on the lake. In 1940, the seawall was in need of repair. The village deeded the boathouse to Syracuse with the agreement that the seawall would be repaired and a new building would accommodate two watershed boats and a fire department boat. In 1990, the boathouse was again renovated.

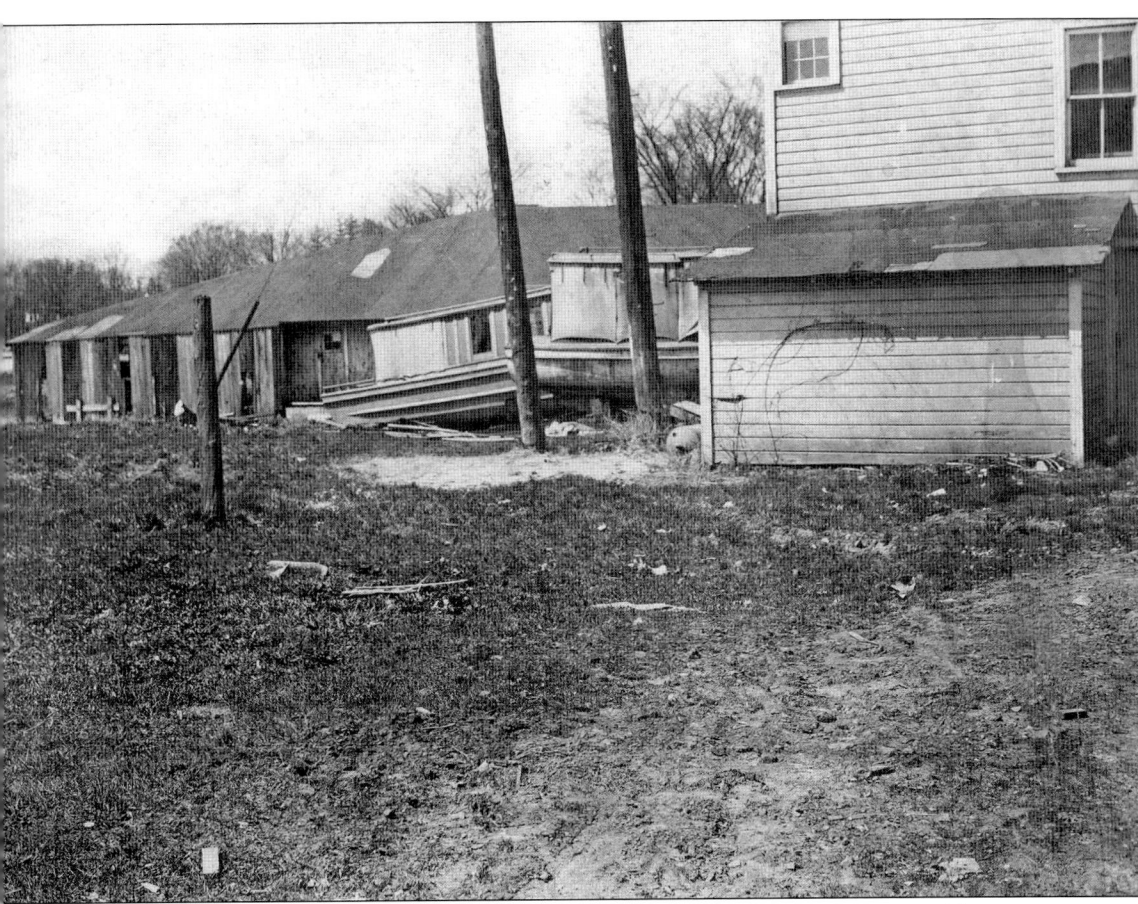

Boathouses, liveries, and docks have always been at the mercy of normal erosion caused by water and destruction from storms. In April 1884, the *Skaneateles Democrat* reported that a "gentle zephyr" blew in from the south. This was a misnomer. "The south wind blew fiercely against the docks and walls at the north end of the lake. People were fearful that the steamer Glen Haven, which lay at the west end of the coffer dam, would be seriously damaged." The steamer was not badly damaged, but the steamboat dock, although strongly built and weighted down with railroad iron, was torn to pieces by the force of the waves. Hurricane Hazel roared into Skaneateles on a Friday night in October 1954. The *Skaneateles Press* reported in October 1954 that "Skaneateles Lake at the height of the hurricane was a sight to behold. The lake was a cauldron of seething foam as the angry winds, reaching a velocity from 65 to 90 miles an hour, raged and lashed through the community. The Stinson boat line's mailboat, being taken out of the water, was blown on the beach and damaged." The photograph is a good depiction of the force of Mother Nature.

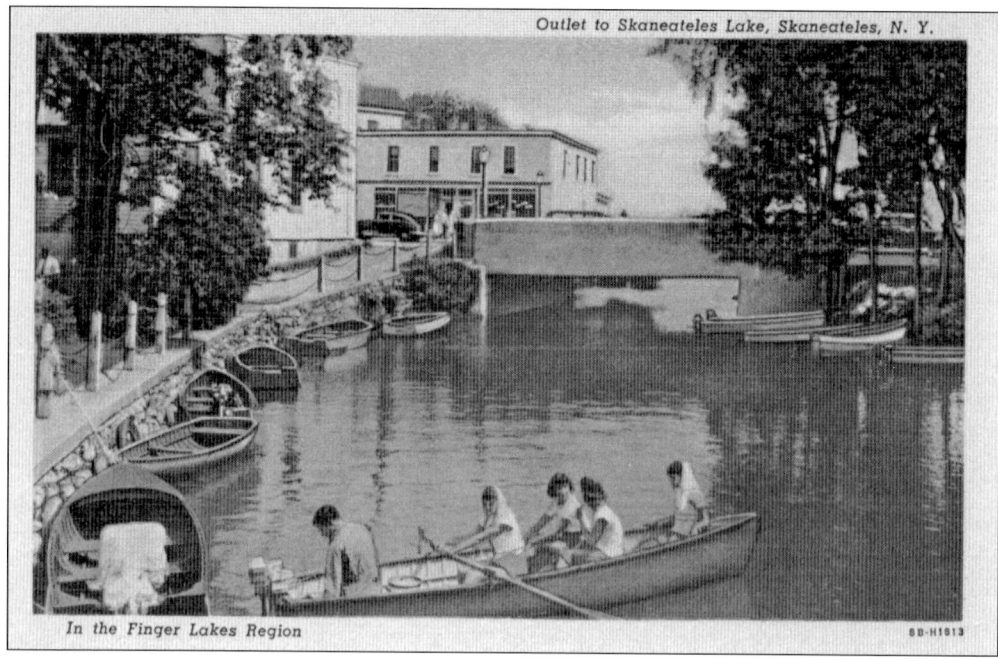

Following the demise of the steamboats, the outlet waters were calmer and less congested. Owners of small boats used the south end of the outlet adjacent to the dam for easy access to the lake and boat storage. In the 1980s, local residents complained about the boat storage by people who did not pay waterfront taxes. The village subsequently banned the outlet boat storage.

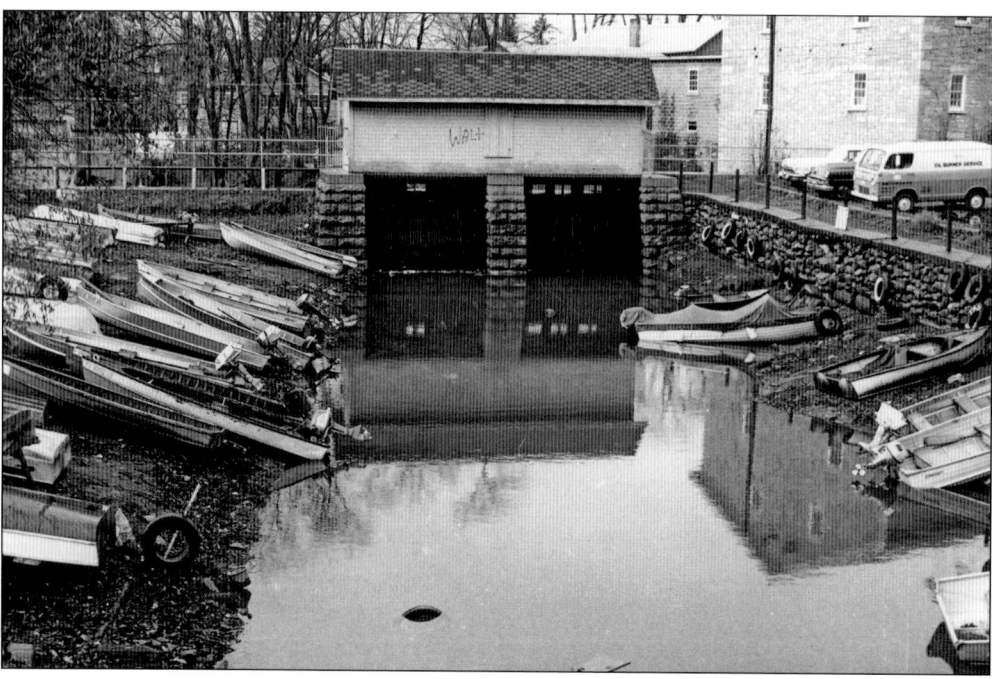

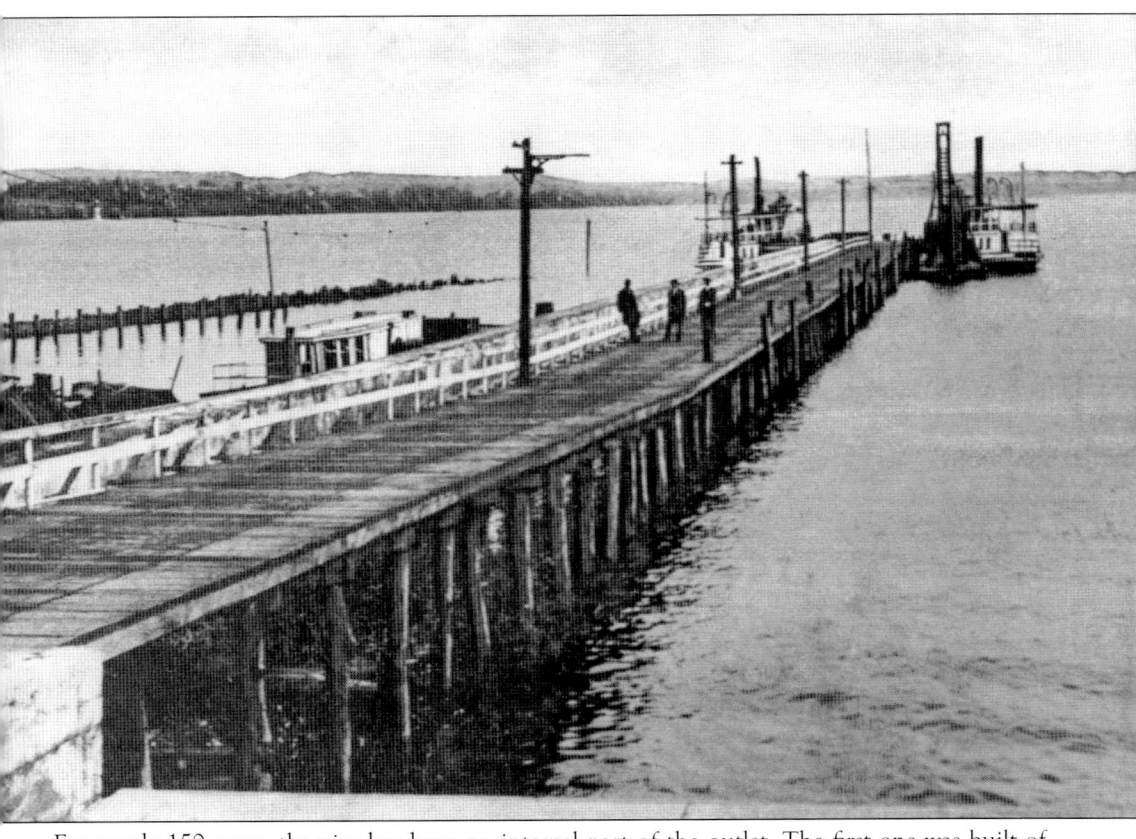

For nearly 150 years, the pier has been an integral part of the outlet. The first one was built of wood in 1876 and was referred to as the "steamboat wharf," where passengers boarded steamboats for trips to their destinations on the lake. It was noted in the *Skaneateles Free Press* in 1906 that "Atlantic City has its boardwalk and Skaneateles its steamboat pier which is fast becoming known as 'lover's lane'. When the evening shades are falling over this good old town of ours, then our young people take advantage of this promenade."

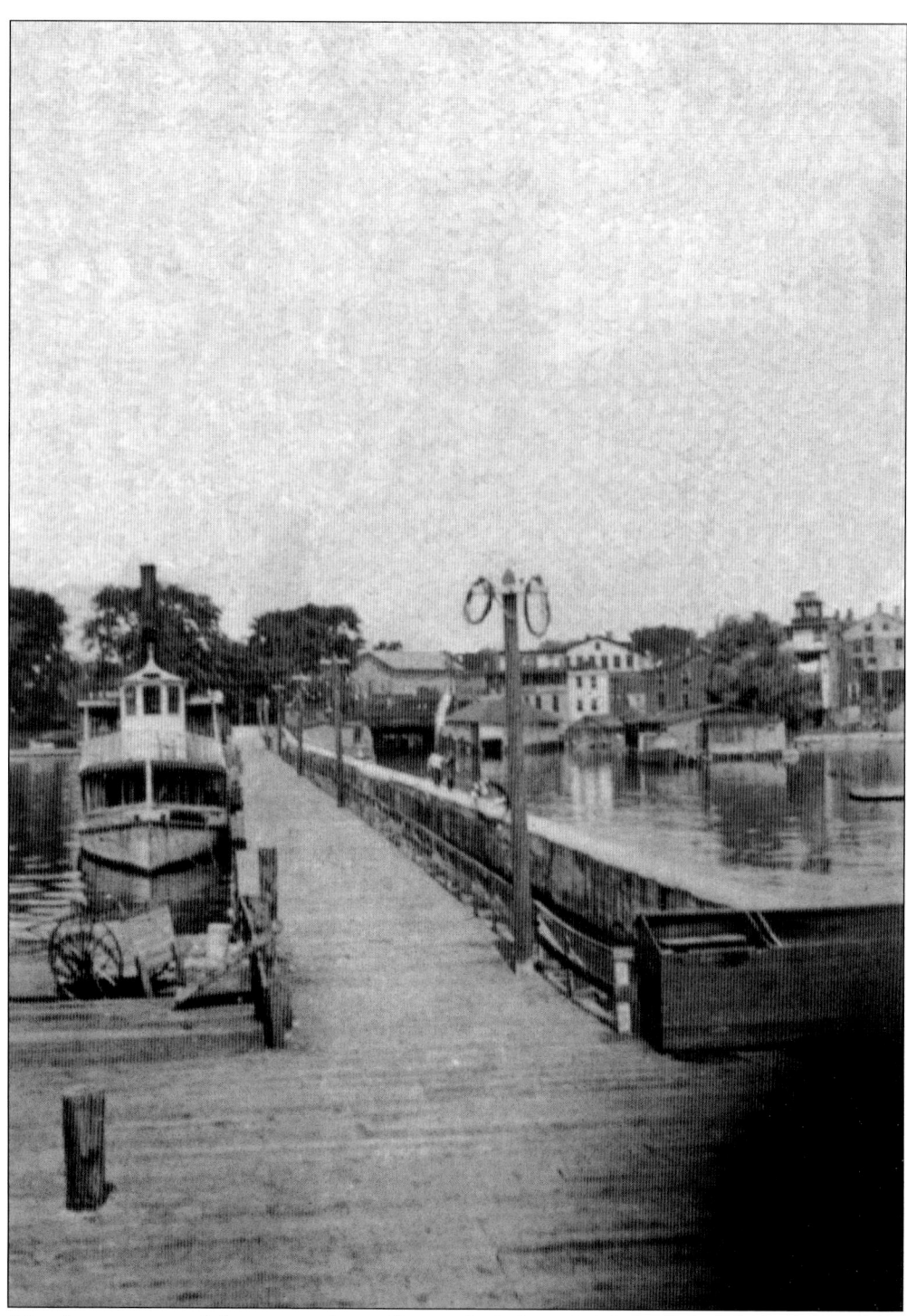
After Syracuse secured the water rights to Skaneateles Lake, a 500-foot concrete and stone jetty was built by the city next to the steamboat wharf in 1906 to prevent silt from filling the outlet. It also provided a place for excursion steamboats to dock. The old wharf became out of use following the demise of the steamboat era in 1920.

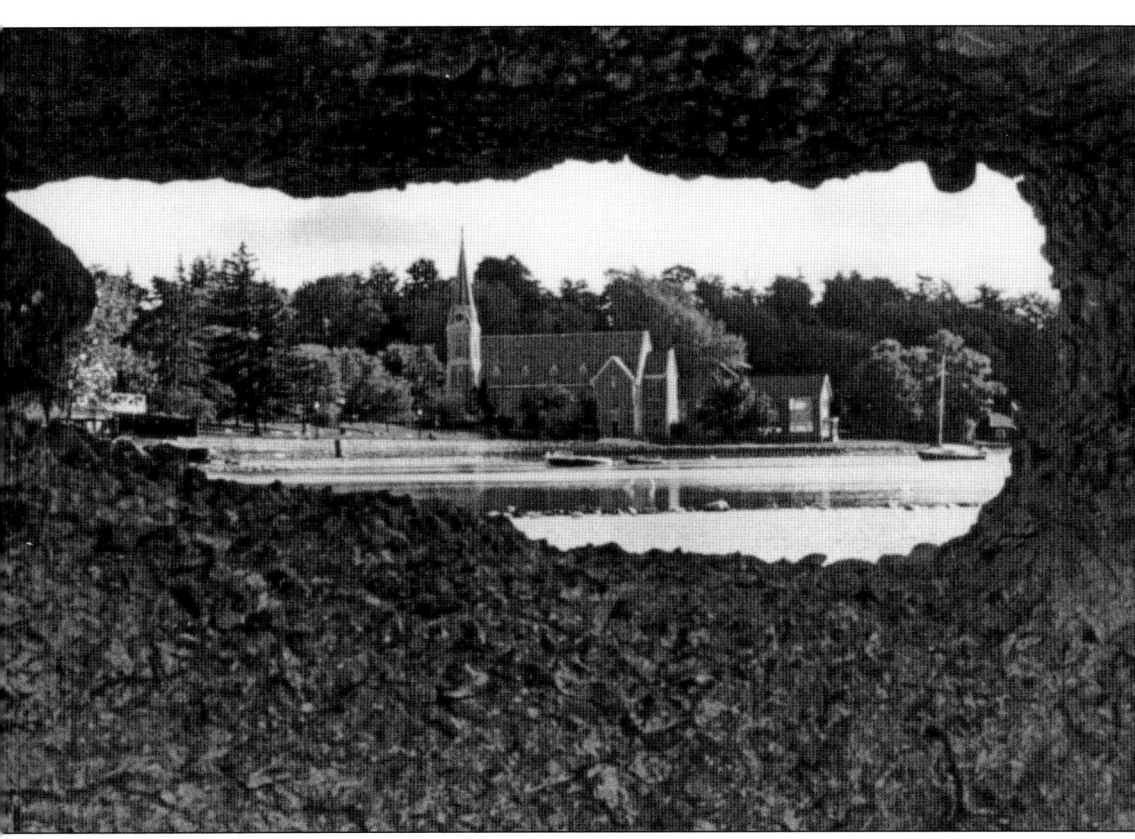

Over the years, the jetty started to crumble, and holes started to develop. The City of Syracuse maintained ownership of the pier but, in the 1960s, was not interested in repairing it as the pier no longer served a purpose. The *Skaneateles Press* reported on November 4, 1963, that the pier could be purchased from the city for $1. However, the liability and cost to the village for repair would impose a tax burden on the village citizens. A proposal for repair was made to the city, which was approved, but the city would assume no financial obligation. The Skaneateles Chamber of Commerce assumed the responsibility of raising funds through voluntary collection from civic-minded citizens. Collection cans were placed in stores and public places. Work was done, but it was only temporary.

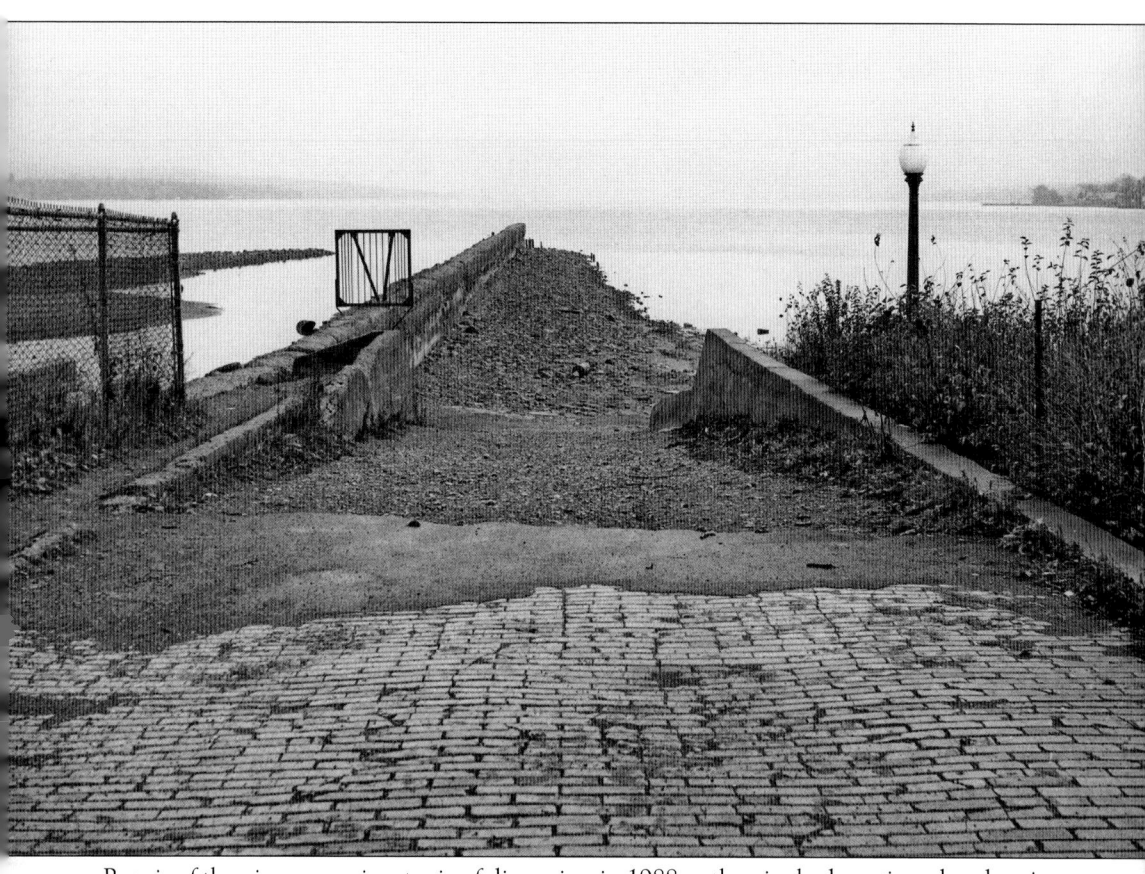

Repair of the pier was again a topic of discussion in 1988 as the pier had continued to deteriorate. A barrier had been constructed to prevent trespassing, but this did not deter avid fishermen and adventurous swimmers. The City of Syracuse was again approached regarding repair and replacement. This time, an agreement was reached; the cost was $390,000.

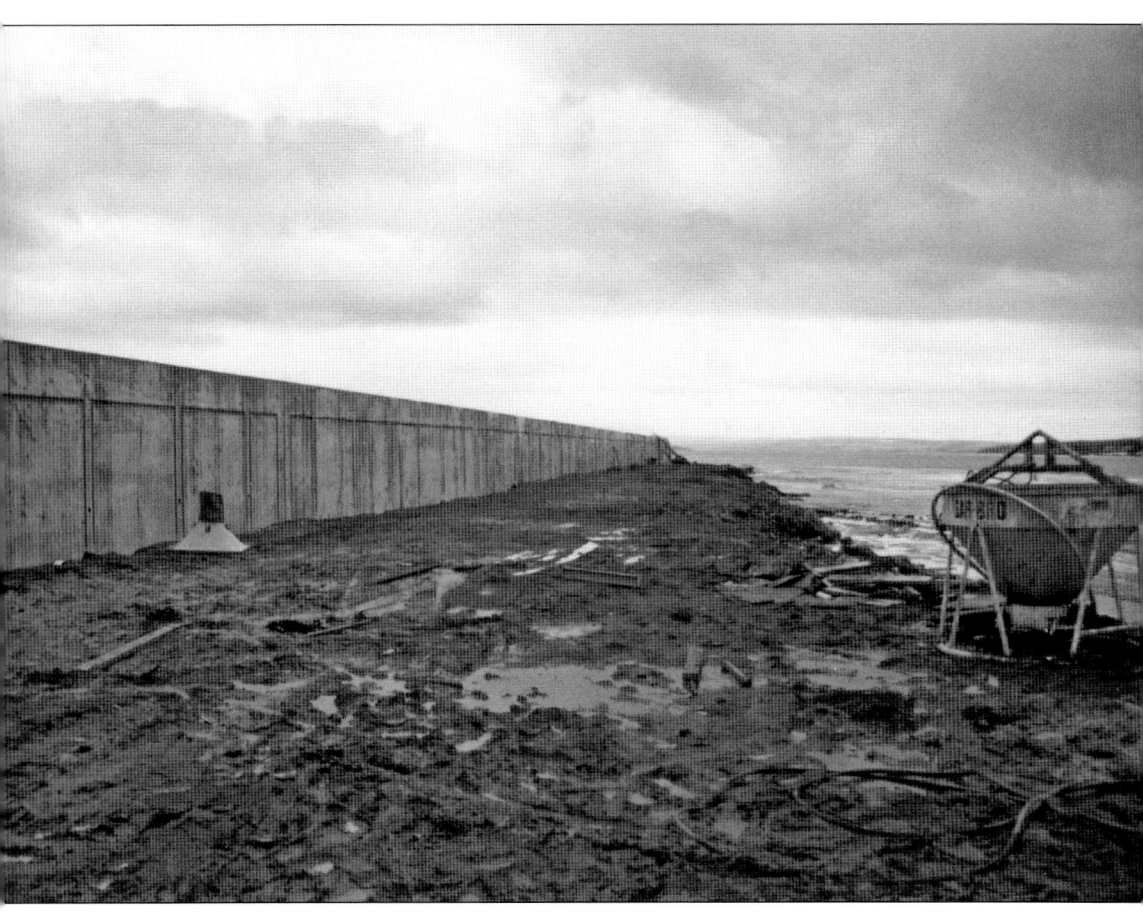
The canal and the shoreline were dredged in early 1989. The new pier was constructed by pouring concrete through wire mesh over the old form that was salvageable. The pier was widened, and handrails were installed. Work was completed in the spring of 1989.

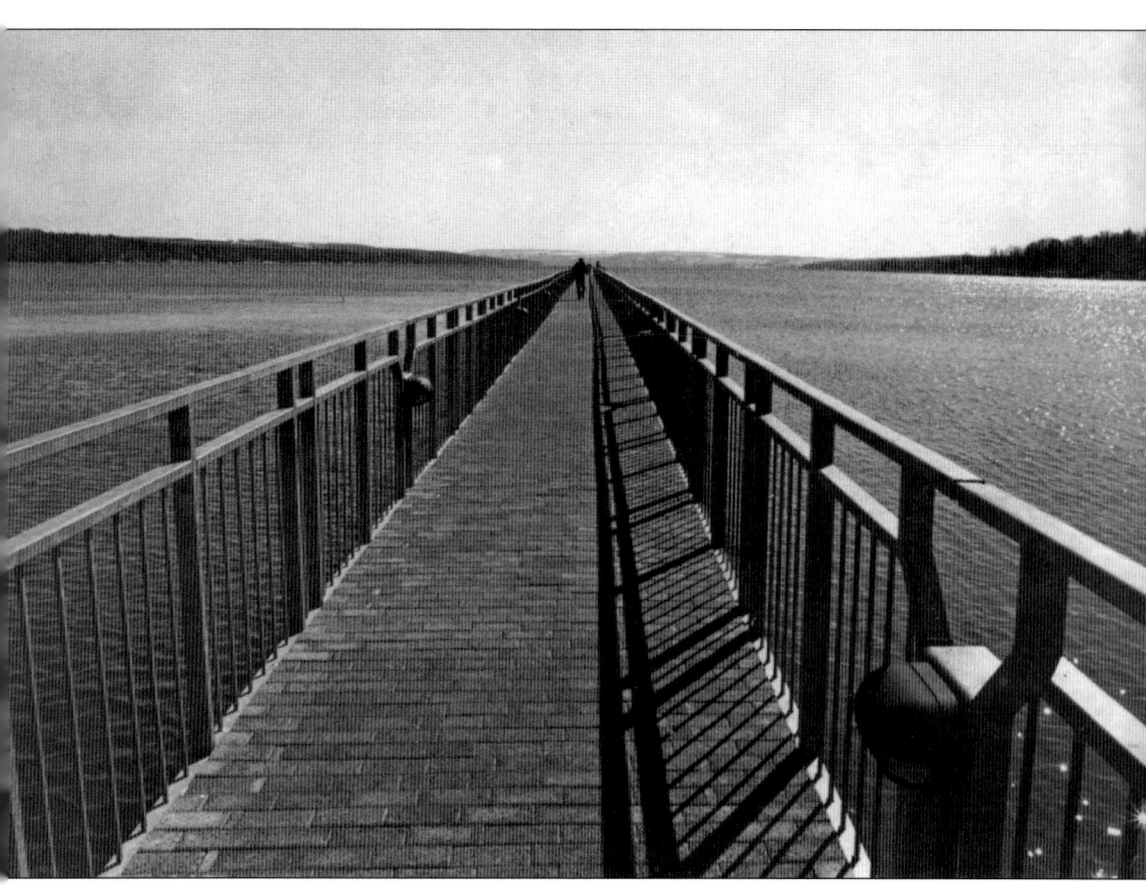

In 2012, the Skaneateles Chamber of Commerce proposed building a $1 million permanent floating dock adjacent to the pier. It replaced the temporary dock that volunteers put in and removed each year. The project had been researched since 2002. Syracuse University civil and environmental engineering students developed design and cost projections for this project, which were approved. Grants and donations provided funding. Today, those who come by boat to the village can park adjacent to the pier. People on foot can walk along the pier, enjoying views of the east and west shores.

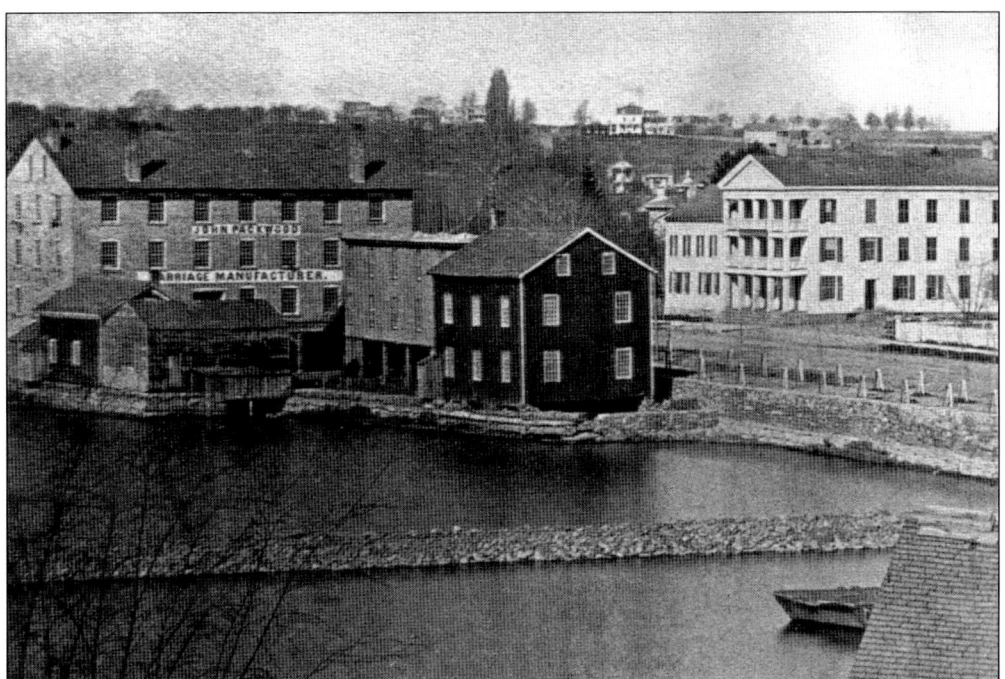

Between 1865 and 1886, the lakeshore property adjacent to the outlet was the site of several business establishments. The most prominent was the Packwood Carriage Factory. The factory was built by John Packwood, who also owned the Packwood House (today's Sherwood Inn). The land along the shore was sold to Joab Clift in 1887. The factory was torn down in 1888.

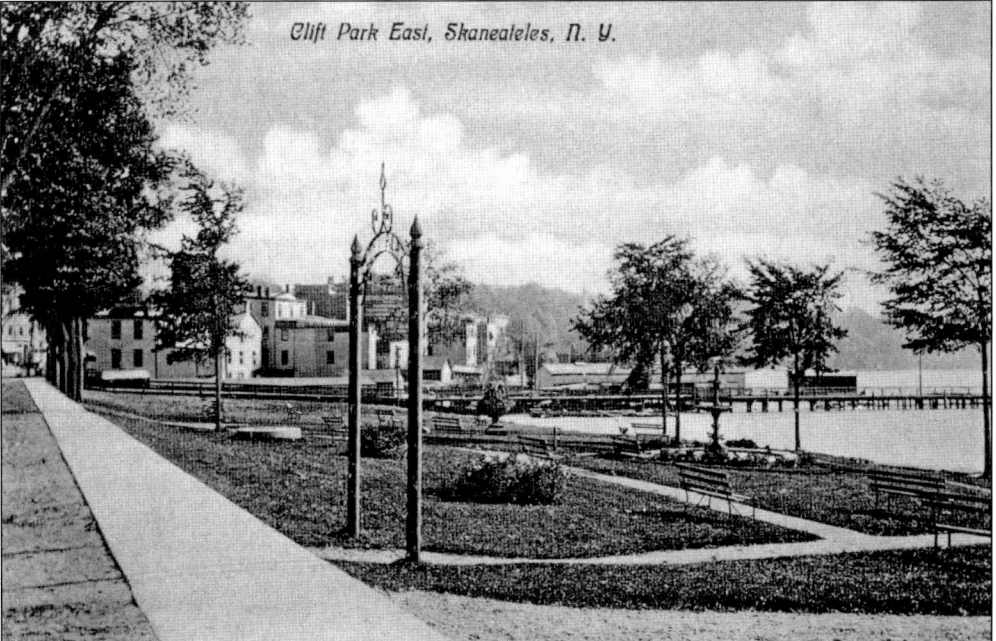

In 1892, Joab Clift sold the land along the shoreline to the village to be used as a park with the understanding that the park would be named for him. Today, Clift Park is a public recreational area offering swimming, boating, and entertainment venues.

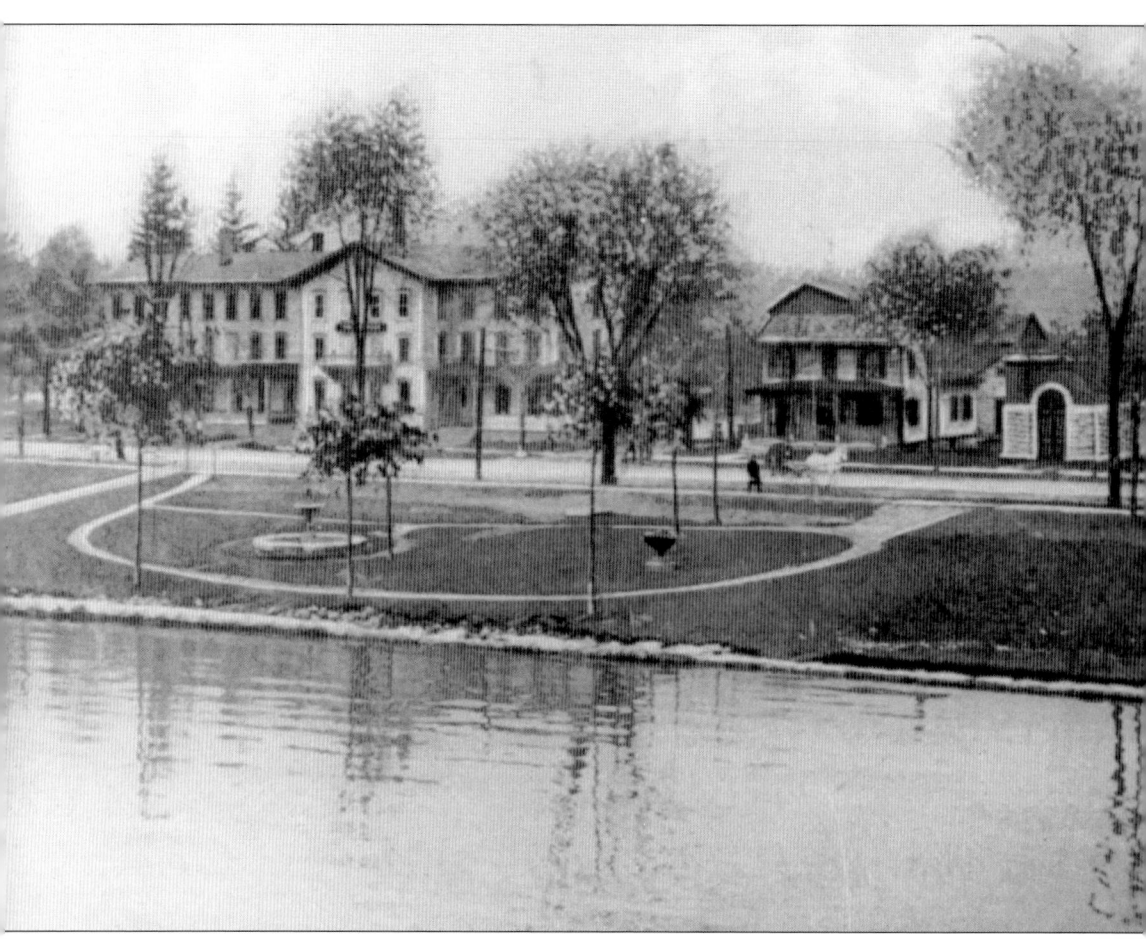

Known today as the Sherwood Inn, the c. 1880 photograph shows the Packwood House. In 1807, Isaac Sherwood built an inn on this site to accommodate his growing stagecoach business. John Packwood, a carriage manufacturer, purchased the property and completely renovated it in 1871. He sold the inn to Edward A. Andrews in 1874. They managed the inn for 45 years. Although the ownership and name of the inn changed many times over the years, the inn once again bears the "Sherwood" name in order to pay homage to the man who built the original Sherwood Inn.

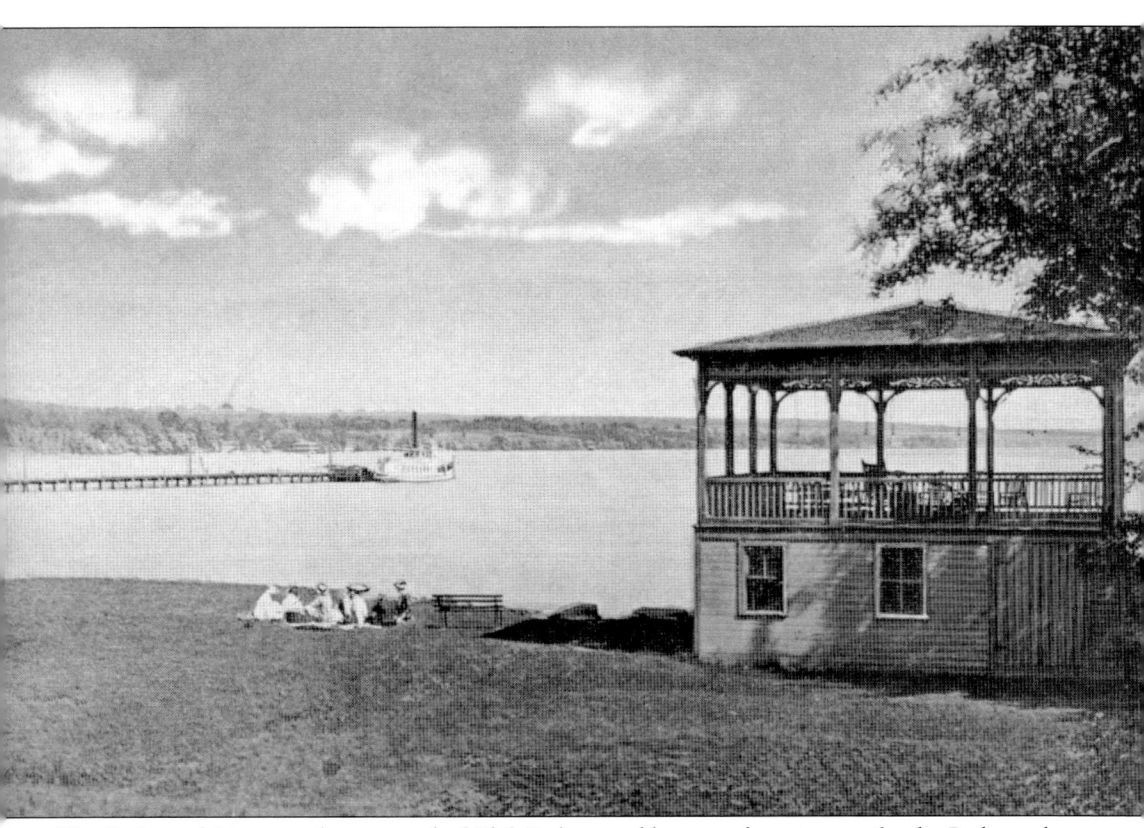

The Packwood Livery, at the west end of Clift Park, stored boats and equipment for the Packwood House. In May 1906, the *Skaneateles Democrat* reported that "after a successful proprietorship for a period of several years, Charles P. Dewitt has sold the Packwood Livery to his brother E.T. Dewitt and Harry N. Blair. The new proprietors will maintain the reputation of the Packwood Livery for fine quality and good service."

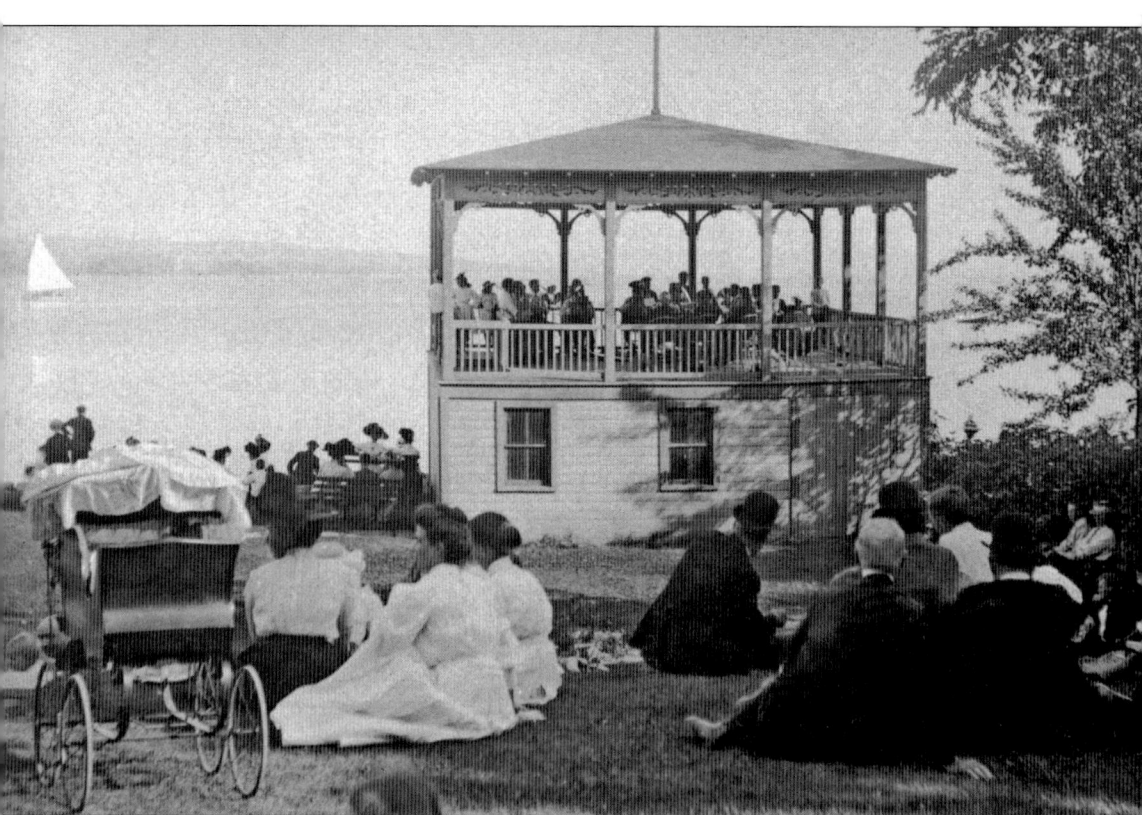

The upper floor of the Packwood Livery was also a venue for band concerts by the lake. In July 1908, the *Skaneateles Democrat* suggested that "The village fathers ought to be kind enough to grant the privilege to the band to have a free arc lamp installed in the Packwood livery for their use at concerts. A band cannot see music in the dark."

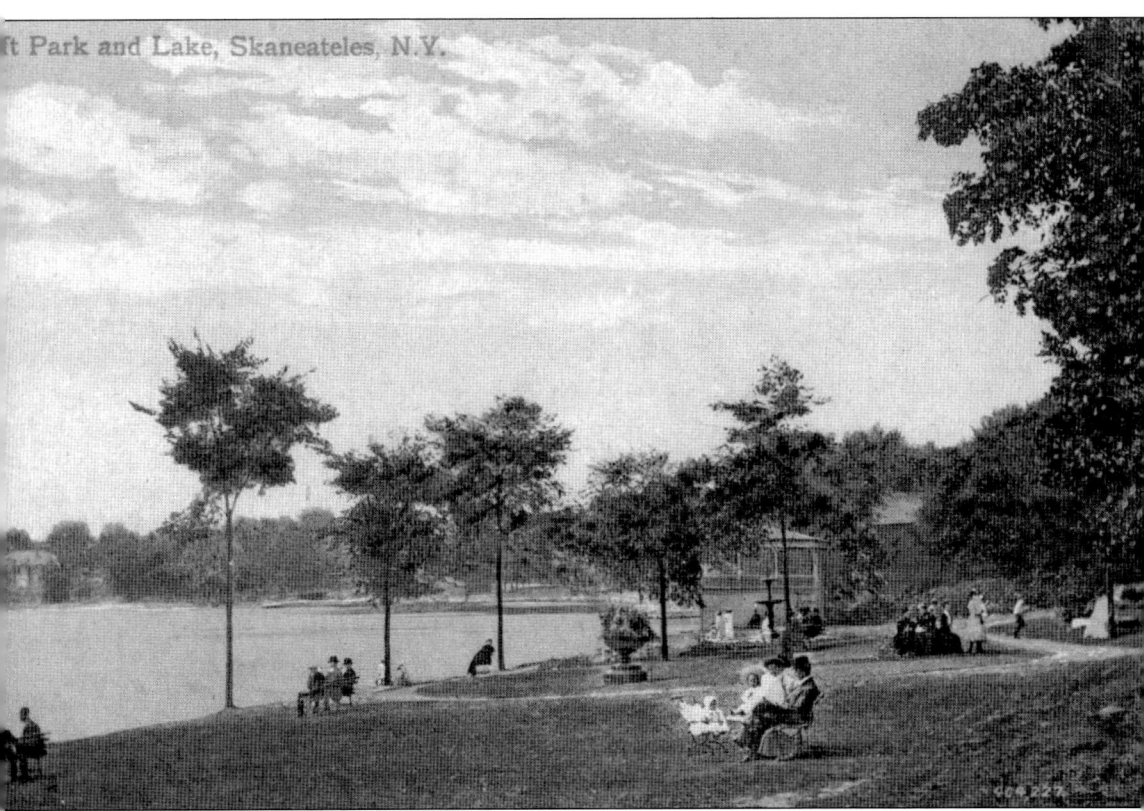

In 1899, the state determined that construction of a seawall was needed along the shoreline of Clift Park and the west arm of the coffer dam on the outlet to prevent the channel from filling with debris. It was reported in the *Skaneateles Free Press* on March 10, 1905, "The state determined that the coffer dam was unsightly and steps should be taken to put the property in harmony with its surroundings." C.D. Beebe, president of the Auburn and Syracuse Electric Railway and owner of the steamboats, placed the only construction bid to build a seawall and make improvements to the steamboat dock. At the state's expense of $12,000, the seawall was built.

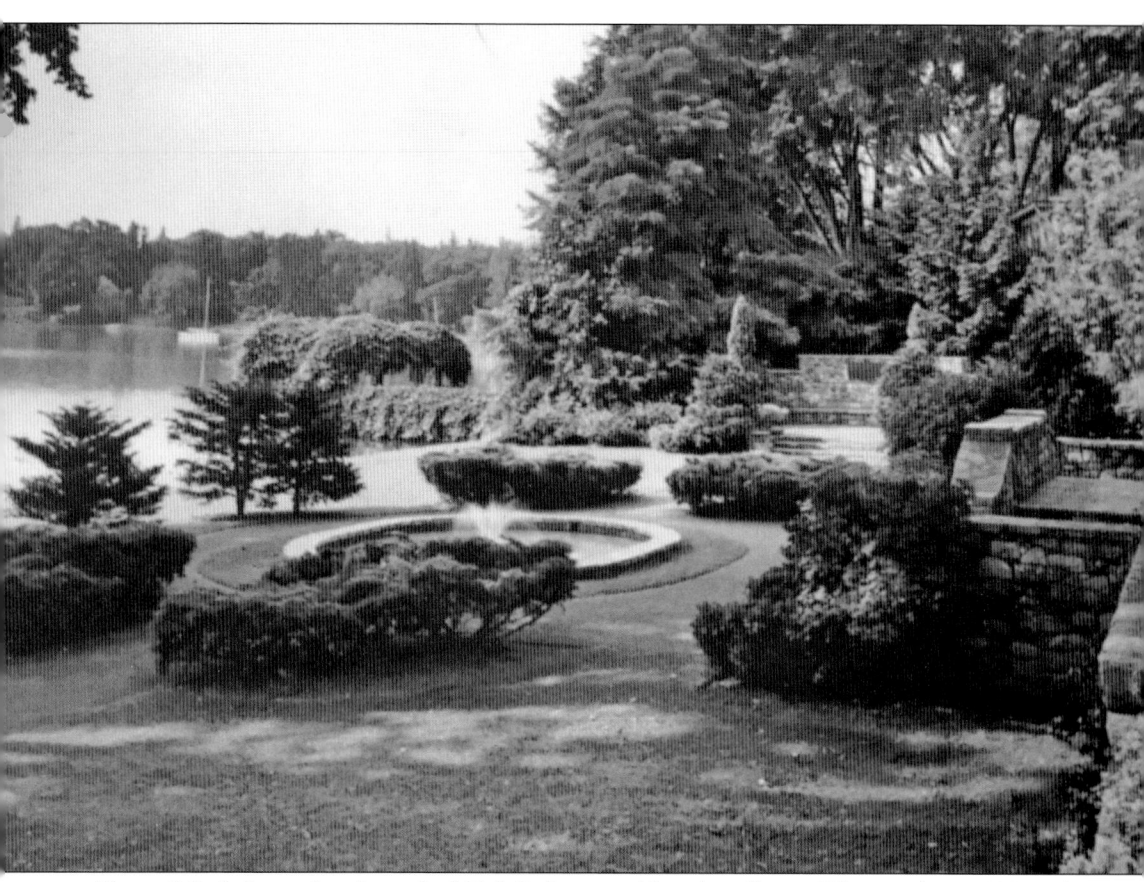

Shotwell Park, located at the end of Clift Park, was sold to the village of Skaneateles in 1934 to be used as a memorial park. Funds to purchase and beautify the park were bequeathed by Florence Thorne Shotwell and dedicated to her late husband, William J. Shotwell, in 1926. Louisa Shotwell, the niece of William Shotwell, later bequeathed funds to maintain the park. On Memorial Day in 1936, the Veteran's Memorial Park was dedicated to those who served in the Spanish-American War and World War I. The park has been rededicated several times, honoring those who have served in subsequent wars.

Four

THE WEST SHORE

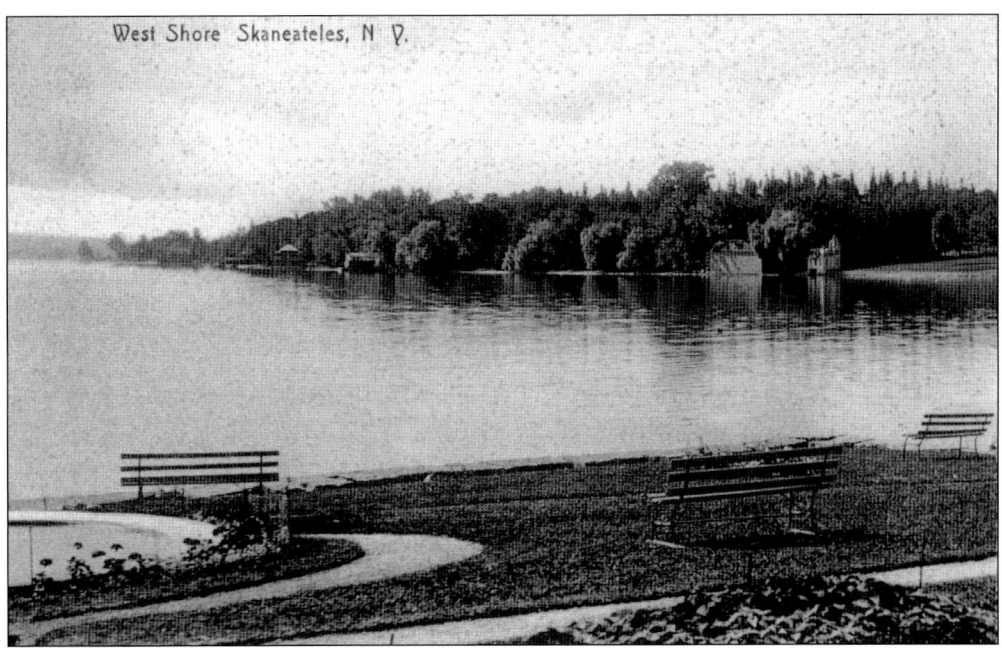

Heading south on West Lake Street from Clift Park is an area known as the Gold Coast, a reference to the elegant homes and boathouses built in the 1800s. John Wheeler and George Barber were the architects and builders of many of the beautiful boathouses. For the next 14 miles south along Route 41A, the landscape is ever-changing. Farmland, vineyards, lakeside homes, waterfalls, small hamlets, and a large conservation area have developed through the 19th and 20th centuries.

The Earll Waller boathouse at 3 West Lake Street was built in 1880 by Julius H. Waller (1857–1882). He and his sister, Julia Waller, inherited the property from their father, a wealthy paper manufacturer in Hartlot, New York.

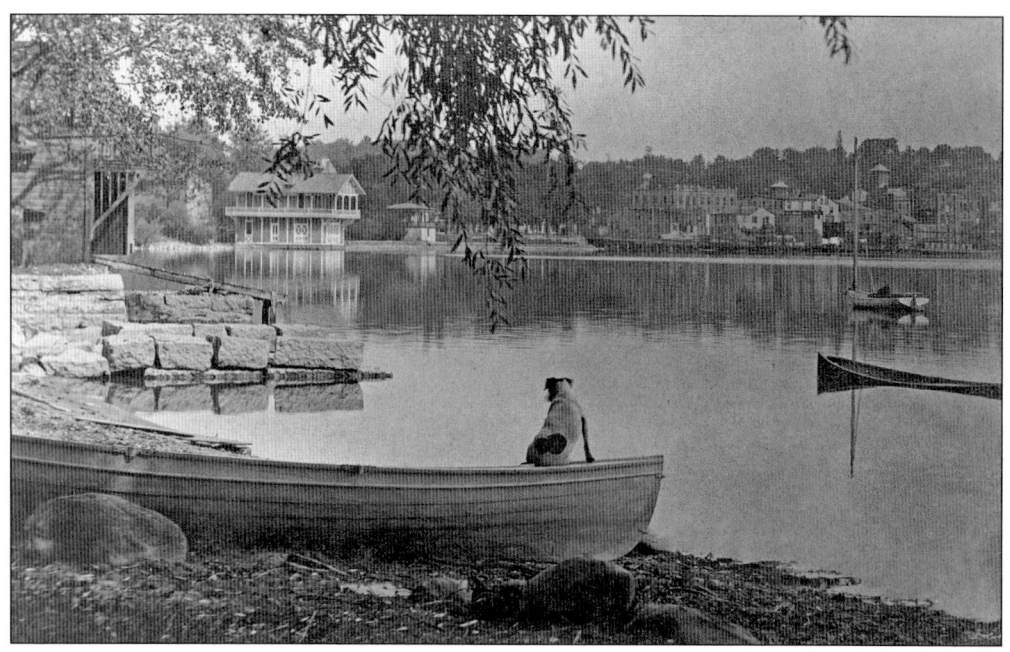

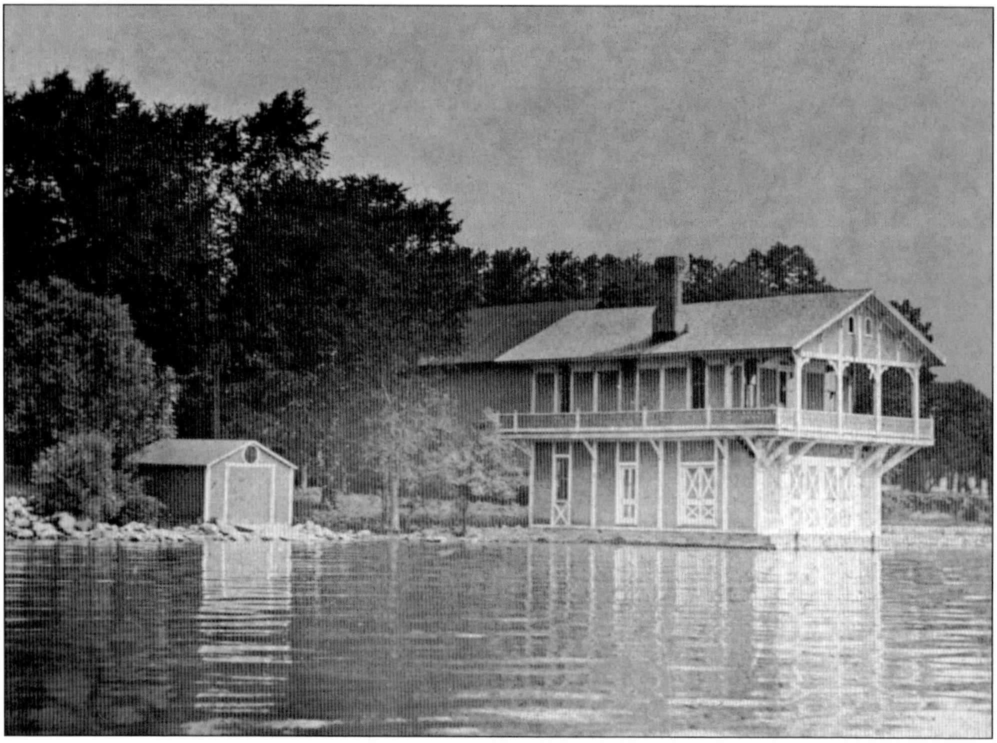

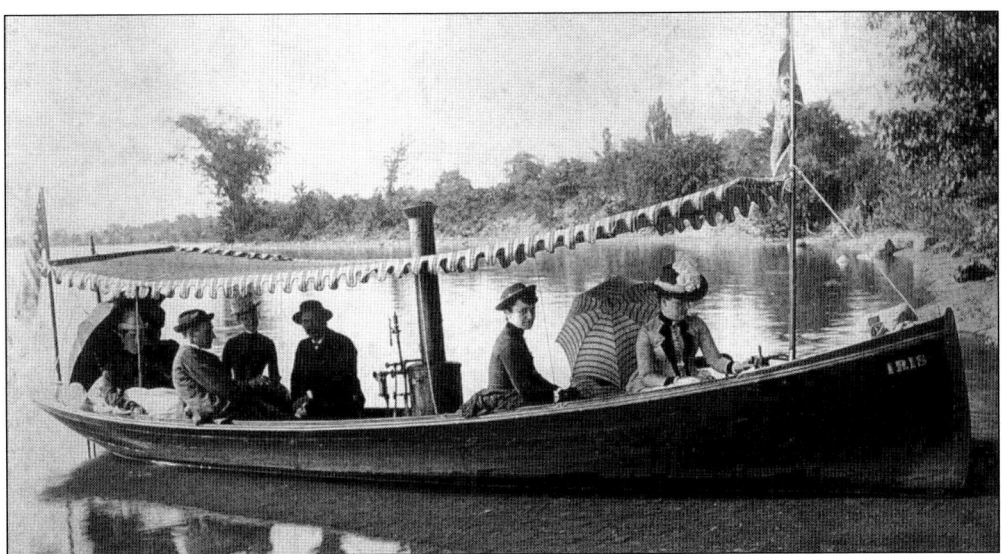

Despite the loss of one eye and his hearing, young Julius Waller was an avid sailor. His steam launch, the *Iris*, seen in the photograph, was one of the fastest power crafts on the lake. In 1882, he was tragically killed in an ice boating accident.

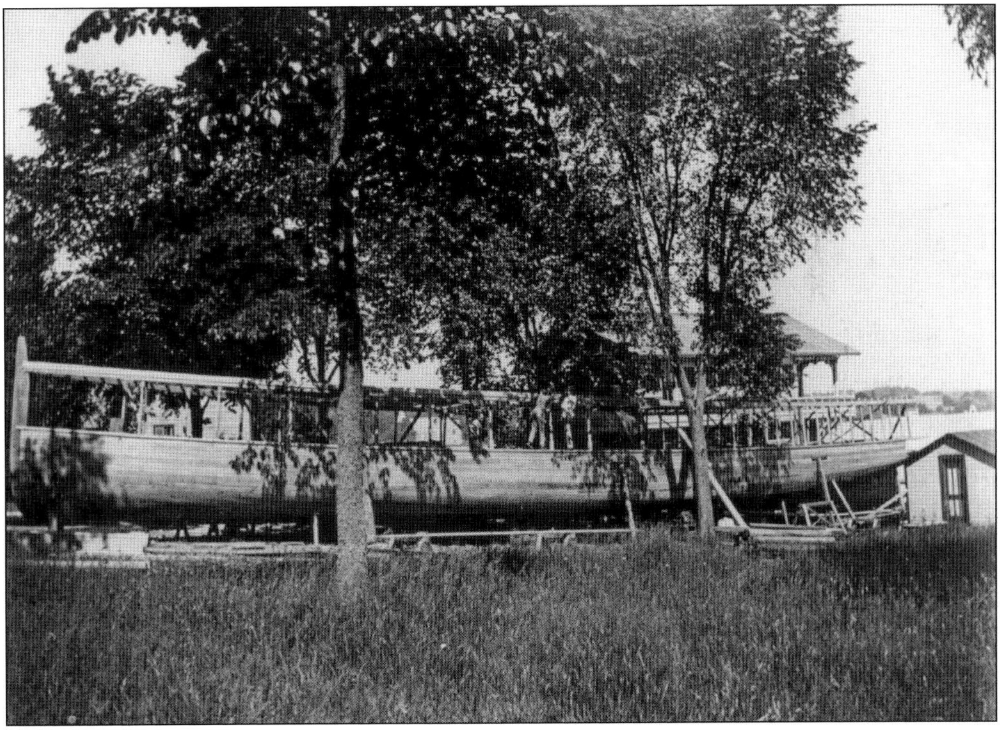

In 1899, the construction of the largest steamboat, the *City of Syracuse*, took place alongside the Earll Waller boathouse. The location of the property near the pier and outlet was the perfect place to launch and test the boat's performance. In 1913, Laura B. Fitch, who owned a portion of the Waller property, including the boathouse, was granted a permit to remodel the boathouse into a residence after it was moved to the street where it stands today.

The Fitch boathouse is perhaps the most iconic boathouse on the west side of Skaneateles Lake. Named for Laura Fitch, a cousin of Theodore Roosevelt, it was commissioned by Lucien Moses to be designed by John Wheeler. In September 1877, the *Skaneateles Democrat* reported, "Workmen have been engaged for the last week in laying a very substantial foundation at the south end of the Lucien Moses lot. Rumor hath it that a very handsome boathouse is to be elevated at said foundation in the n'ee style, two stories in height, the second story is to be fitted as a luxurious lounging place for its genial proprietor." A follow-up in the 1887 *Democrat* reported, "Thanks to Mr. Moses for his attempt to add to the beauty of our shore and view from the village . . . Mr. Moses will keep his beauty pure white, the only paint that agrees with a wooden structure." A main house had been planned but never built. It is interesting to note that when the lake level rose, Moses could not park his boat in the boathouse. The boathouse still adds beauty to the west shore today.

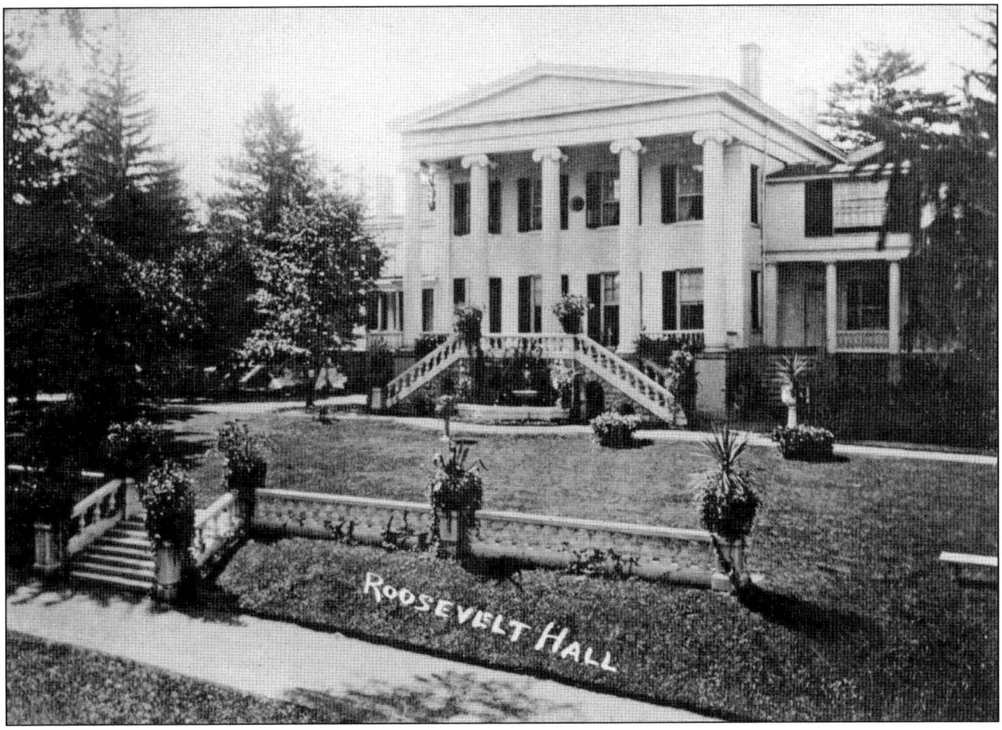

Originally from Westbury, Connecticut, the Willetts were a wealthy Quaker farming family. The family owned a great deal of land, extending from West Lake Street in the village to the town of Niles, nine miles southeast of Skaneateles. Sometime after the 1846 death of William Willett Sr., his widow, Annie, married Anson H. Lapham, who owned the 'Lake Home," later known as Roosevelt Hall. In 1872, William Willett Jr. purchased his magnificent home from his mother's estate and lived there until he sold it for $2000 in 1892.

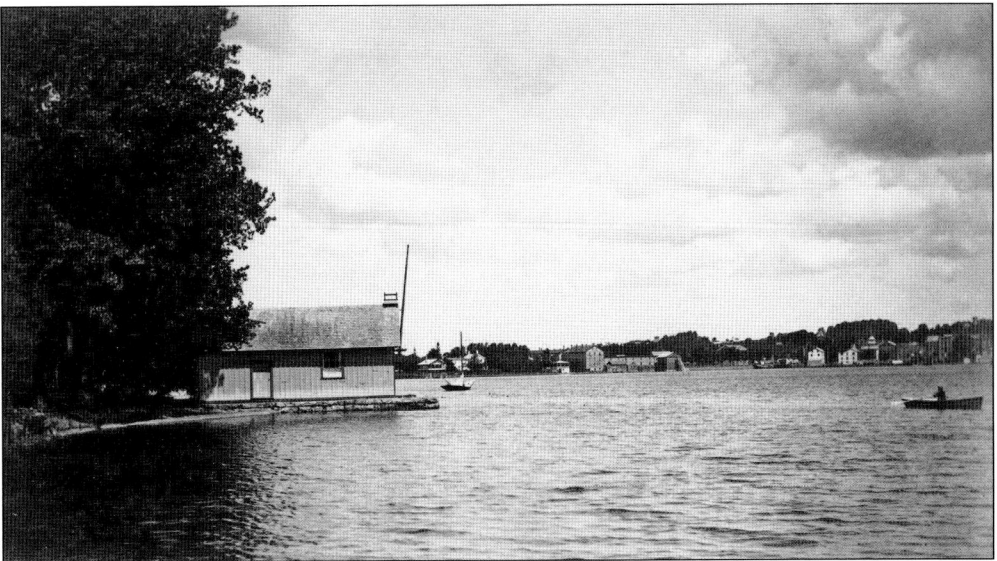

The Willetts boathouse was part of the Lake Home estate (Roosevelt Hall) and has since been torn down.

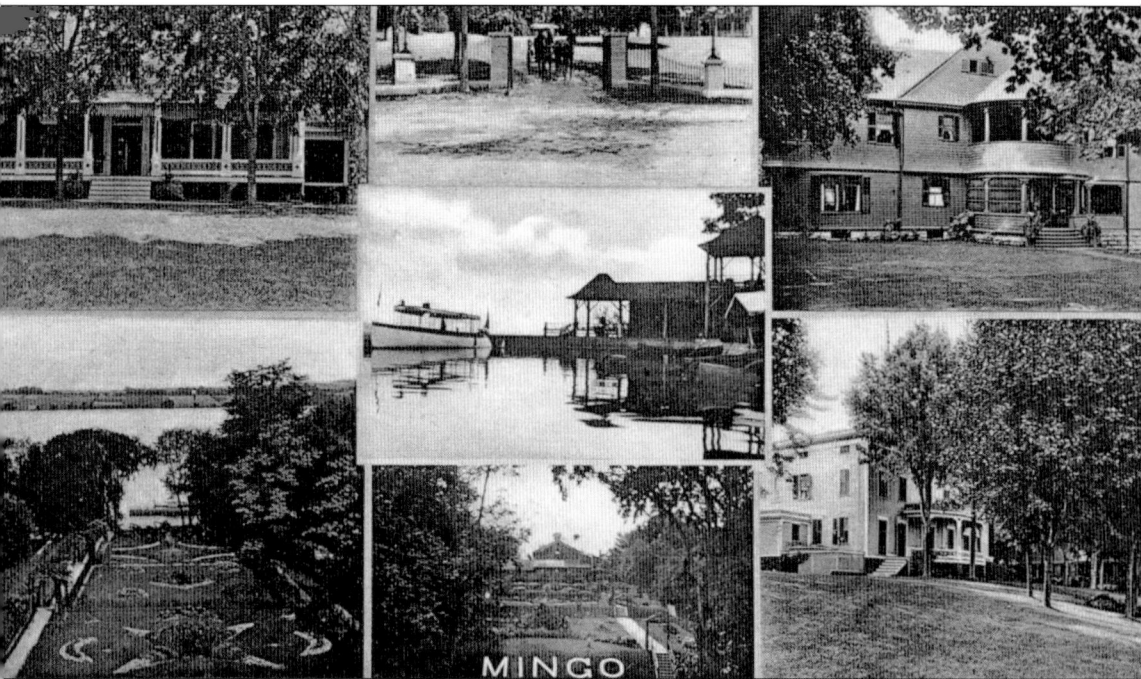

Between 1867 and 1870, Daniel Cook Robbins of New York City purchased land next to Roosevelt Hall. His wife, Matilda Frost, was sister to Annie Lapham of Roosevelt Hall. The wealthy Robbins family and estate grew. A main house was built, and an annex was added, designed by the architectural firm McKinney and Mead in 1879. Daniel died in 1888, and the estate was sold to five Syracuse businessmen who incorporated it as Mingo Lodge. (The name "Mingo" is derived from the group of Seneca and Cayuga Haudenosaunee who banded together and moved to the Ohio Valley in the 19th century.) Reunions and social events were held for relatives and friends of the five Syracuse families. In 1910, the Mingo Estate was sold to a Syracuse attorney, Howard P. Dennison, for $12,000. Dennison divided and sold the property. The house became known as Mingo Manor, today known as Westgate. The annex remained Mingo Lodge. Various owners have passed through the properties. Today, the Mingo Annex is gone.

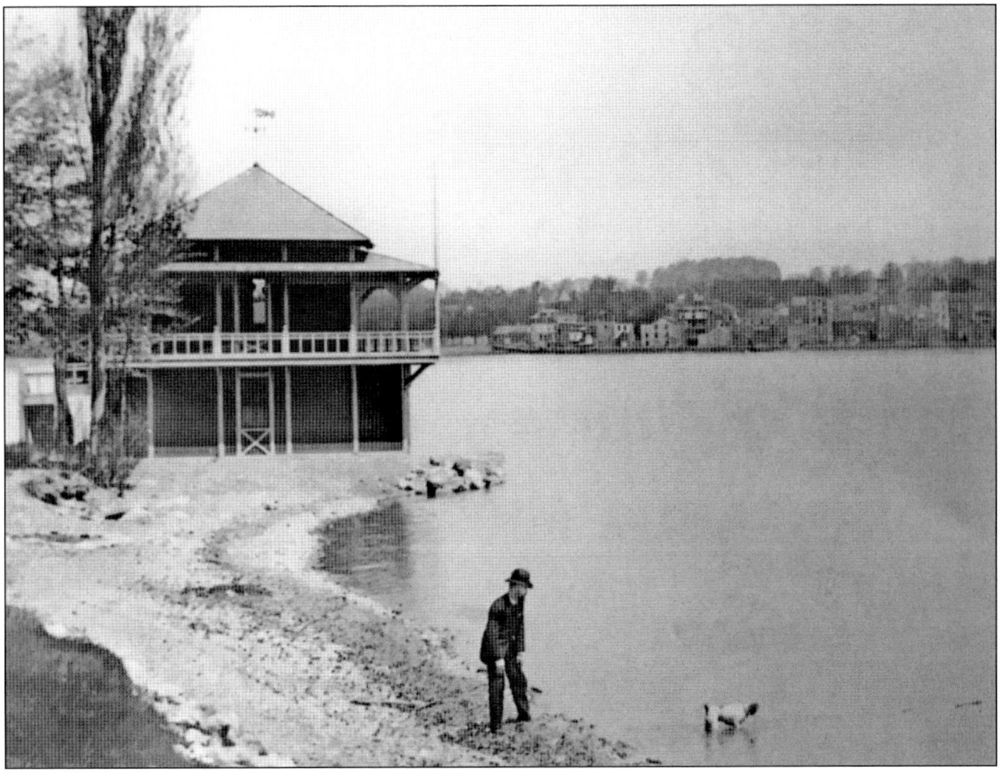

The first mention of a Robbins boathouse was in the *Syracuse Post Standard* in 1897: "The pretty boathouse at the water's edge is well equipped with the finest St. Lawrence boats. The second story, with a veranda, is a charming retreat for an afternoon with a book or fancy work." These photographs capture two different angles of the boathouse.

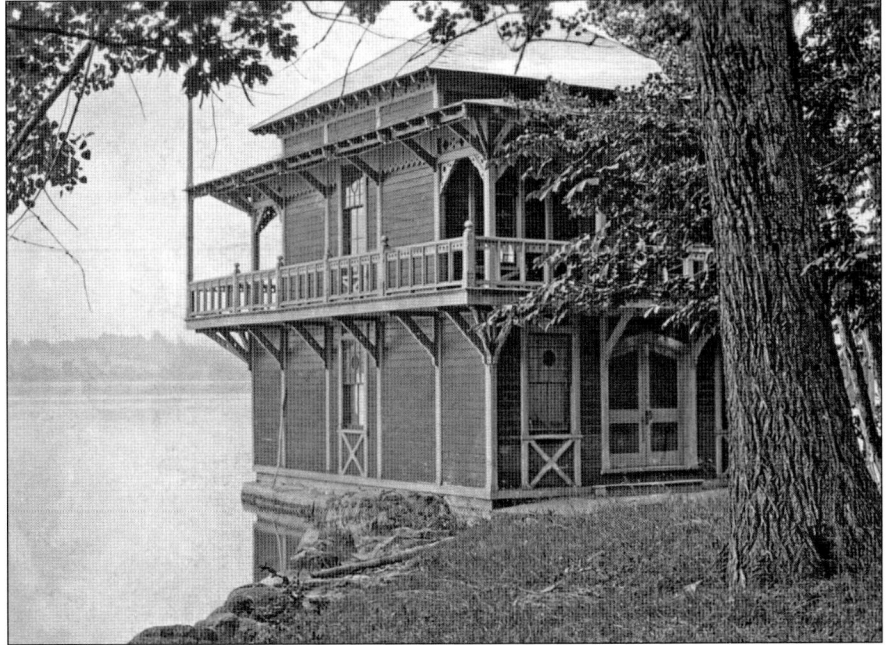

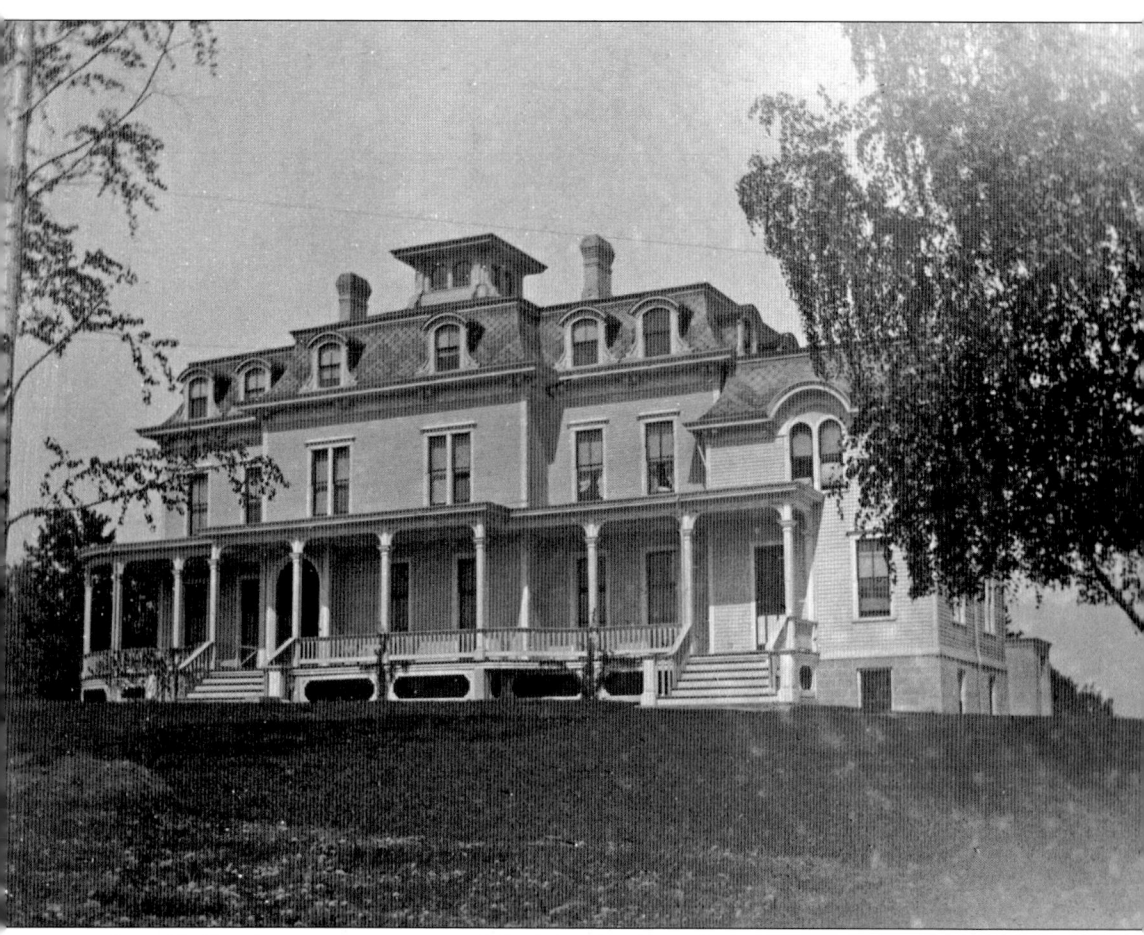

On a bluff with a panoramic view of the lake, Dr. Samuel Hurd purchased 27 acres of Military Tract 37 in 1877 and built a home. According to the Skaneateles Press in 1915," a most hospitable one with all that can make a home attractive." Dr. Hurd died in 1897, and the house was sold to William Fitzgerald of Chicago, a hardware salesman who made his fortune after the 1872 Chicago fire. He came to Syracuse and contracted to build a sewer and make improvements on Onondaga Creek in the city. It was a bad investment, and he lost most of his fortune. Fitzgerald filed a lawsuit in 1908 against the state for property damage when the lake level was raised to provide Syracuse with water. The *Syracuse Herald* reported on May 27, 1908, that there would be a case "if it could be shown that the city (Syracuse) was liable for high water on the account of the raising of the dam two feet when it secured the water rights." His was the first legal case but was lost so that a precedent could not be set with other lakeside properties. After Fitzgerald died in 1913, the house named Geraldine, as seen in the photograph, was foreclosed in 1914.

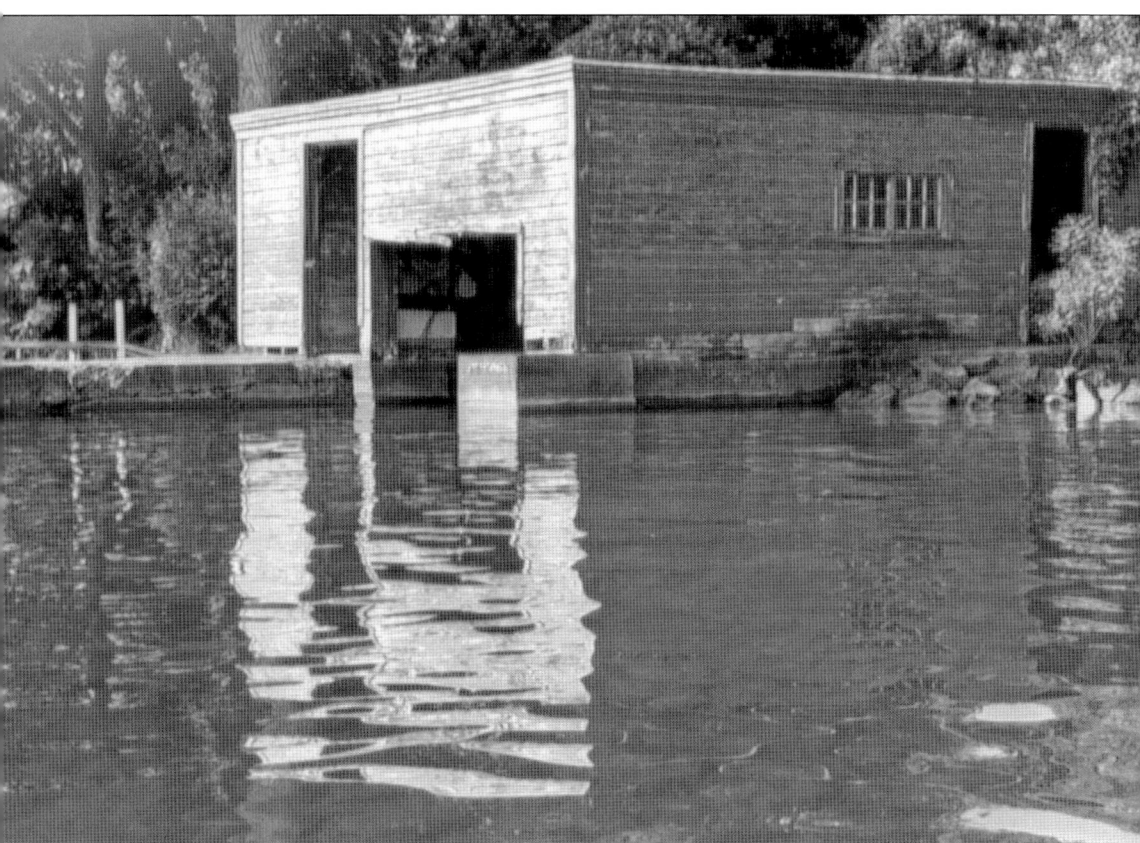

In 1917, John G. Hazard, director of the Solvay Process Company, bought the Geraldine from the Syracuse Trust Company and renamed it Westmoreland. Hazard died in 1918. John's widow, Ada, and their three children continued to enjoy the property as a summer home. Ada died in 1930. Although she died without a will, the children were heirs to their father's trust, so Westmoreland stayed in the family. As with many boathouses, the modest boathouse, which exists today, was not listed in wills or deeds. It was possibly built during the 1940s when there was a shortage of building supplies following the Depression and World War II.

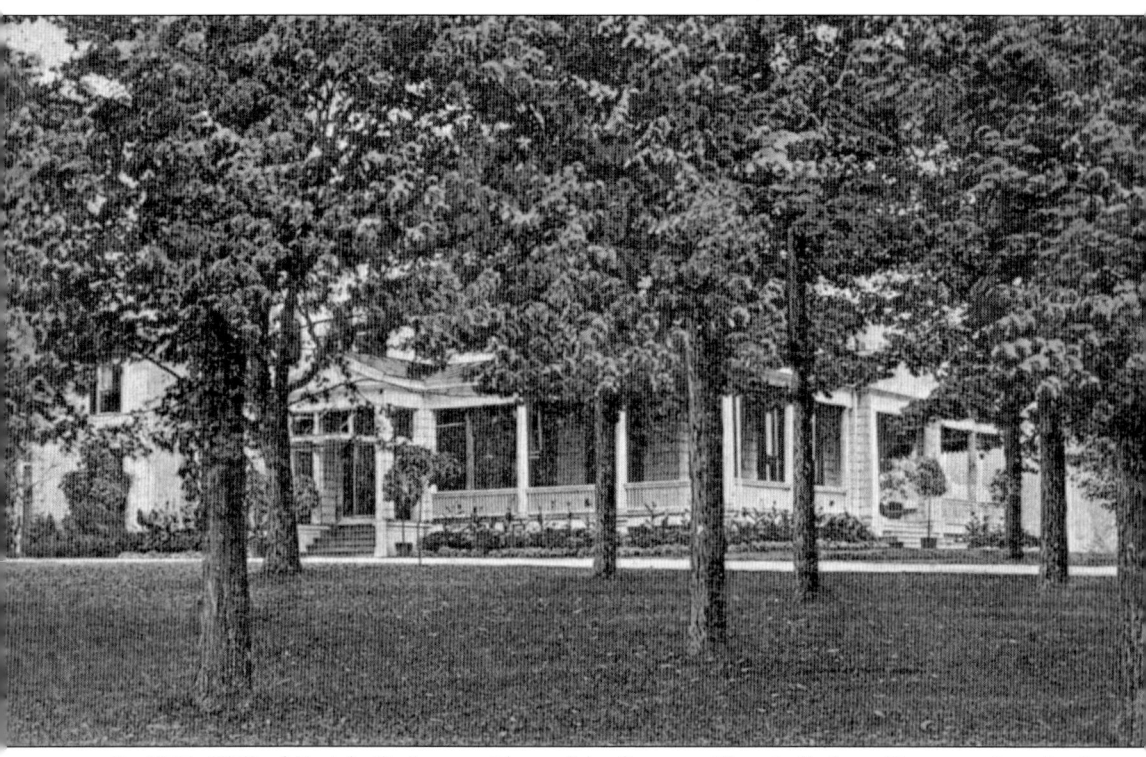

In 1901, Clifford Dwight Beebe, president of the Syracuse Electric Railway Company, bought the west shore property extending from the Westmoreland estate south, including today's Skaneateles Country Club. He named his summer home "Lone Oak." In 1915, fifty-two acres of the Beebe property were incorporated as the Skaneateles Country Club. Lone Oak was sold to Madeline and Morris Foley in 1929. They were prominent Auburn citizens interested in raising and showing horses. Lone Oak became Lone Oak Stables. In 1945, the widowed Madeline sold the estate to Dwight W. Winkelman, president of D.W. Winkelman Construction Company, who renamed the estate "Lakelawn." The buildings were remodeled and modernized. The property was sold to the Rustons in 1978. Following a failed attempt to develop the property, the aging structures were torn down, and the property sold for $11 million in 2014.

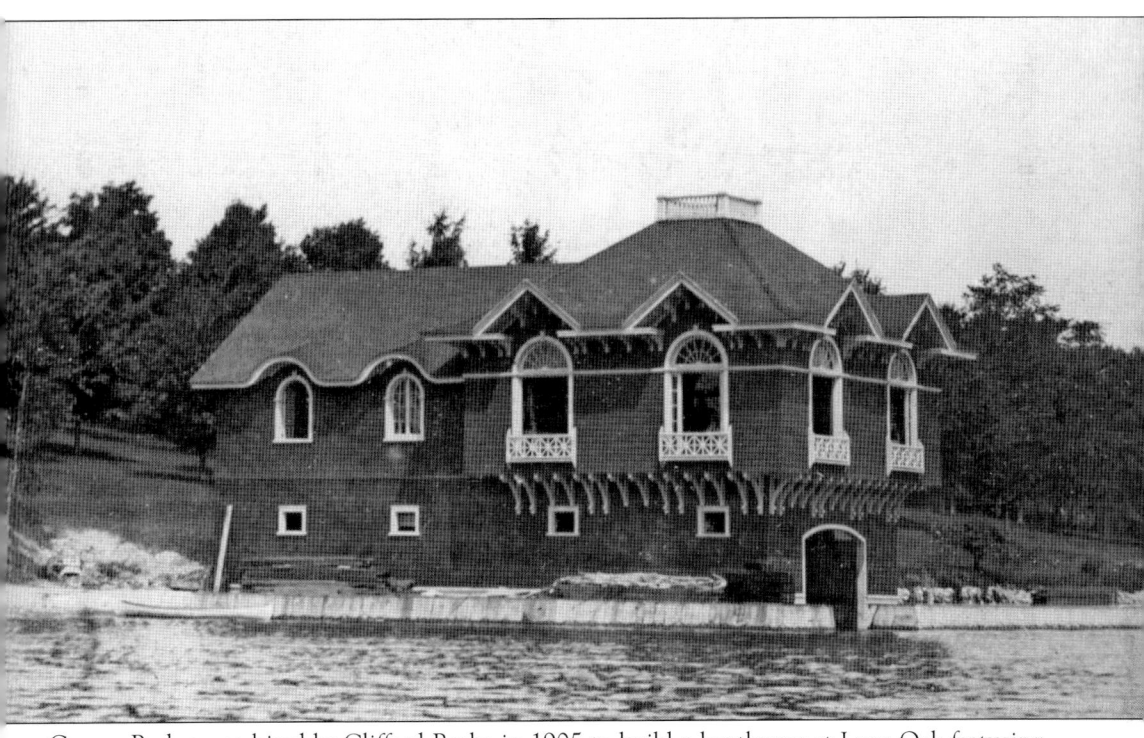

George Barber was hired by Clifford Beebe in 1905 to build a boathouse at Lone Oak featuring a billiard room, two bedrooms on the first floor, and servants' quarters on the second floor. A dance in the boathouse was described as a "brilliant affair" in the *Auburn Citizen* (August 1908). "The moon rising over the boathouse with its beautiful illuminations and the strains of soft music produced an effect that was entrancing." Audrey Arthur was a girlfriend of Mary Ann Foley, who spent many summers on the lake with the Foleys. Her favorite recollections were of the boathouse, recorded in her diary: "The boathouse was our hangout that summer of 1939. It had big windows all around the main room that jutted out over the lake. Several white polar bear rugs on the floor and a terrific record player that was stocked full of Benny Goodman's records. The country club was next door. We would spend the afternoon hanging out on the dock with the record player full blast so that everyone at the club would know where we were."

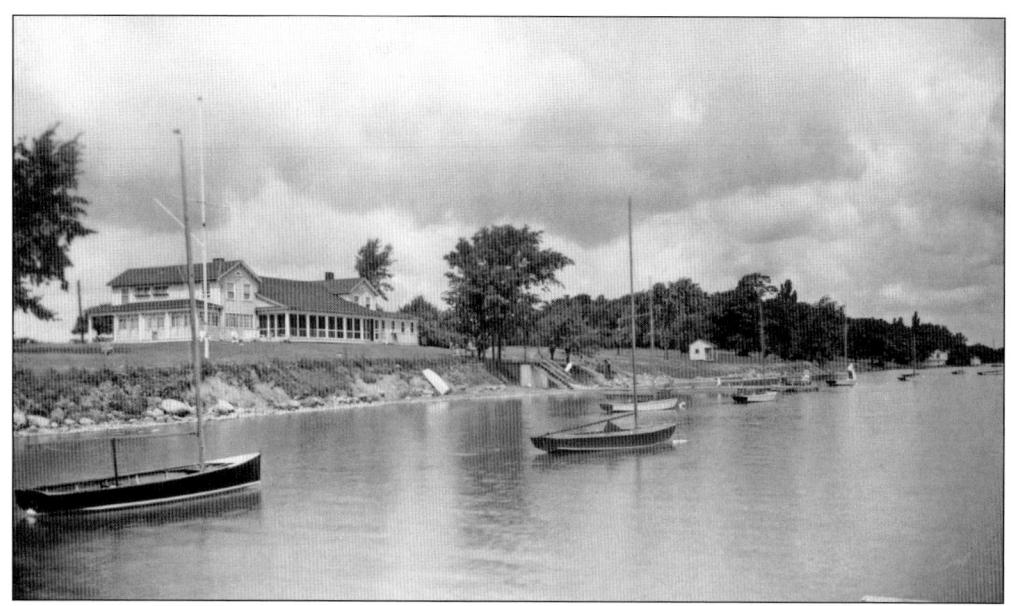

During the summer of 1915, a group of Syracuse and Skaneateles men met with Beebe to discuss the possibility of a country club and golf course being built on 52 acres of his property. The *Syracuse Post Standard*, August 6, 1915, reported that "on the property there is ample room for a nine-hole course, with a clubhouse facing the lake. The establishment should be a popular one with Syracuse, Auburn, and Skaneateles families." On October 21, 1915, plans to lease the land for this purpose from Beebe were approved.

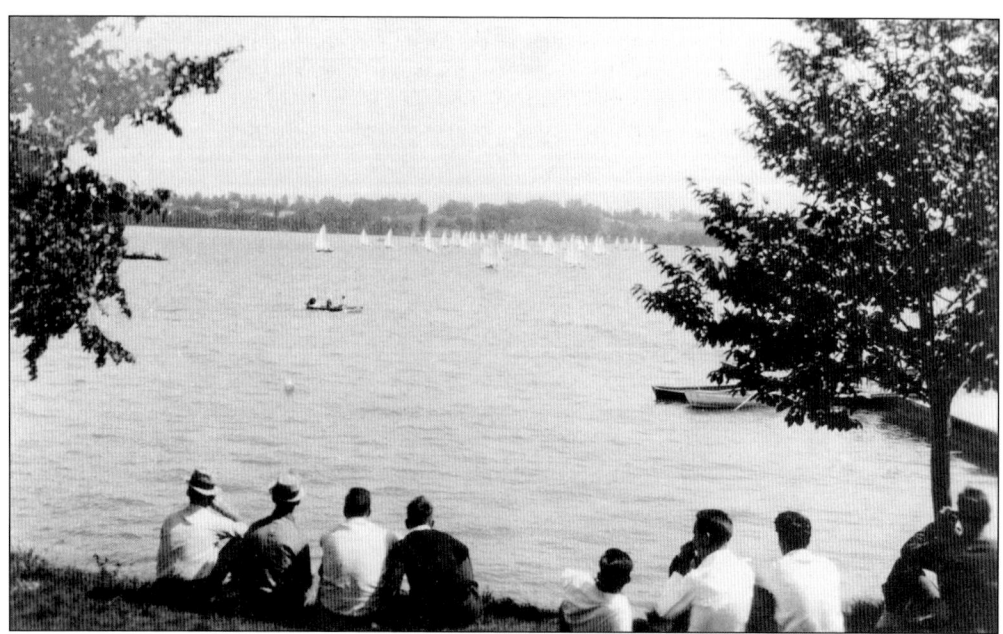

The first sailing regatta was held in 1938. This c. 1930s photograph shows some enthusiastic spectators enjoying the competition of a regatta from the country club shore.

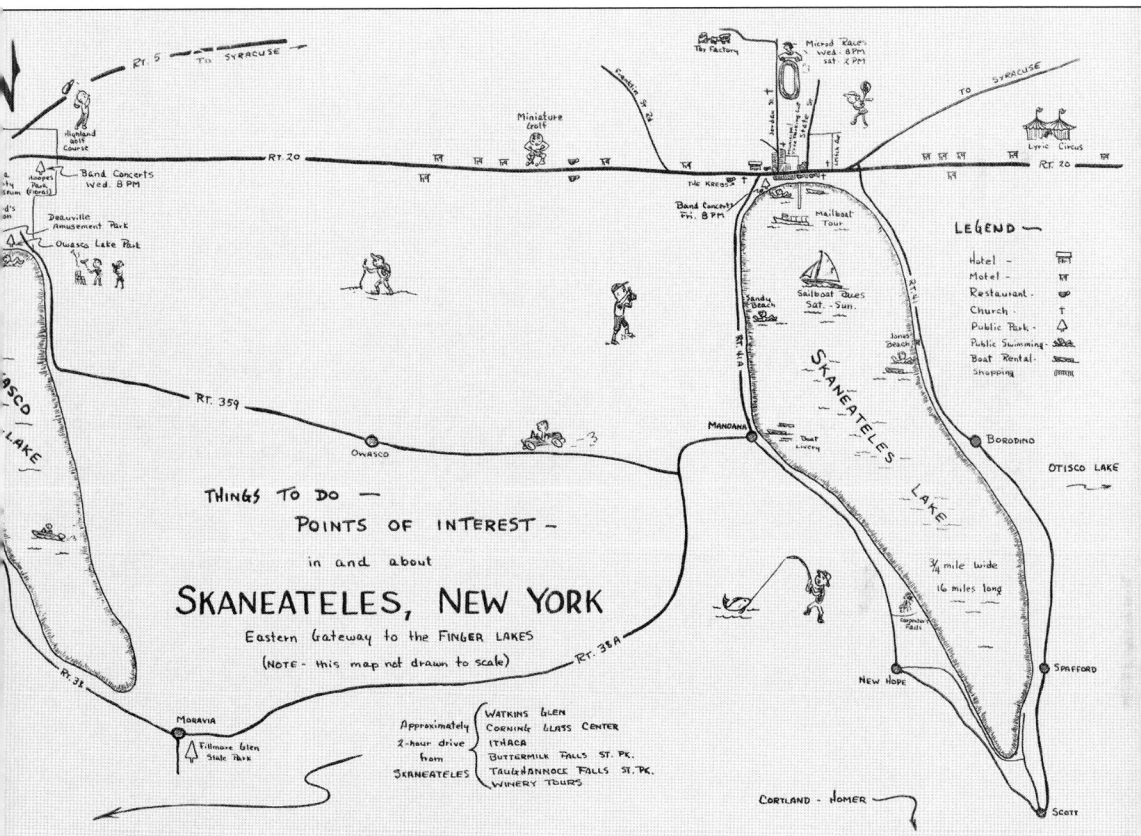

A left turn from West Lake Street onto New York State Route 41A continues along the west shore of the lake. This route travels above the west shore through the small hamlets of Mandana, located in the town of Skaneateles, and New Hope Landing, located in the town of Niles, Cayuga County. Bear Swamp, a New York State conservation area, extends southwest to the end of the lake. The west shore of the lake is connected to the east shore via Glen Haven Road.

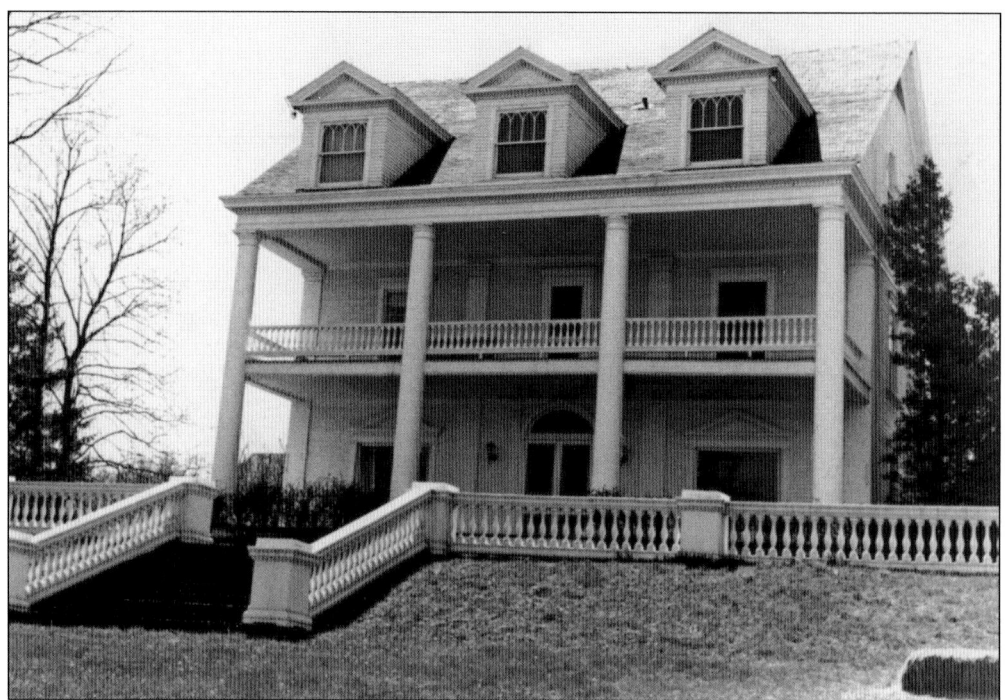

Brook Farm was part of Military Tract 57, covering about 126 acres. The land was originally owned by Russell Frost in 1817 and then owned by the Willetts, Anne Lapham, and John Guy Owsley. John Owsley was a wealthy Syracuse resident who married into the prominent Yates family of Syracuse and built a home on the property in 1902.

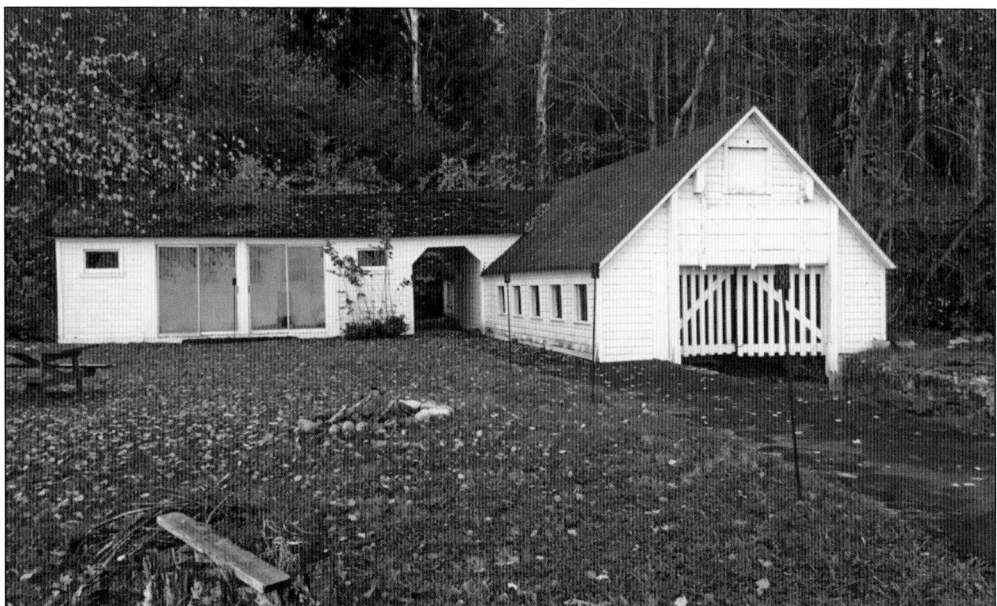

An L-shaped boathouse was added shortly after the house was built. According to Rob and Claire Robinson, former owners, "There was a grand lit pathway leading to the beach with peony bushes and arbors. A staircase at the end led to the boathouse. Boats were stored in water within the boathouse, which was the practice of old boathouses." (Photo courtesy of Julie DiBagio.)

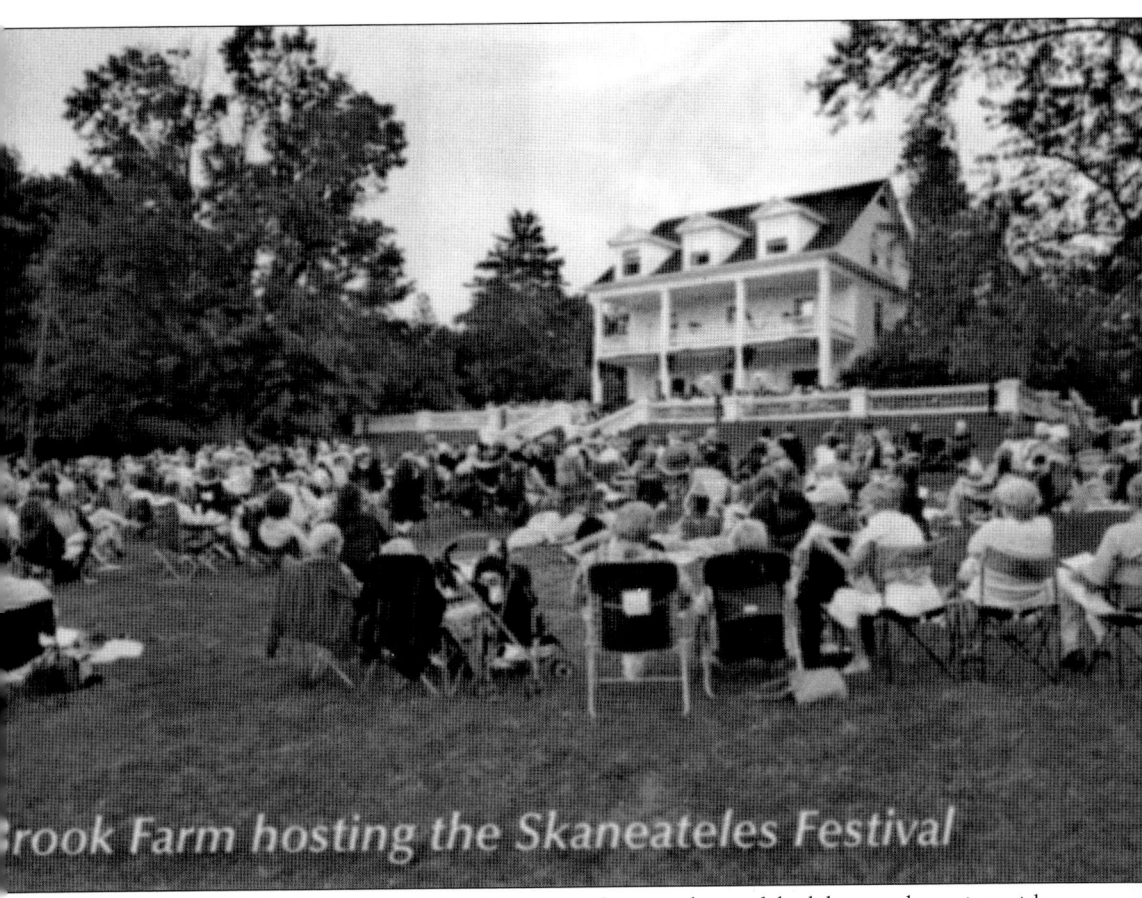

Brook Farm hosting the Skaneateles Festival

From 1980 to 2016, the hills around Brook Farm on the west shore of the lake were booming with lively sounds of music each Saturday in August. The music was the idea of Dr. David and Louise Robinson. The Festival Chamber Music by the Lake was known in the music world throughout the United States. Musicians came from all over the United States and overseas to play and stay in Skaneateles for the month of August. The Robinsons hosted some musicians at their home during the festival. Churches also provided a venue for the festival, but Saturdays belonged to Brook Farm.

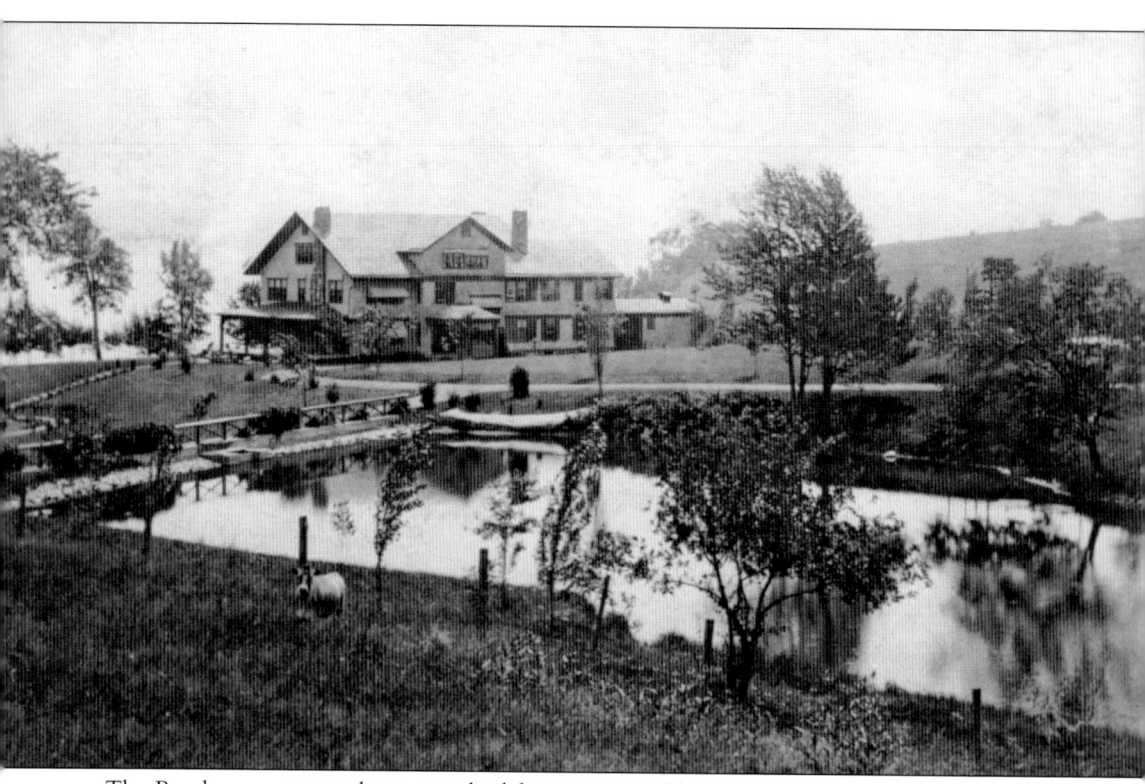

The Beeches, a summer home on the lake, was owned by Edward Needles Trump in 1905. The Trumps were a prominent family living in Syracuse and Skaneateles. Trump was the chief engineer of the Solvay Process Company. He was elected the first president of the Skaneateles Country Club.

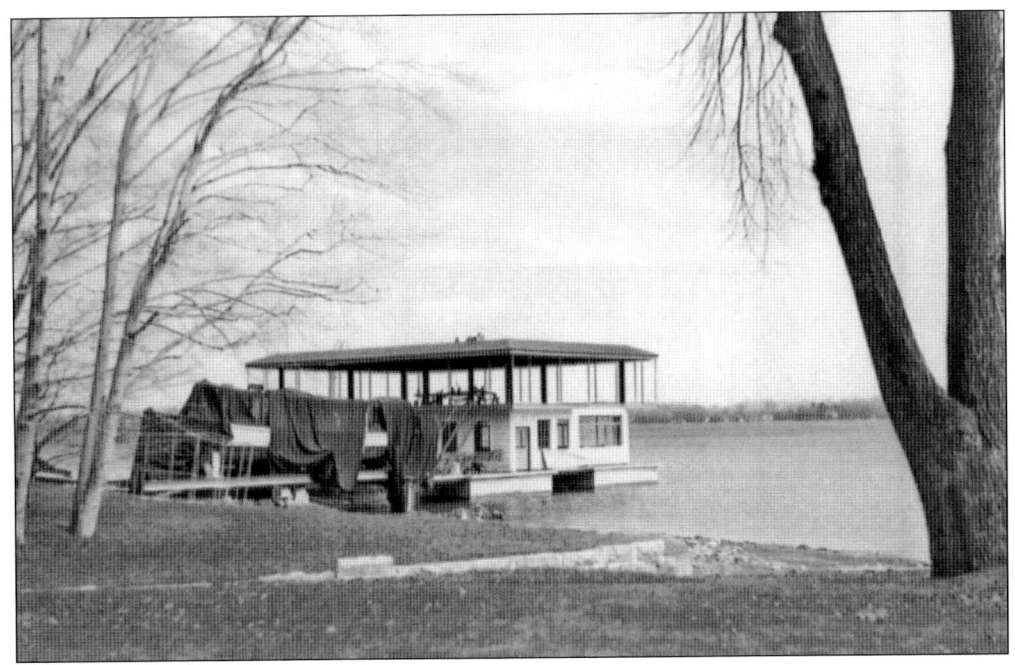

The Trump estate was purchased by A.S. Wikstrom, owner of the Wikstrom Construction Company, located in the old Sinclair factory in Mottville, New York. In 1959, A.S. Wikstrom bought a 48-foot steam-powered boat, the *Phoebe*. His son Steven was smitten and quickly learned to navigate the waters. He said that the boat was a "chick magnet." It also led Steven to a maritime career around the world. Meanwhile, A.S. Wikstrom was at work on a boathouse to house the Phoebe. Construction was of wood with a copper roof. The windows were discards from the Syracuse airport. The last run of the Phoebe was in 1975. Unfortunately, A.S. Wikstrom was killed in an airliner crash on the lake in 1976. The boathouse was torn down in 1985.

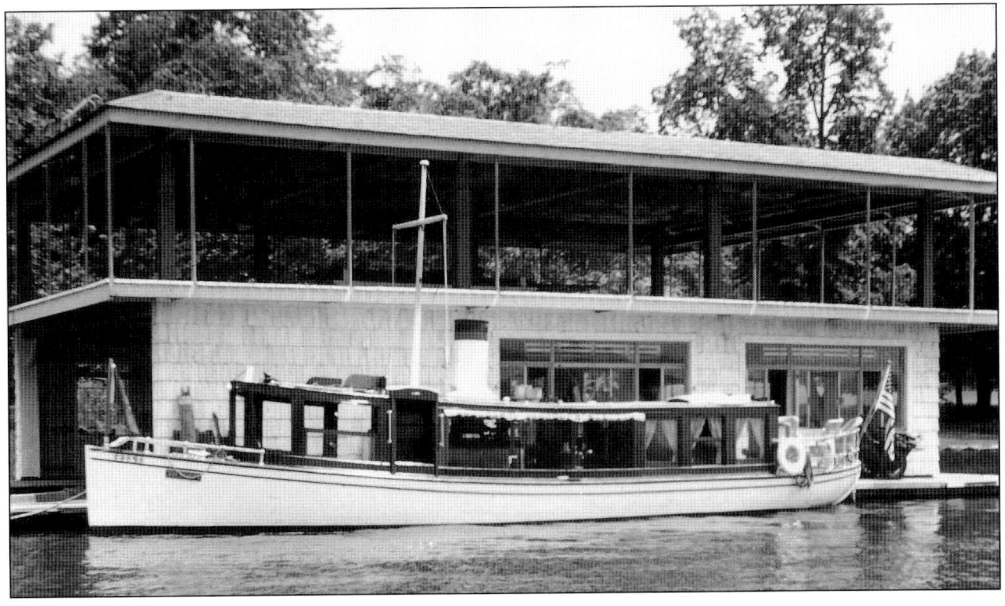

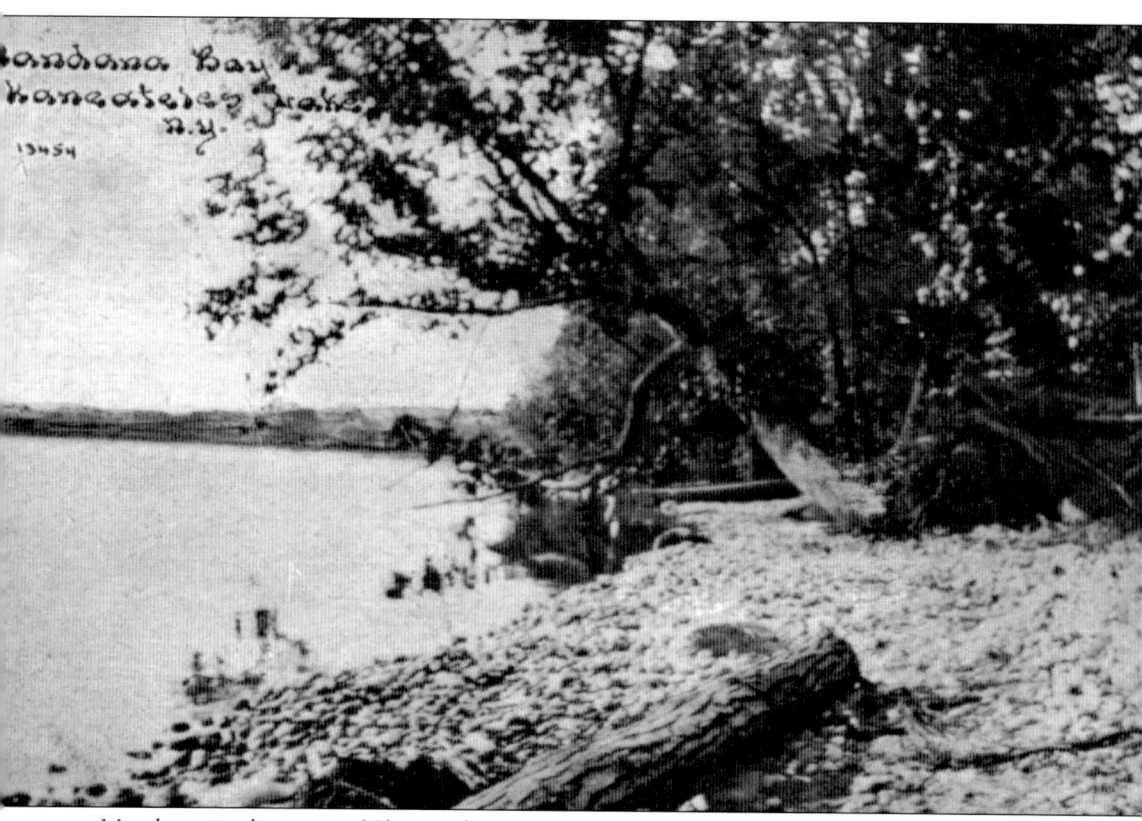

Mandana, in the town of Skaneateles, was a small, thriving settlement in the early 1800s. The earliest settlers were there following the War of 1812. There was a log schoolhouse, a blacksmith, and a store. An early tavern was established in 1835, the site of today's Mandana Inn. A steamboat landing was a destination for travelers on the lake.

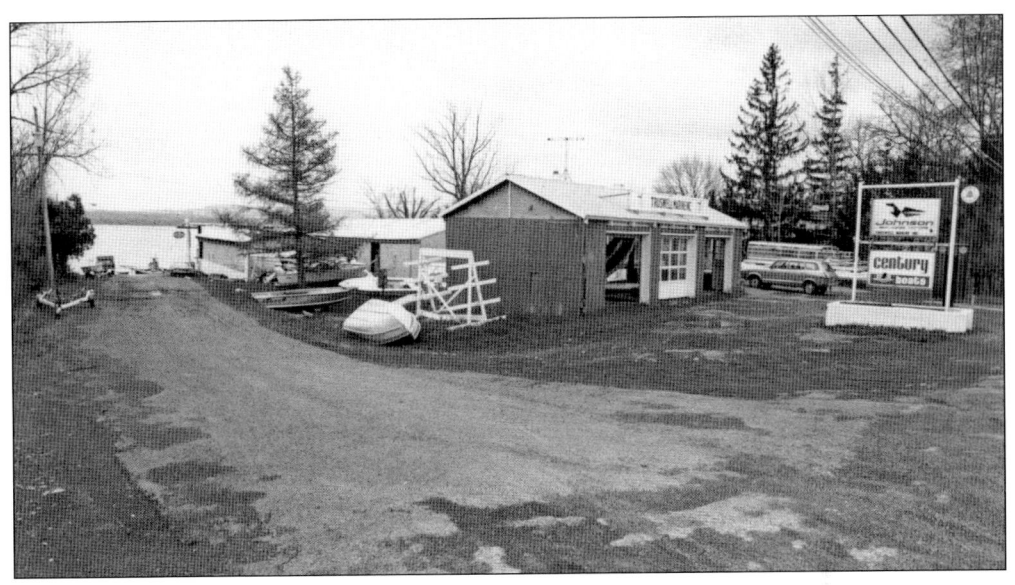

The Truswell Marina was established by Roy and Katherine Russell directly across from the Mandana Inn in 1948. A total of 130 boats could be stored there during the winter months. The boats were repaired and restored for the upcoming season. The Marina provided a docking and livery facility and a complete line of maritime products, including boats, accessories, marine hardware, and paint. The Truswell Marina was sold in 1968.

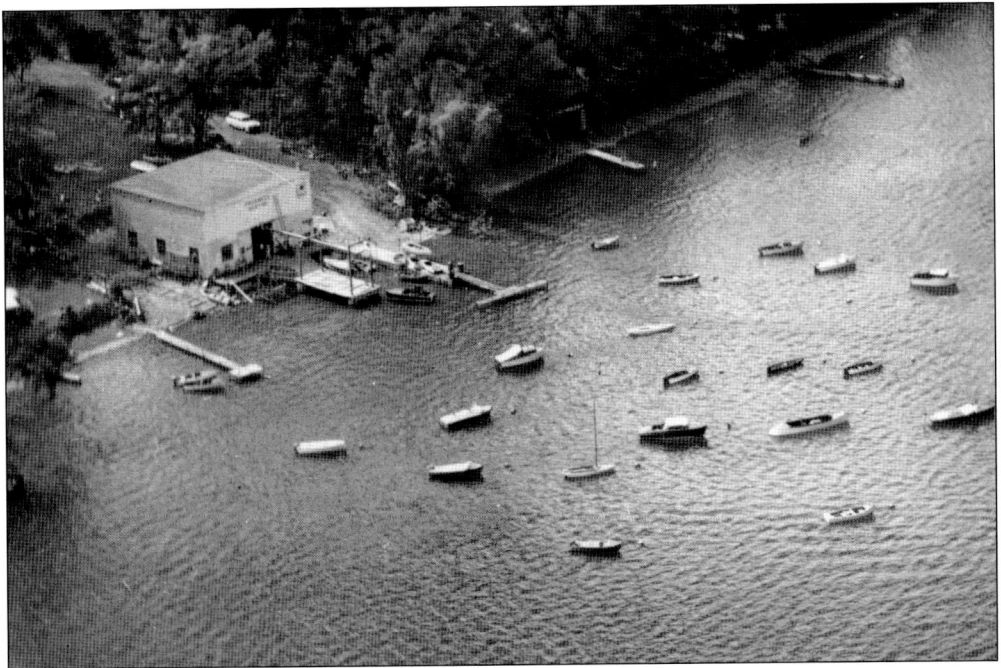

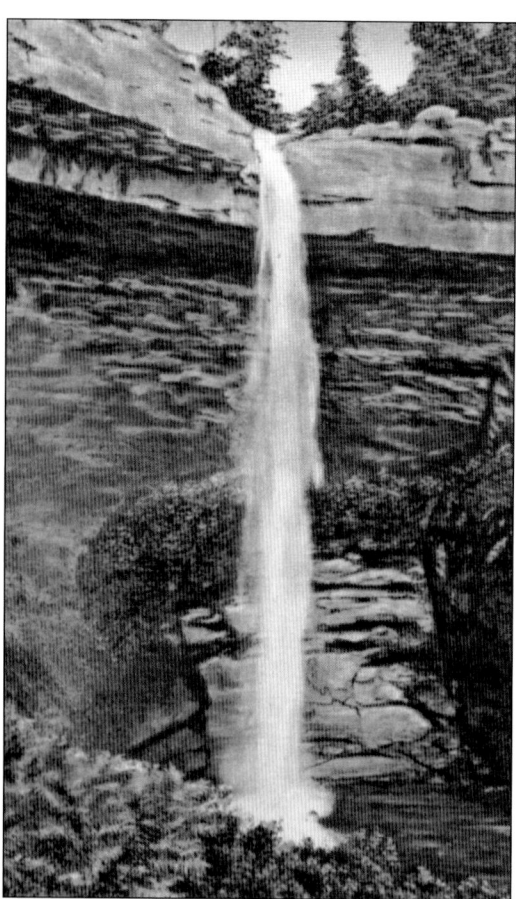

Carpenter Falls is one mile inland from the southwest shore of the lake. The Bear Swamp Creek, a major tributary of Skaneateles Lake, flows through a ravine, cascading over four waterfalls that flow into the lake.

A projection of land into the lake near Carpenter Falls is known as Carpenter Point or Apple Tree Point due to the many apple trees planted there by early settlers. Cottages were built, and a steamboat landing was a destination for residents living on the point.

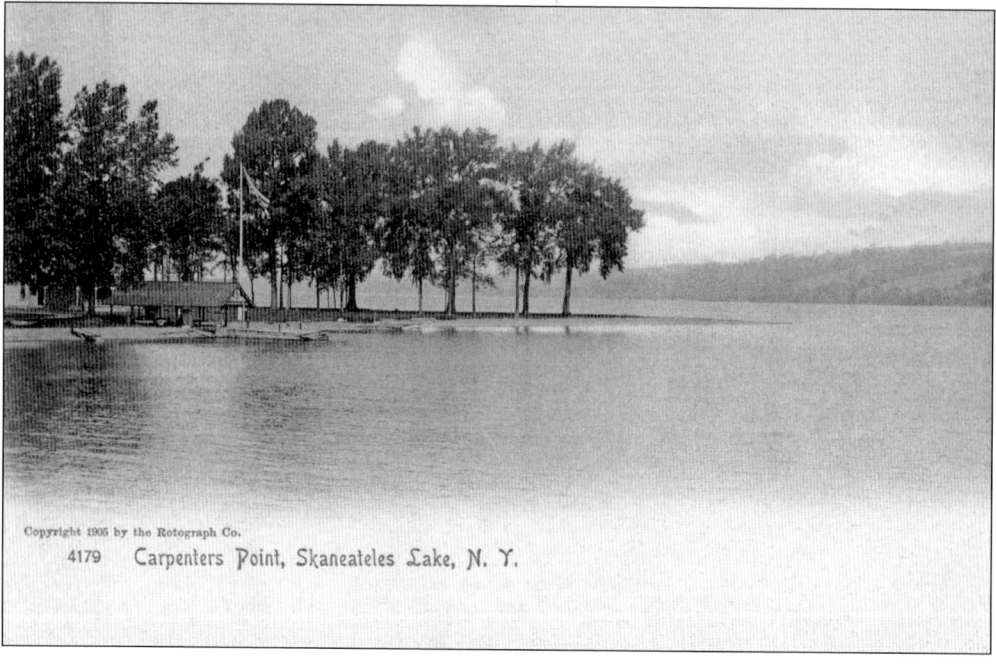

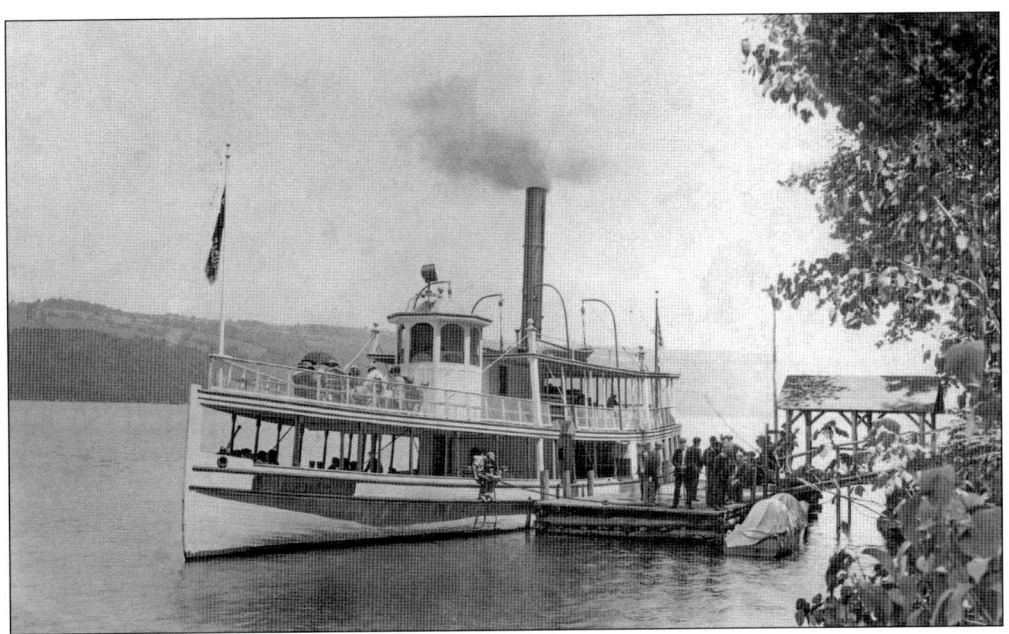

According to *Elsie Gutchess Memories of the New Hope Landing*, "G.B. Gutchess grew up enjoying summers at the end of Skaneateles Lake where his father had purchased the site of a sawmill which had supplied lumber for the building of the Glen Haven Sanitarium. G.B. owned a lumber company in Cortland, New York, which was struggling following the Depression. He purchased 100 acres of tract lumber south of Carpenter Point extending to the lake. The timber was hard to harvest because of the ravines on the property. He quickly cleared the shoreline and built a two-story cabin for his family." This was the site of the New Hope steamboat landing seen in the photographs. This landing provided access to lake transportation and mail delivery for the residents of New Hope, a small hamlet in the town of Niles.

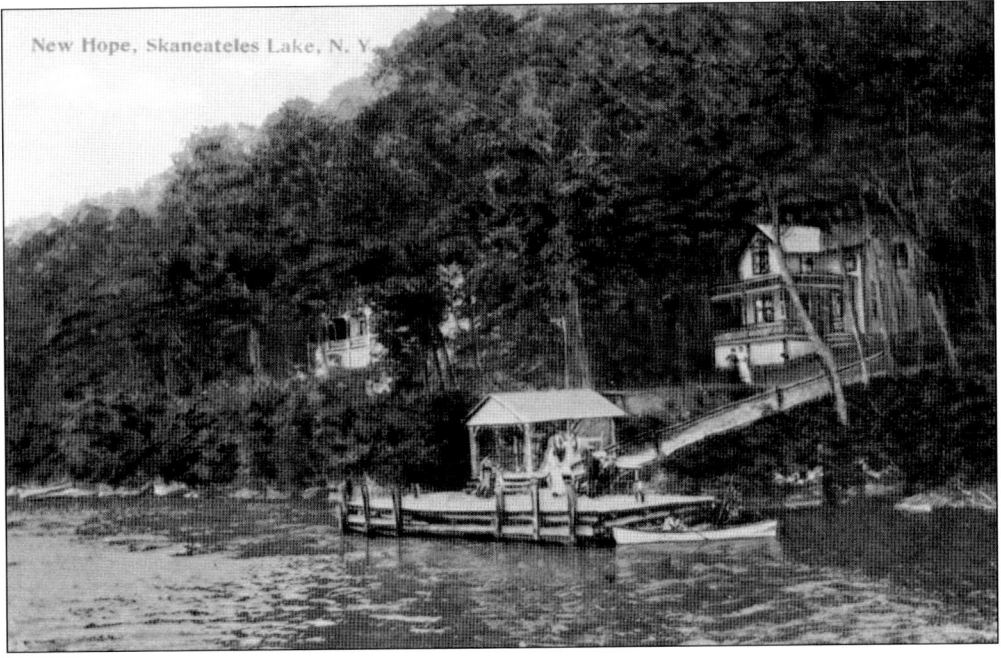

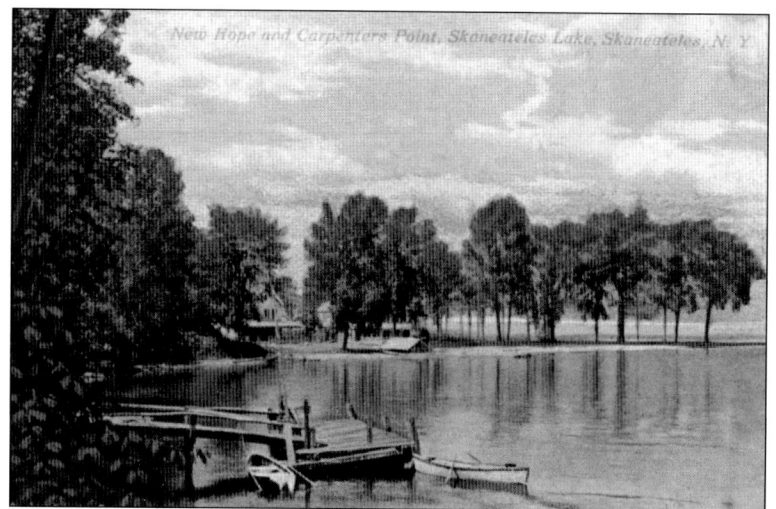

Carpenter Point Landing and New Hope Landing were in close proximity. Eventually, both landings succumbed to winter storms and ice.

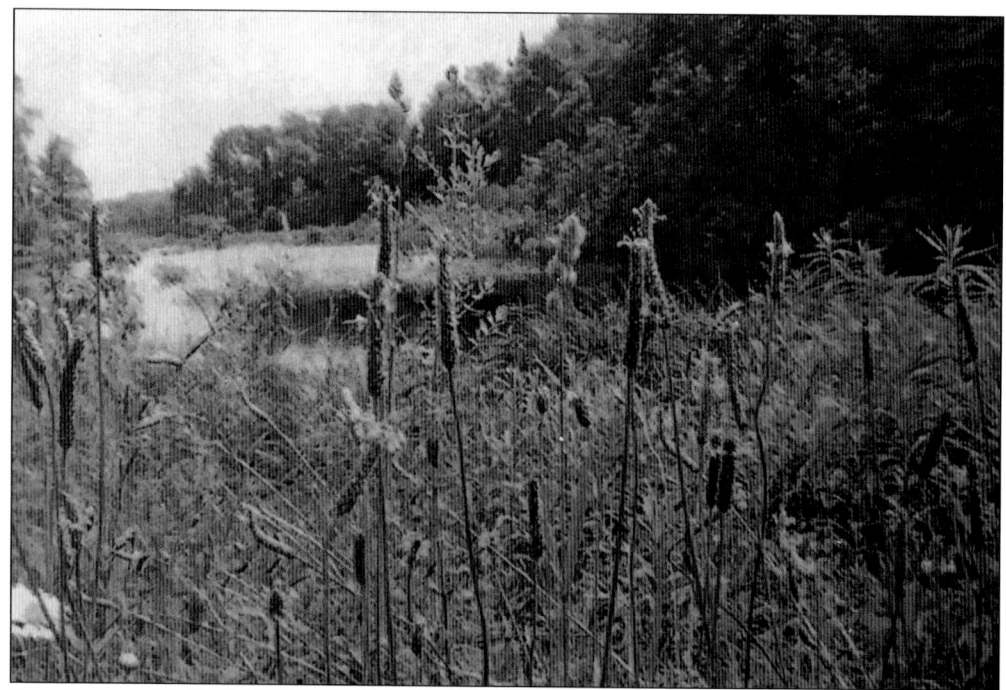

Bear Swamp is a large wetland 800 feet above the west end of Skaneateles Lake in the town of Sempronius, Cayuga County. Early settlers came from Ireland in 1863. The soil was poor but they established farms. All that remains today are stone foundations and hedgerows of these early farms. According to Charlie Major, whose ancestors settled in Bear Swamp, the name may have originated because there were bears there or because there was nothing there (bare). All settlers were gone by 1920. Bear Swamp is an important part of the Skaneateles Lake watershed. It is a designated state forest owned by the state of New York. During the Depression, the Civilian Conservation Corps planted trees to hold and replenish the soil.

Five

THE EAST SHORE

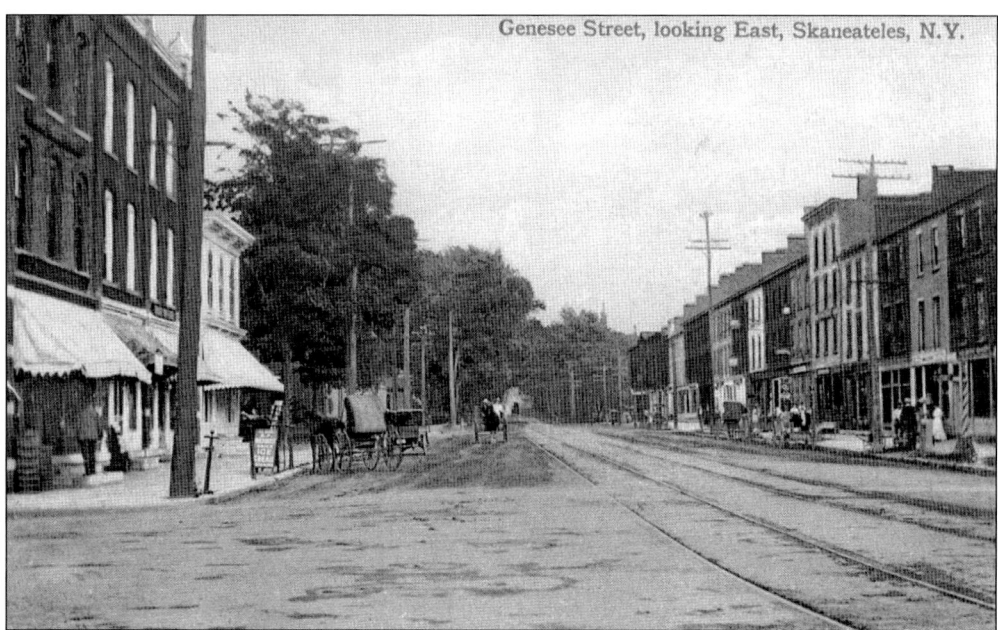

The "Great Genesee Road," or Genesee Street, as it is known today, runs east and west through the Skaneateles village. It was also known as the Seneca Turnpike by settlers coming from the east. The area immediately east of the village was heavily forested but desirable for building due to its elevation. The Genesee Road follows the northern shore of the lake through the village until the lake bears south, and the road continues at the intersection of Route 41, known as the East Lake Road or the Homer Road. The road follows the shore into the town of Spafford, the hamlets of Borodino, and Spafford Landing, ending at the head of the lake in Fair Haven, Cortland County.

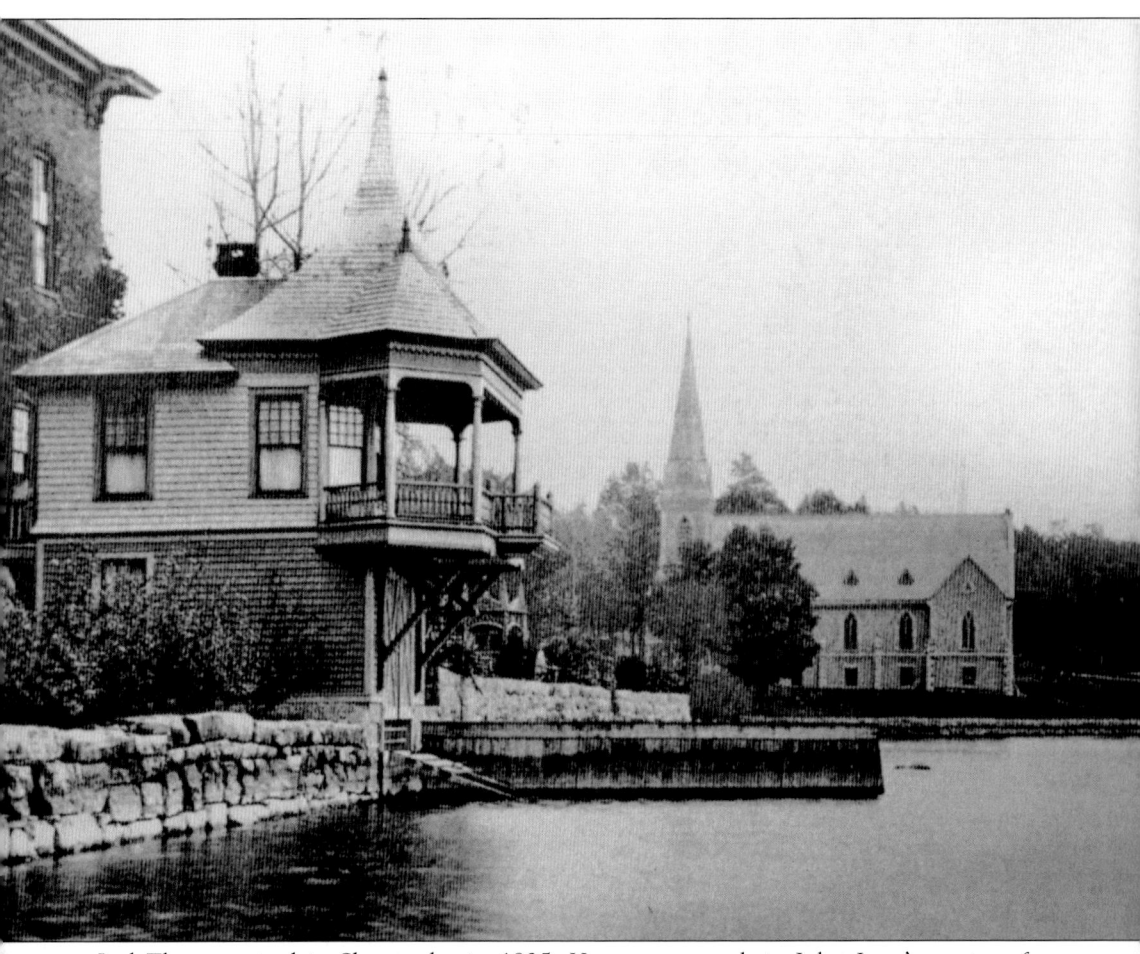

Joel Thayer arrived in Skaneateles in 1835. He went to work in John Legg's carriage factory at the east end of the village on Genesee Street. Together, the two civic-minded businessmen accumulated fame and fortune. Thayer married Legg's daughter, Juliette. In 1866, he rebuilt Legg Hall and named it for his father-in-law. In 1868, a boathouse was added to the back of Legg Hall, as seen in the photograph. At some point, it was removed.

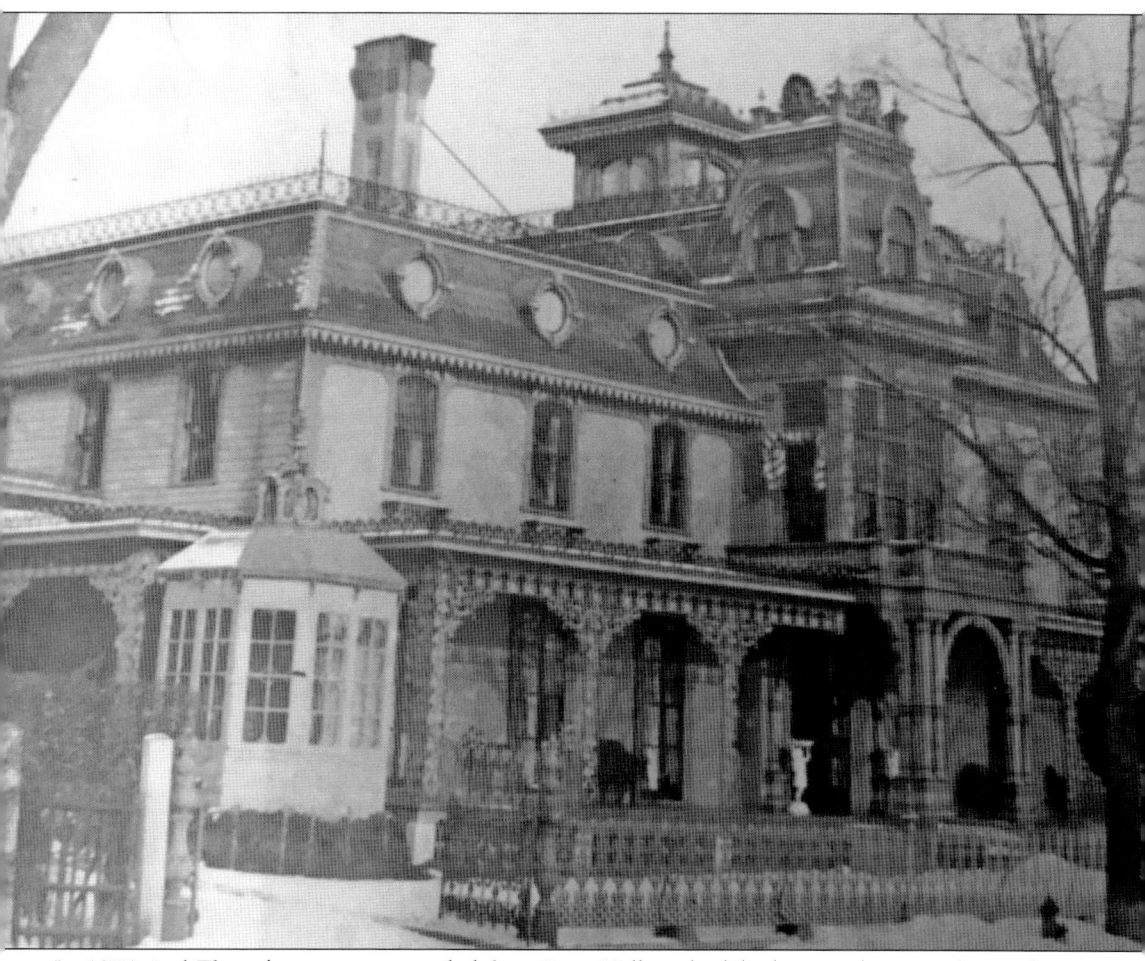

In 1874, Joel Thayer's property extended from Legg Hall to the lakeshore and east to the newly built St. James Episcopal Church. He and his family lived on the northern side of the property, which was one of the original village lots. The elegant Italianate-style home was built about 1830 by John Legg. Following Legg's death in 1857, Joel Thayer inherited the property and remodeled the house into a showplace, which remains on site today.

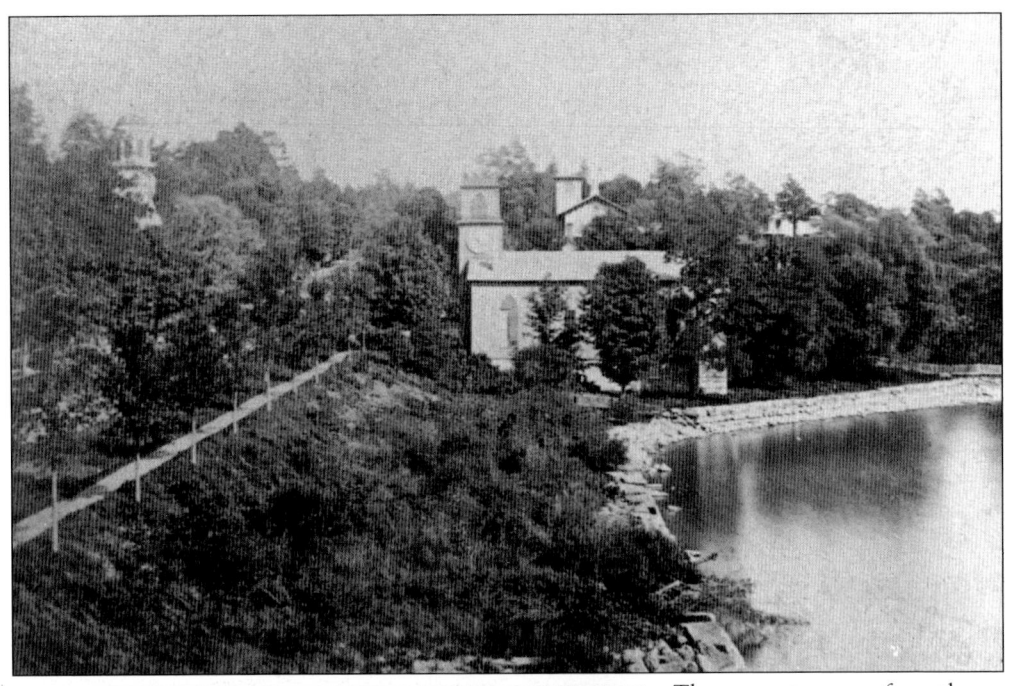

The property across from the Thayer mansion extending east along the lakeshore to St. James Episcopal Church was overgrown.

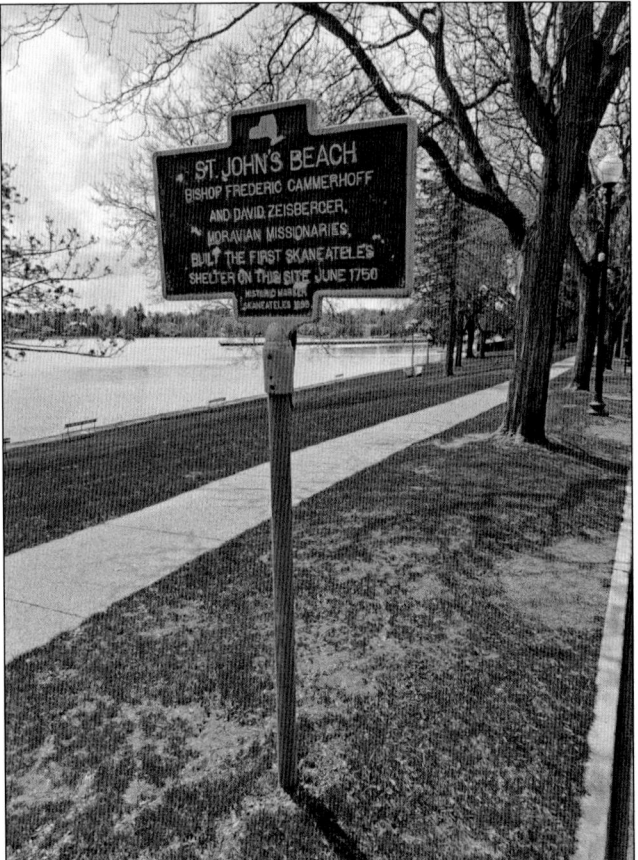

A marker on this site recognizes the two 18th-century Moravian missionaries from Bethlehem, Pennsylvania, who landed in this area and proclaimed it St. John's Beach.

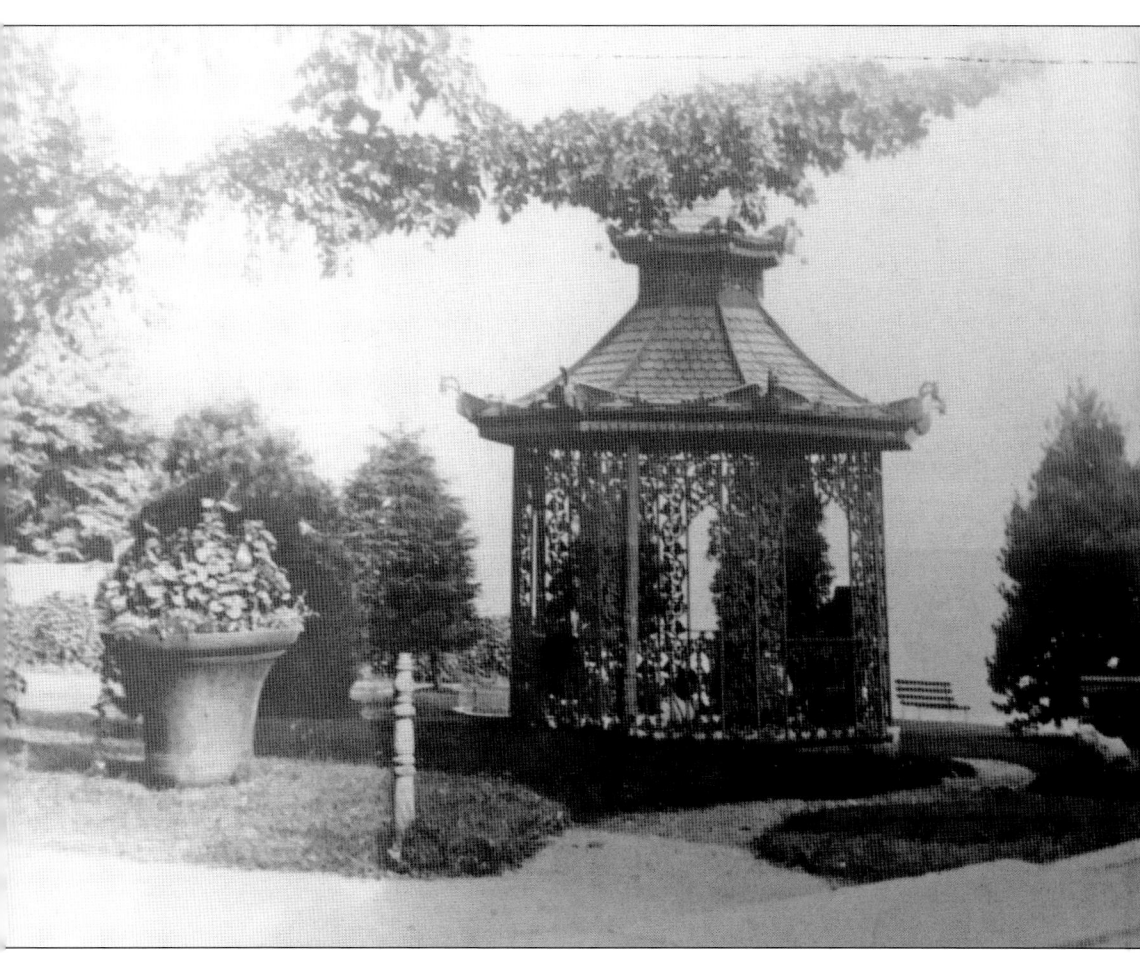

In 1874, a portion of the Thayer property was turned into a park for all to appreciate. Joel died in 1881. Marie and Eva Webb, heirs to the Thayer estate, formally deeded Thayer Park to the village in 1922.

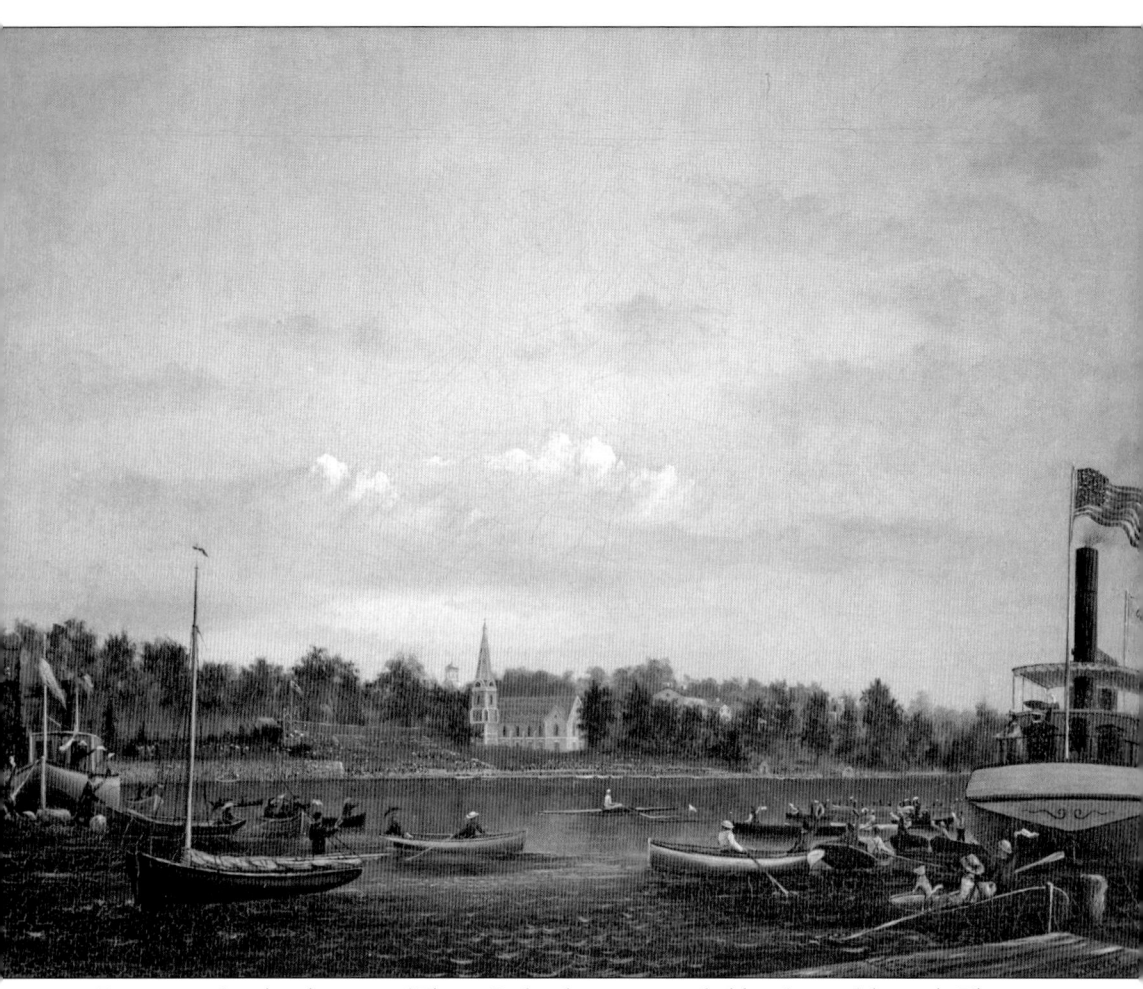

Four years after the planning of Thayer Park, a boat race was held in front of the park. The race was captured by artist Henry J. Saunter (1850-1900) in an oil painting titled *The Great Skull Race of July 4, 1878, at Skaneateles*. A crowd of onlookers can be seen in the background, sitting along the hill by St. James Episcopal Church. Two steamboats, the *Glen Haven* on the right and the *Echo* on the left, were stationed among the competing skulls, probably providing seats for passengers interested in the race. The race was won by Charles E. Courtney of Union Springs, a nationally known rower. The original painting is in the collection of the University of Rochester's Memorial Art Gallery. The painting was reprinted and donated to the Skaneateles Historical Society collection by Kihm Winship.

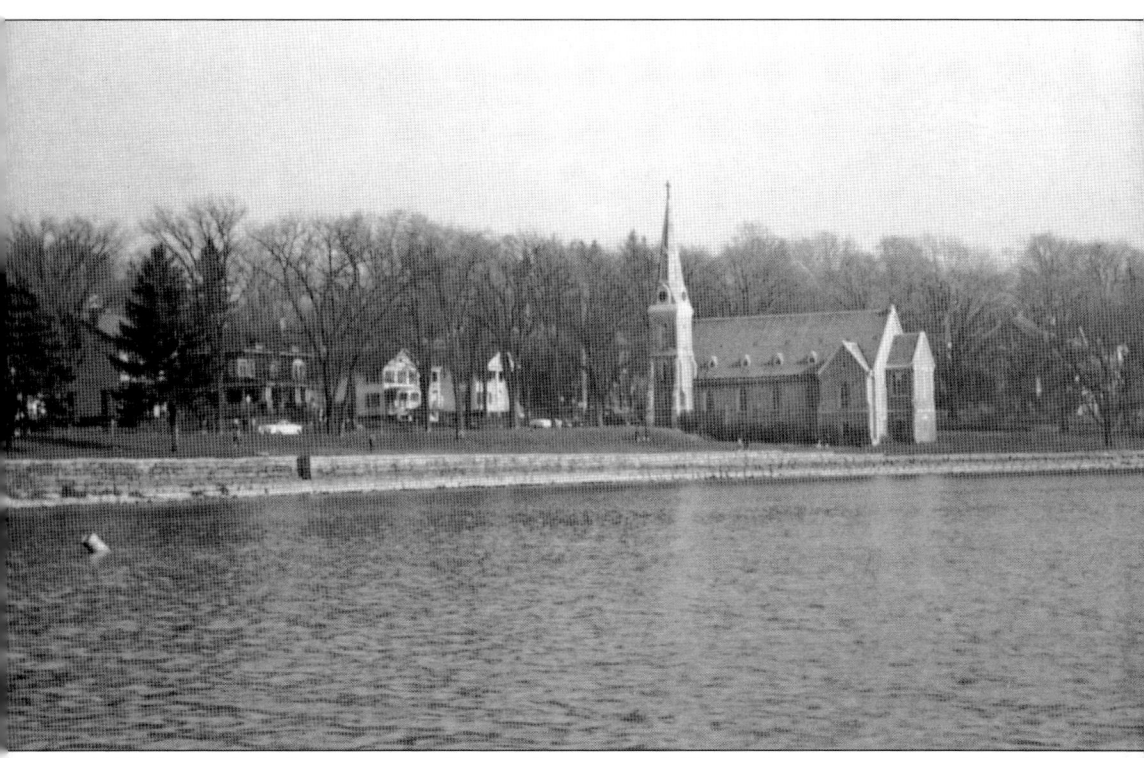

In 1922, Frederick Carleton Austin, a Skaneateles native and Chicago businessman, noted that the area between Thayer Park and St. James Episcopal Church remained overgrown. Austin purchased the property in 1923. At the same time, he gave a $25,000 endowment to the village to maintain the land and build a seawall. Six years later, the village had not made any progress in building the seawall. In 1829, Austin stated that there would be no endowment if the project was not completed within the next five years. Austin died in 1931. The project was completed in 1935. Today, the land between St. James Episcopal Church and Legg Hall is a sprawling grassy park thanks to the generosity of the Thayer-Webb families and F.C. Austin.

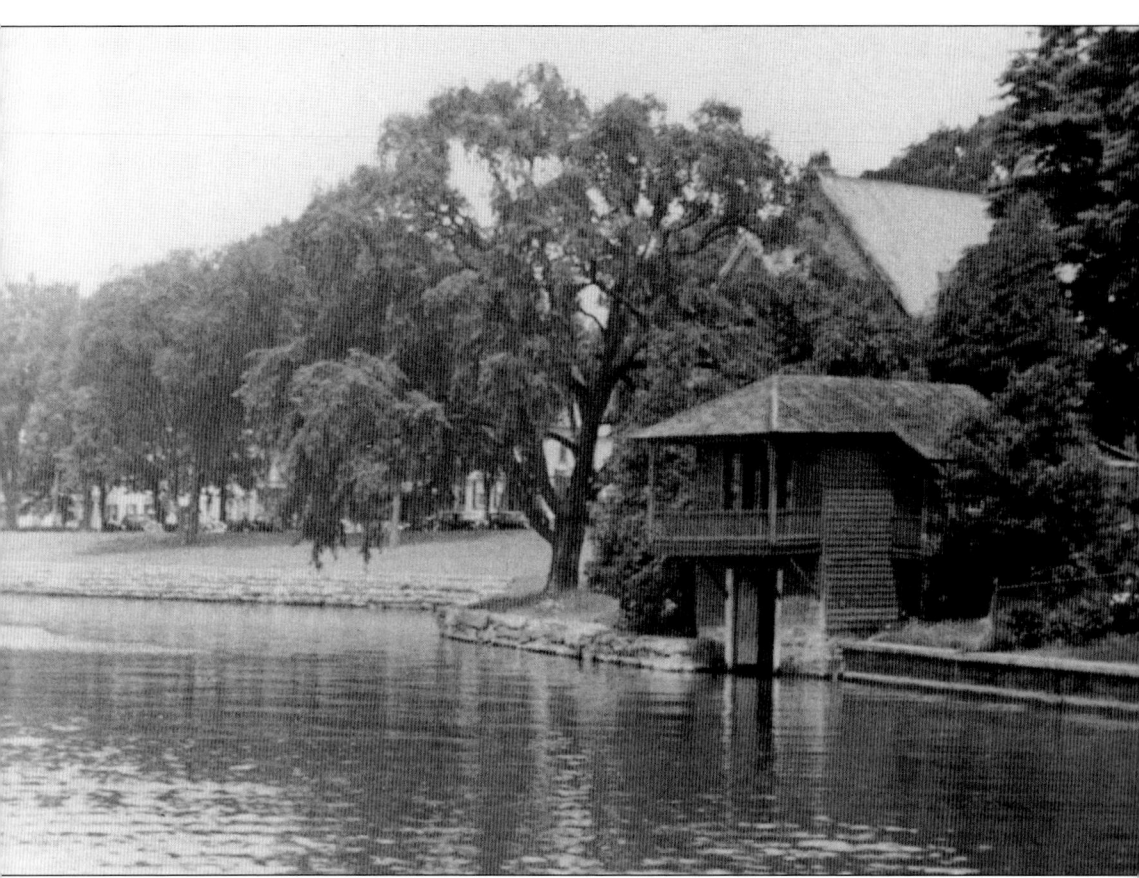

The house just east of St. James Episcopal Church was known as the Porter home. In 1907, Edith Porter sold the property, which included the boathouse seen in the photograph, to the church for a rectory; it is still in use today. The Porter boathouse was torn down prior to 1933.

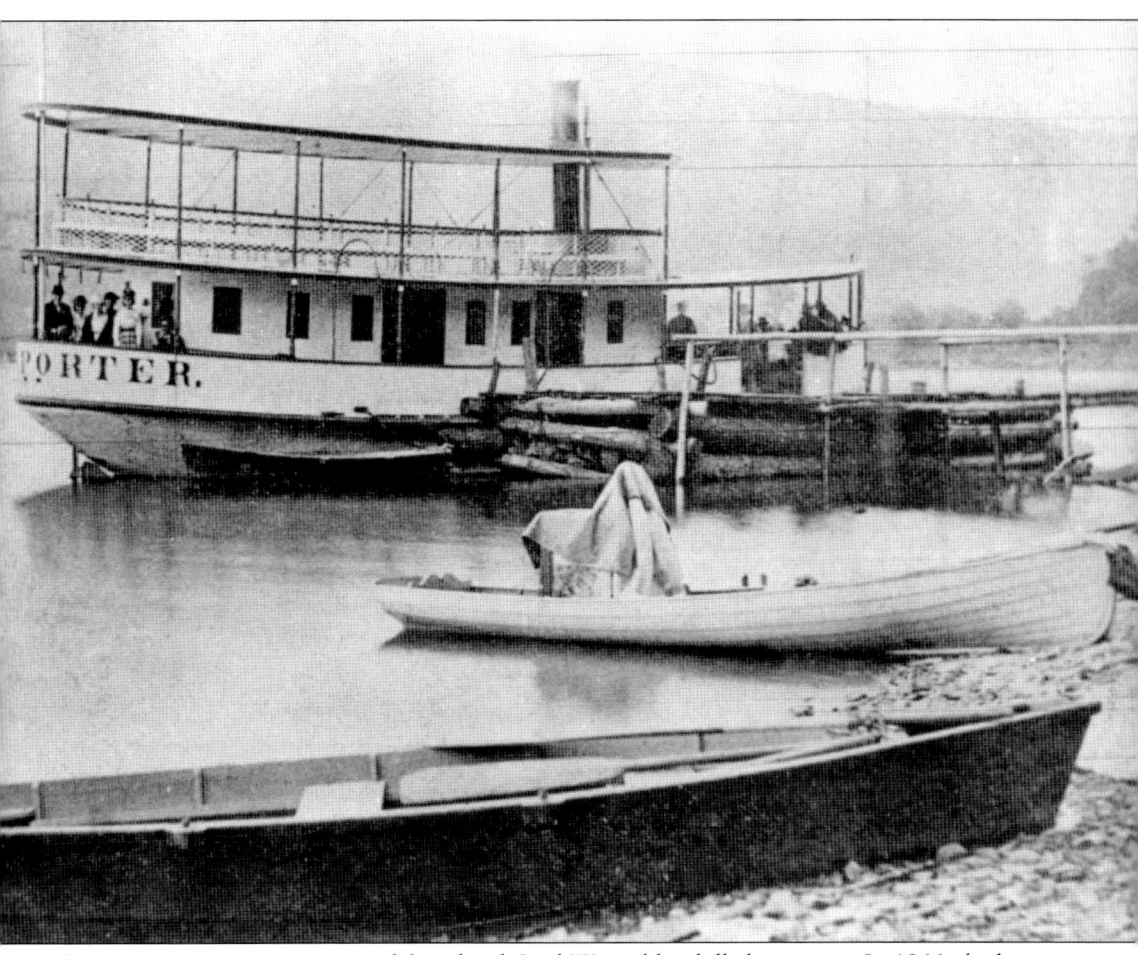

The *Ben Porter* steamer was named for a local Civil War soldier killed in action. In 1866, the boat was christened by young Edith Porter before heading on its maiden voyage from behind the Porter home. The *Ben Porter* was primarily used for hauling supplies, carrying lumber from the south end of the lake to the village, and moving Genesee Street sidewalk stones by raft from Spafford to the village. The demise of the boat is unclear. According to sources, a former deckhand claimed that in 1875 the *Ben Porter* was transported to Cayuga Lake, where it was used as a wood boat. Others believe the steamer sank off Spafford Point and was used as a dock.

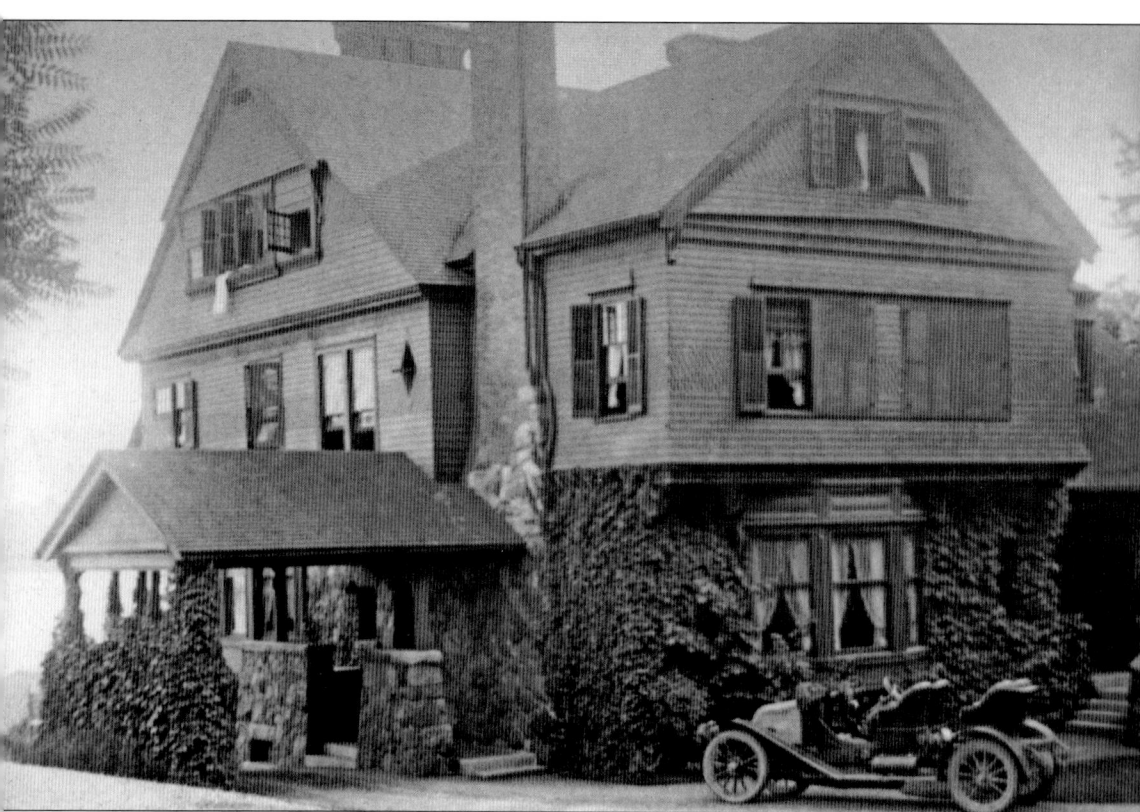

The Boulders on East Genesee Street are distinguished by the large stones that make up the first level of the house and the boathouse. The house, built in 1883, was the inspiration of Joseph C. Willetts, who personally selected the boulders on his property for construction. Willetts was the son of William J. Willetts of West Lake Road. He grew up in a farming family and earned his wealth from farm-related business.

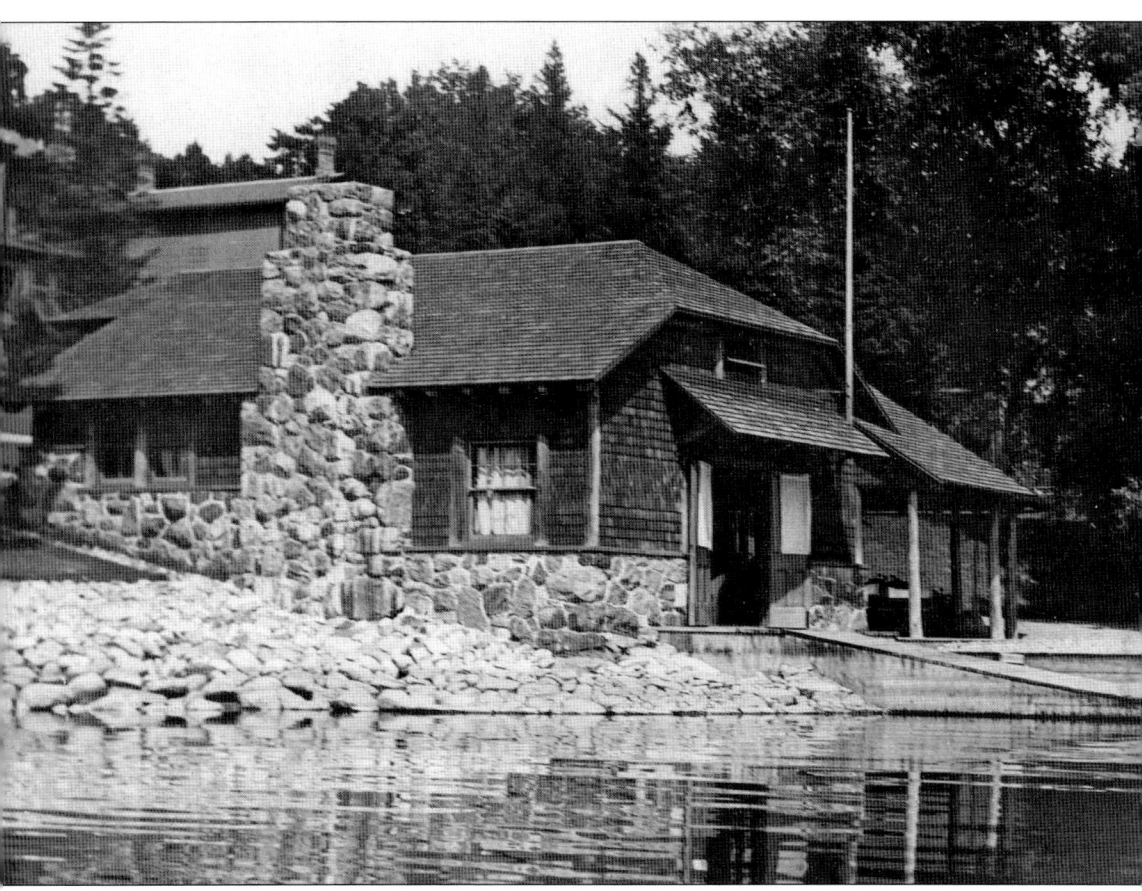

The Willettes enjoyed long summers sailing and entertaining in their boathouse. The property was sold in 1919 and has changed owners several times. At one time, the house was converted into several apartments. Today, the home has been restored to its original grandeur, and the boathouse remains, as has its name.

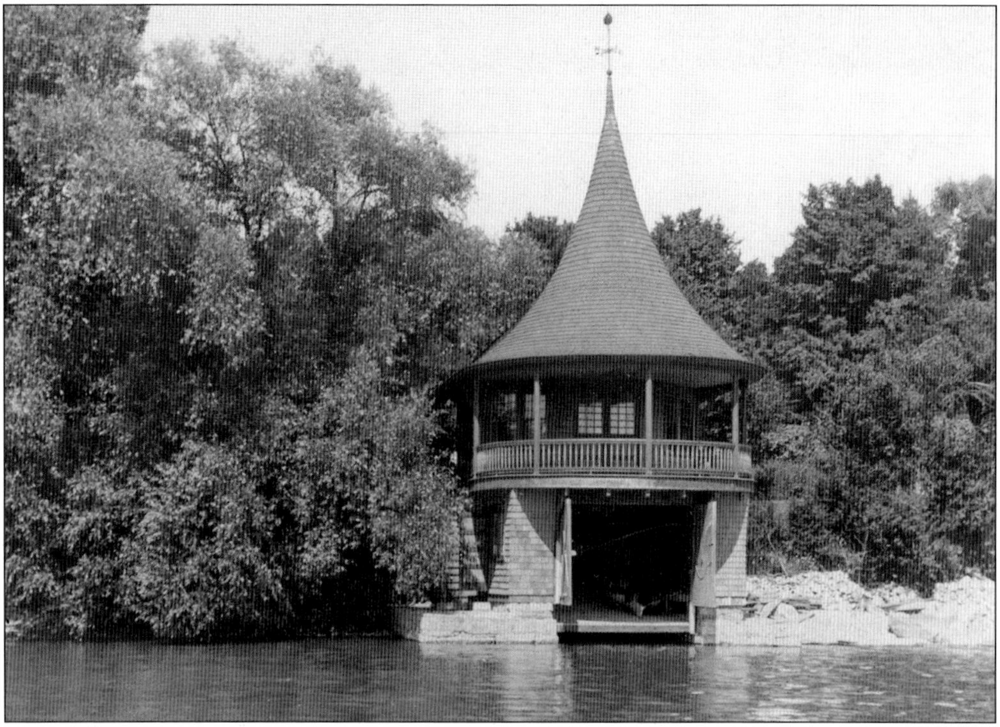

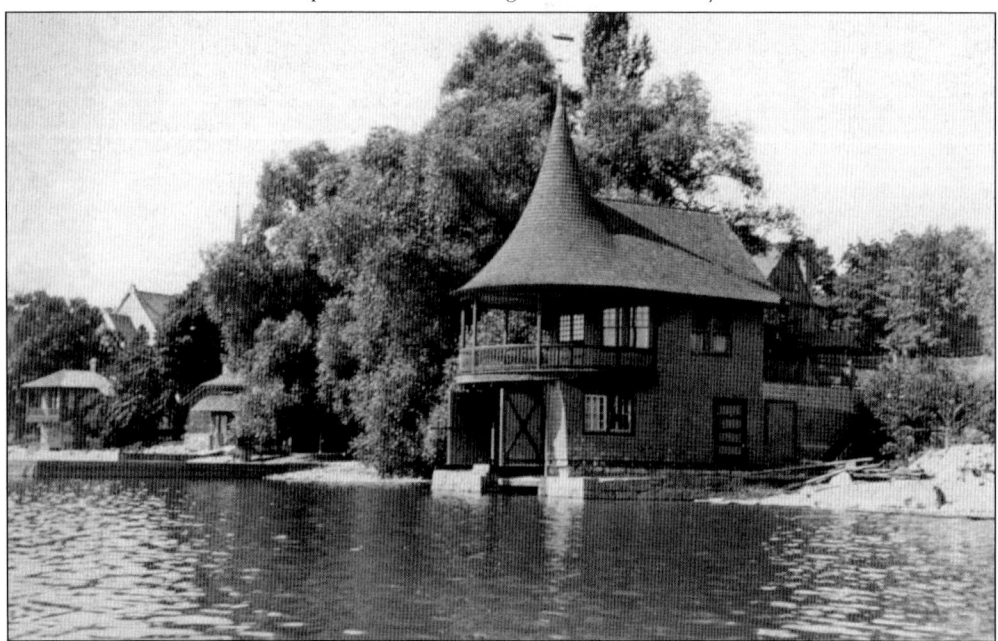

The beautiful summer home next to the Boulders on East Genesee Street was facetiously known as the "Poor House." It was a wedding gift to Cornelia Tyler Longstreet and her husband, Charles Henry Poor II, from Cornelia's father in 1871. Unlike its nickname, it was an elegant house, legally known as Willowbank, with beautiful grounds stretching to the lake. Charles Poor II, son of an admiral, served 23 years in the Navy. He was an avid sailor, hosting regattas during summers spent on Skaneateles Lake. The unique boathouse that graces the lake today was built in the 1800s.

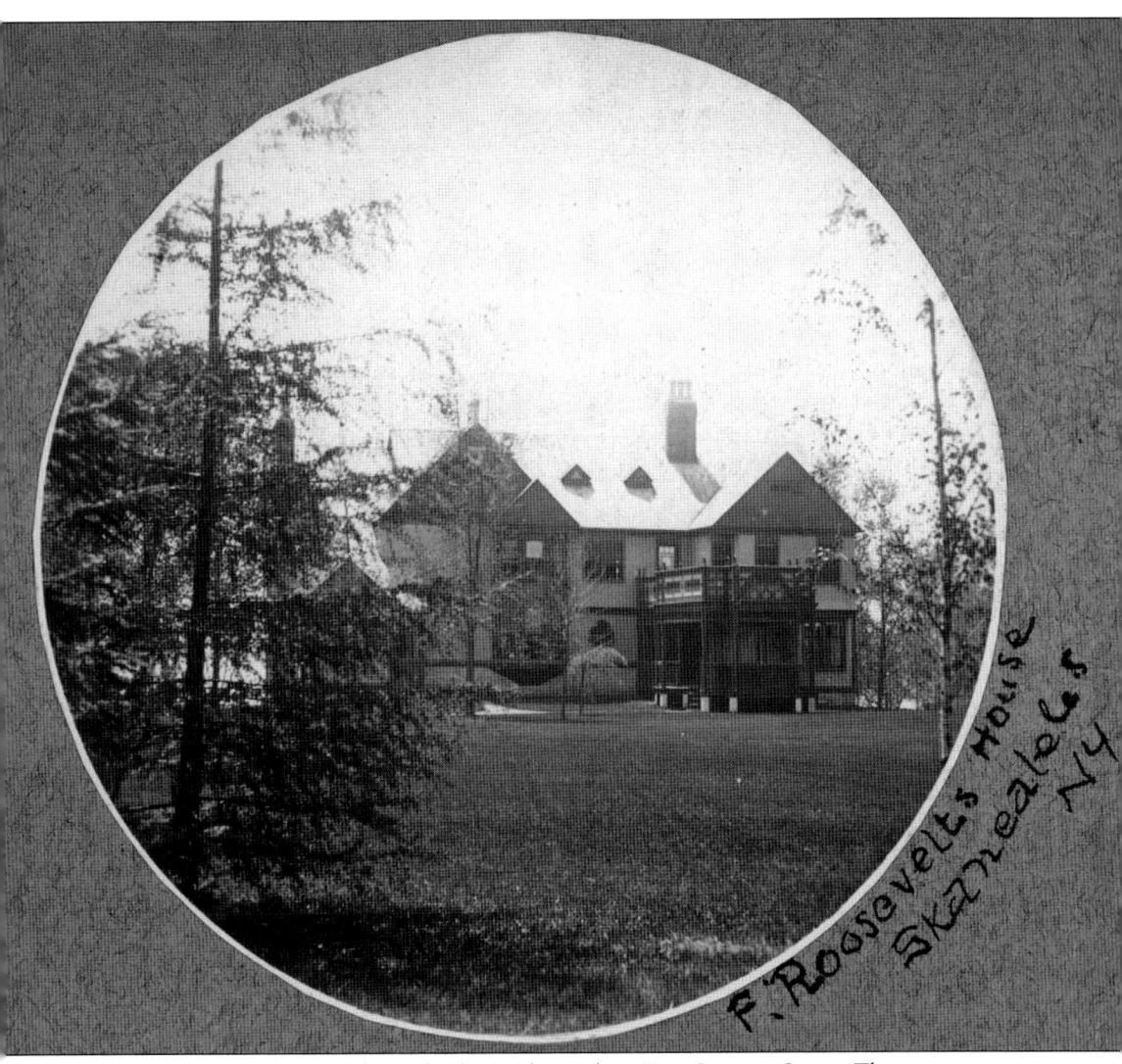

The property, originally named Roseleigh, was located on East Genesee Street. The property was purchased by Frederick Roosevelt of New York City and his wife, Mary Loney of Hazelhurst, in 1879. They wanted a "summer cottage" and hired a well-known architectural firm from New York City, McKinney and Mead, who designed the house seen in the photograph.

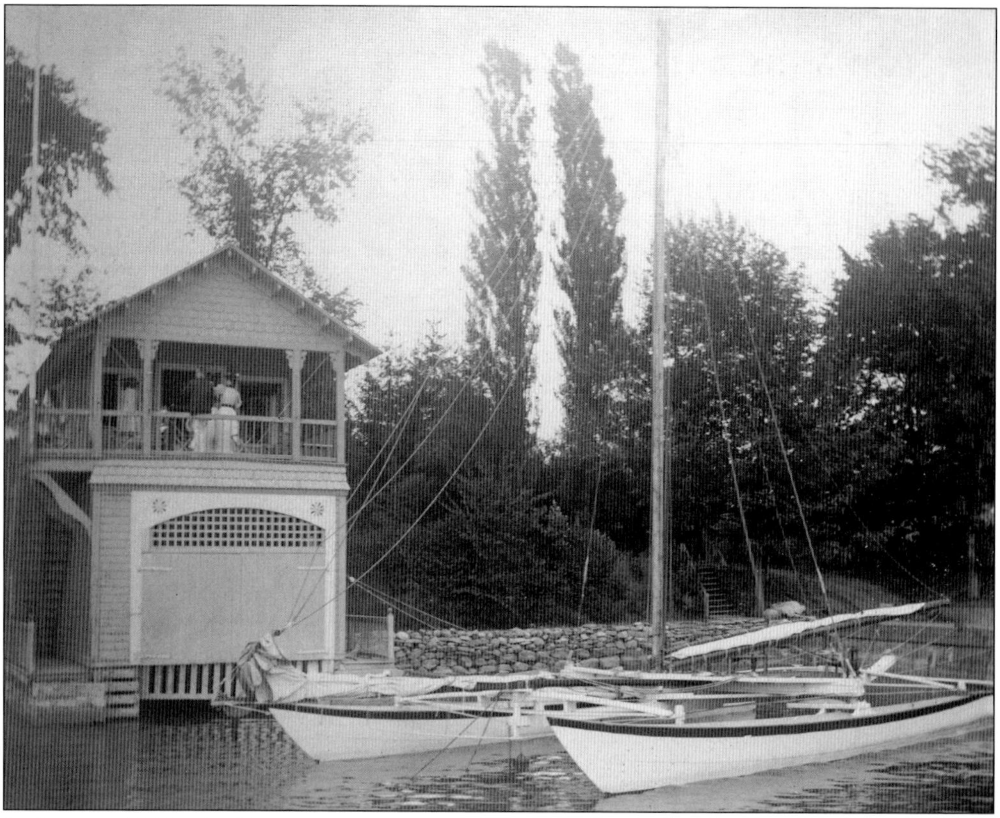

In January 1880, the *Skaneateles Free Press* reported, "During the past summer, Mr. Frederick Roosevelt of New York built a spacious house just east of the village at a cost of nearly $20,000. The lot stretches down to the lake, where a handsome boathouse and substantial dock have been erected. The owner has a fine sailing boat and a staunch little steamer. During the summer, a fair day seldom passes without finding Mr. Roosevelt and his many friends on the lake." In 1917, the Roseleigh property of 10 acres, the house, and the boathouse were sold to Burns Lyman and Smith of the Smith Corona typewriter company. In 1952, Lyman's daughter Flora sold the property to the Sisters of St. Francis of Syracuse to be used as a retreat house, Stella Maris. In 2014, the property was sold. The house was structurally unsound and demolished.

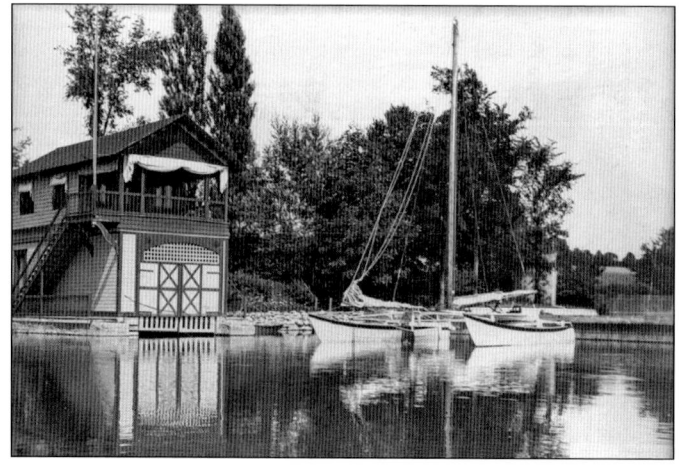

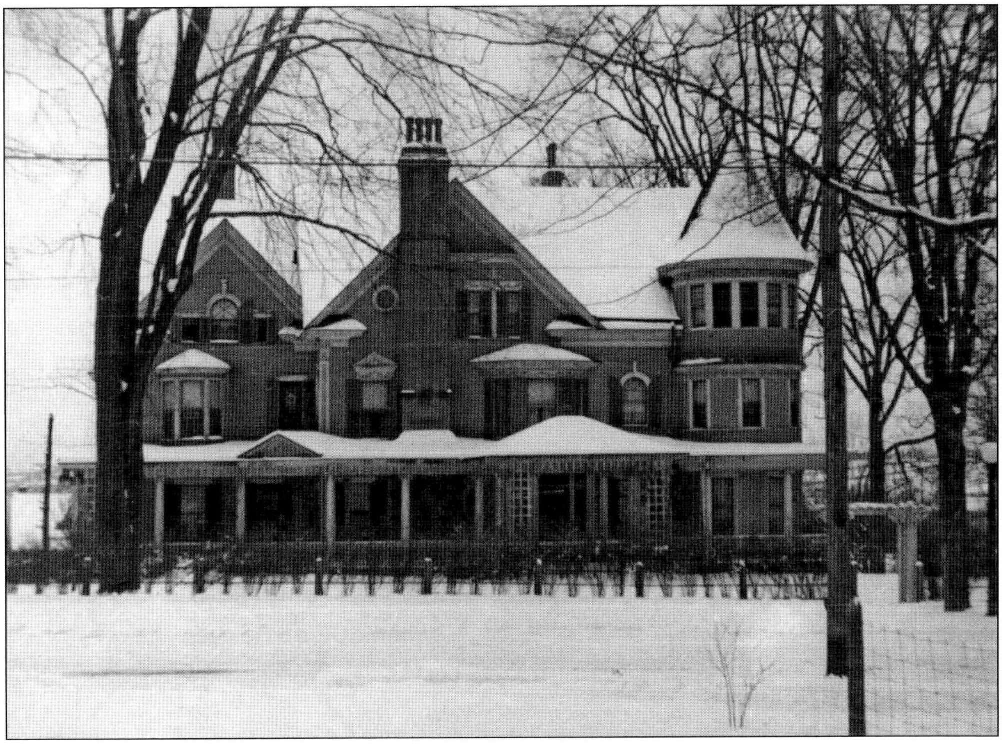

Hazelhurst, located on East Genesee Street (next door to Roseleigh), was built in 1866 by William Loney as a summer residence. It was purchased in 1899 by Theodore Specht, a wealthy German American merchant who came to Skaneateles when his New York City firm bought the Glenside Woolen Mill in Skaneateles Falls. The Specht family is pictured below. The home was remodeled into a year-round home in 1905. The home became a senior living community in 2007.

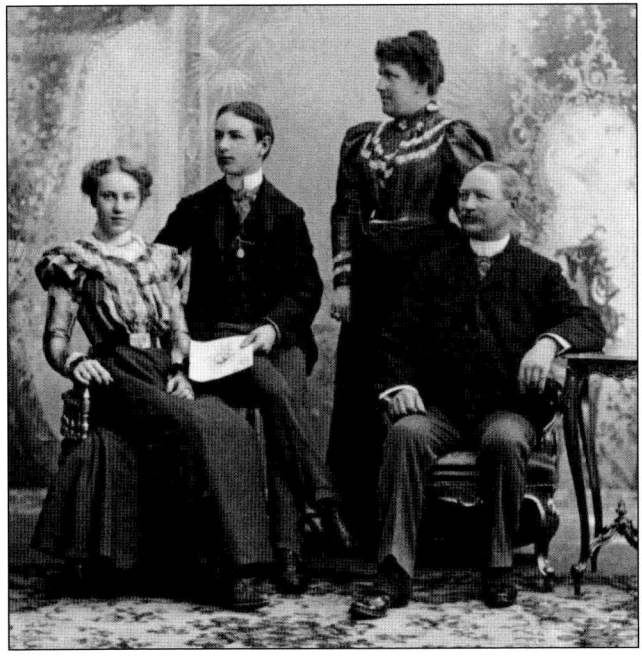

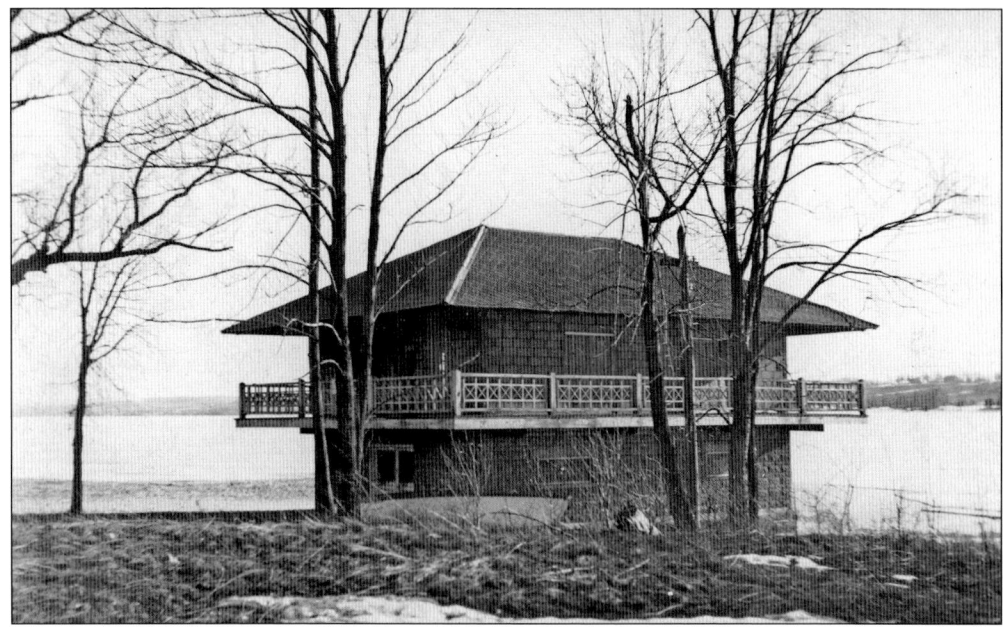

The Specht boathouse was built in 1906, taking advantage of the lake's low level at that time. It was 24 by 26 with space for 007, the fastest speed boat on the lake. The upper floor was used for guests. Today, the boathouse is gone.

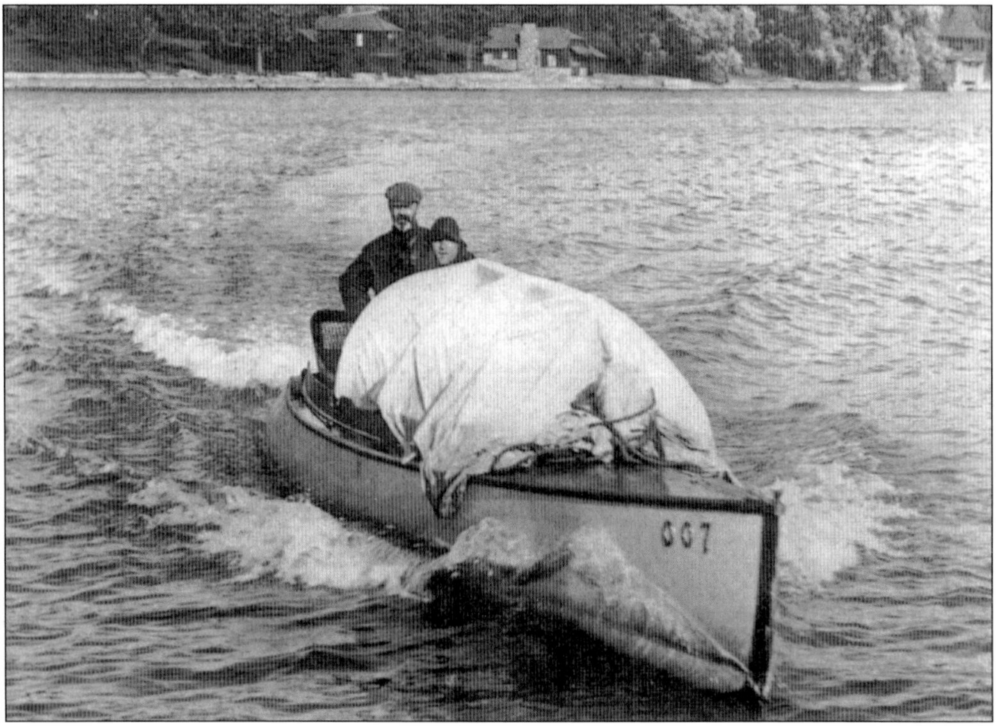

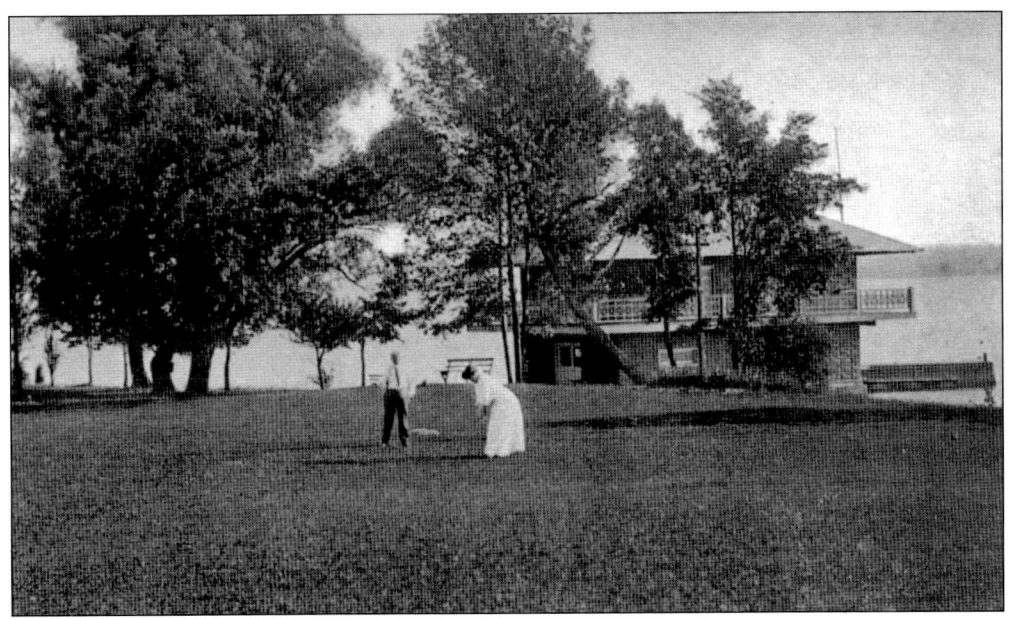

The Spechts were noted for their love of entertaining. The sweeping lawn to the lake accommodated an outdoor bowling area and a small golf course where, in the photograph, Theodore Specht and his daughter are playing golf. The property remained in the Specht family until the 1940s. The estate was sold, and the sweeping lawn was divided into building lots in the 1960s, now known as Lakeview Circle.

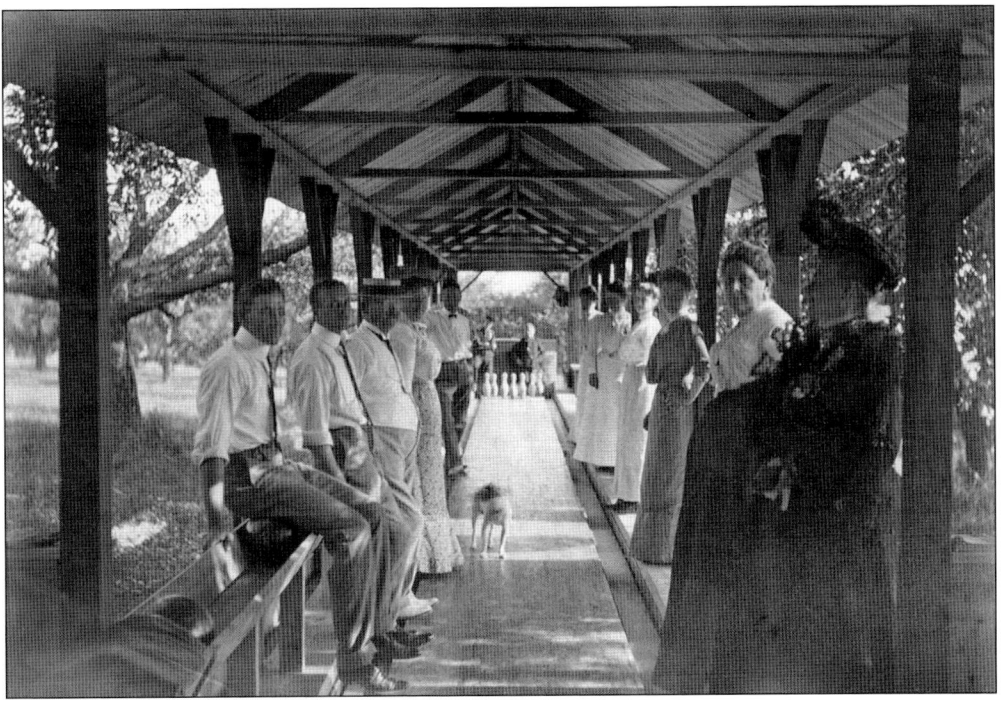

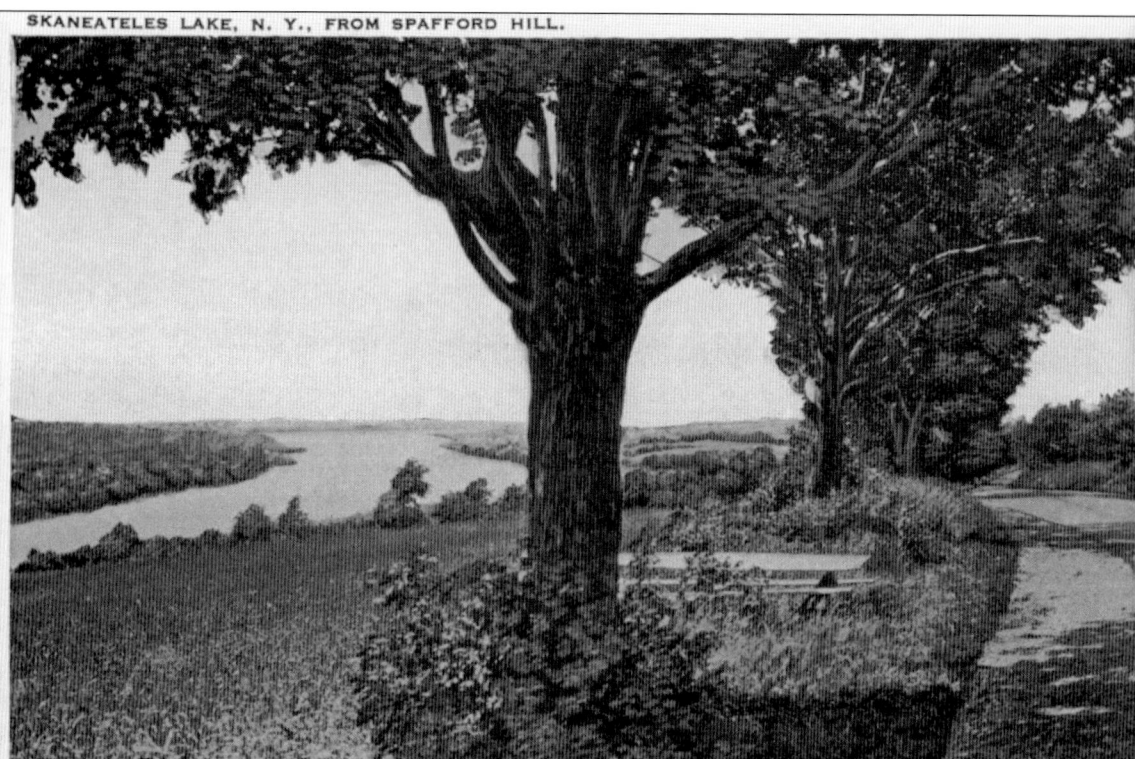

SKANEATELES LAKE, N. Y., FROM SPAFFORD HILL.

Leaving the village of Skaneateles, East Lake Road (Route 41), also known as the Homer Road, follows the eastern lakeshore through rolling hills, providing magnificent views of the lake. Approximately five miles south, still in the county of Onondaga, is the town of Spafford, situated between the eastern shore of Skaneateles Lake and the western shore of Otisco Lake. The town's area is 32.8 square miles of land and 6.4 square miles of water. An early Haudenosaunee trail connected the two lakes.

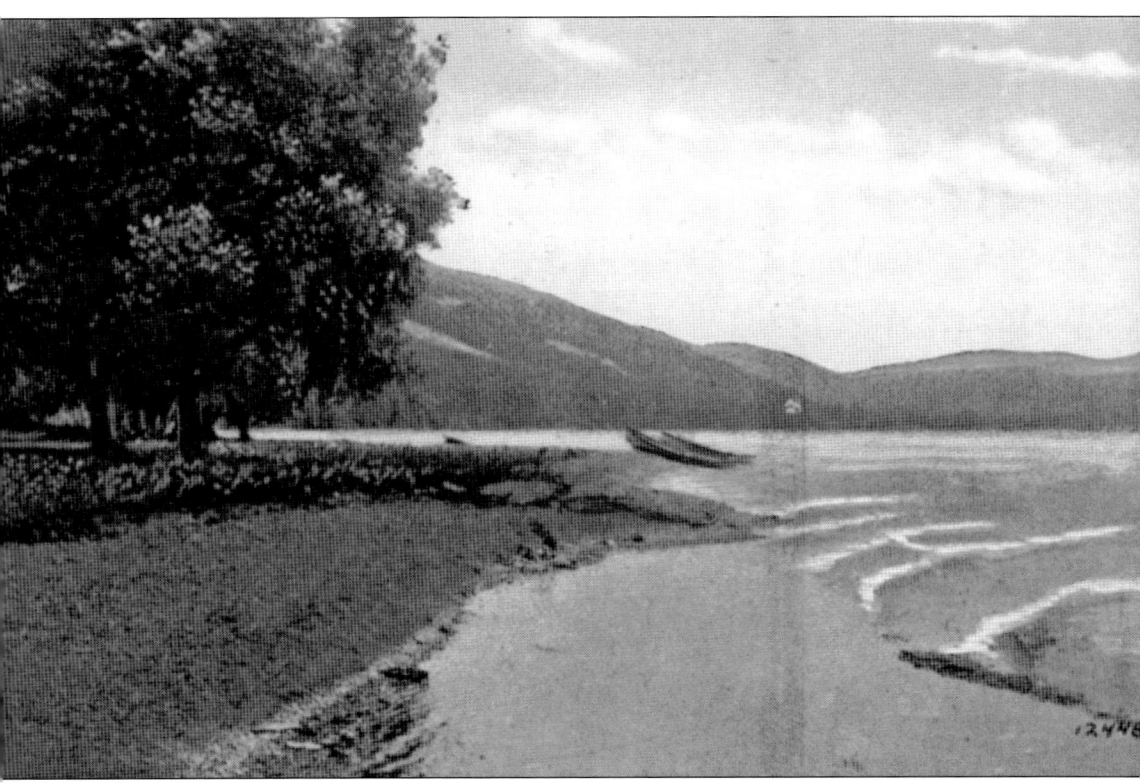

Spafford was originally part of Military Tract 57, located in the larger towns of Marcellus, Sempronius, and Tully. Many of the military tracts in this area were awarded to soldiers from the Hudson Valley and New England who fought in the American Revolution. Gilbert Palmer was the first settler in 1794 from Westchester County. He was followed by some colorful and industrious New England men who settled the area. The town of Spafford was established in 1811 and named for the Honorable Horatio Gates Spafford, author of the first *Gazetteer* of the state of New York. In return, Spafford donated a library for public use. It is noteworthy that between 1811 and 1842, disagreements raged between Marcellus and Skaneateles over the northern boundary of Spafford. A compromise was reached in 1842.

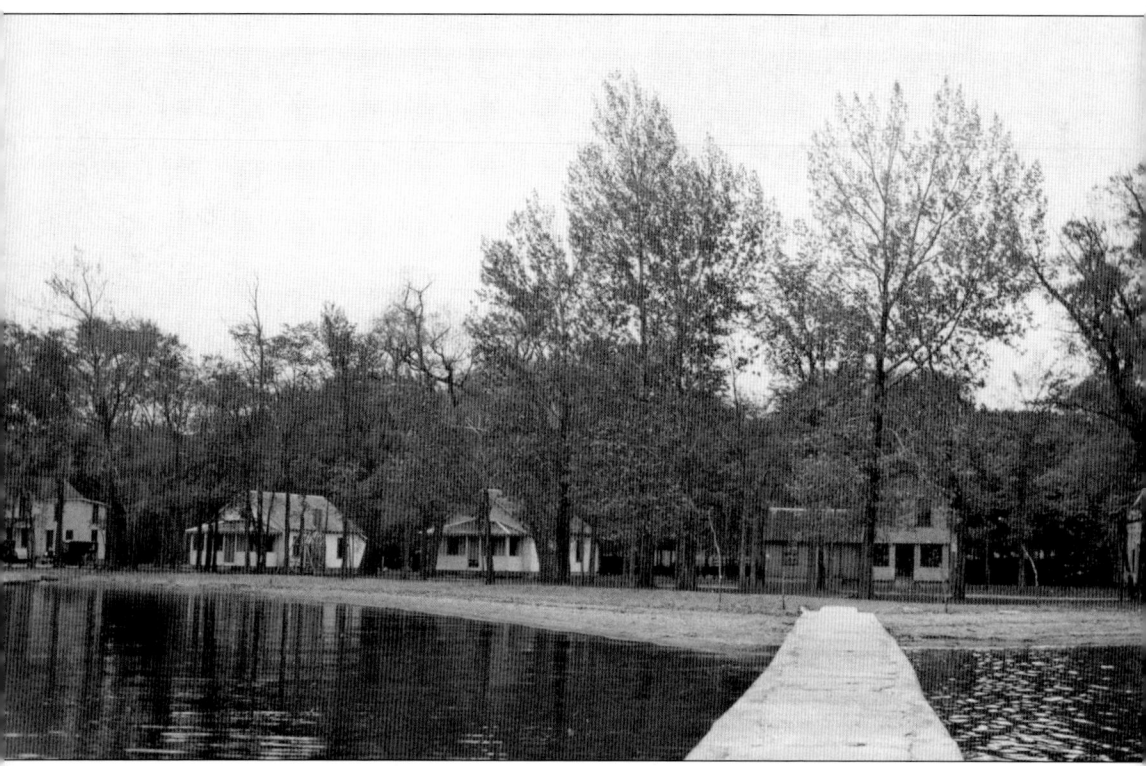

Five Mile Point, in the town of Spafford, has also been known as Factory Point, Edgewater, and Edgewater Park. There, the lake is sandiest and widest at one-and-a-half miles. In the early 1800s, Amos Miner's Wheelhead Factory was located on the point. There was also a cider mill. In 1896, fifteen acres of the point were purchased by Charles M. and Elizabeth Goodspeed of Skaneateles. A hotel and rental cottages were built, as seen in the photograph. In 1902, the Goodspeeds' brochure advertised Edgewater Park as a summer resort on Skaneateles Lake that could be reached by steamboat and car.

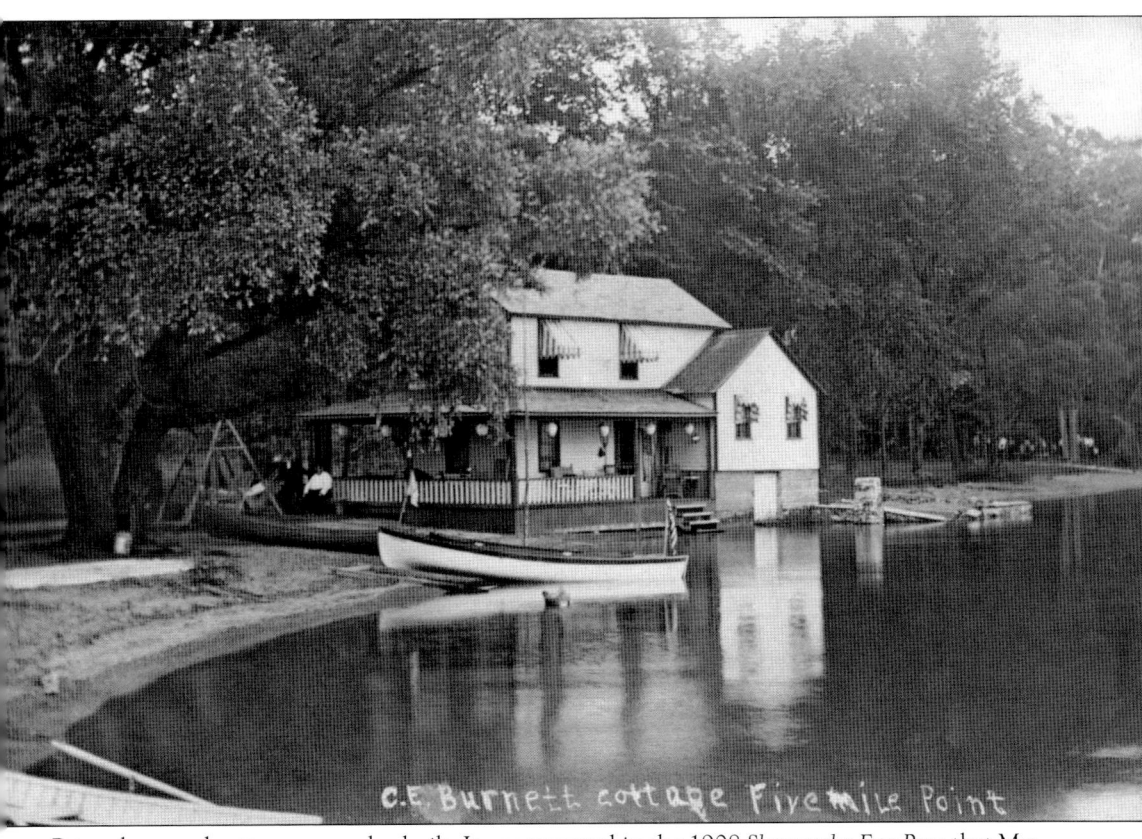

Privately owned cottages were also built. It was reported in the 1908 *Skaneateles Free Press* that Mrs. C.E. Burnett of Rochester enjoyed a picnic at their cottage, which featured an attached boathouse.

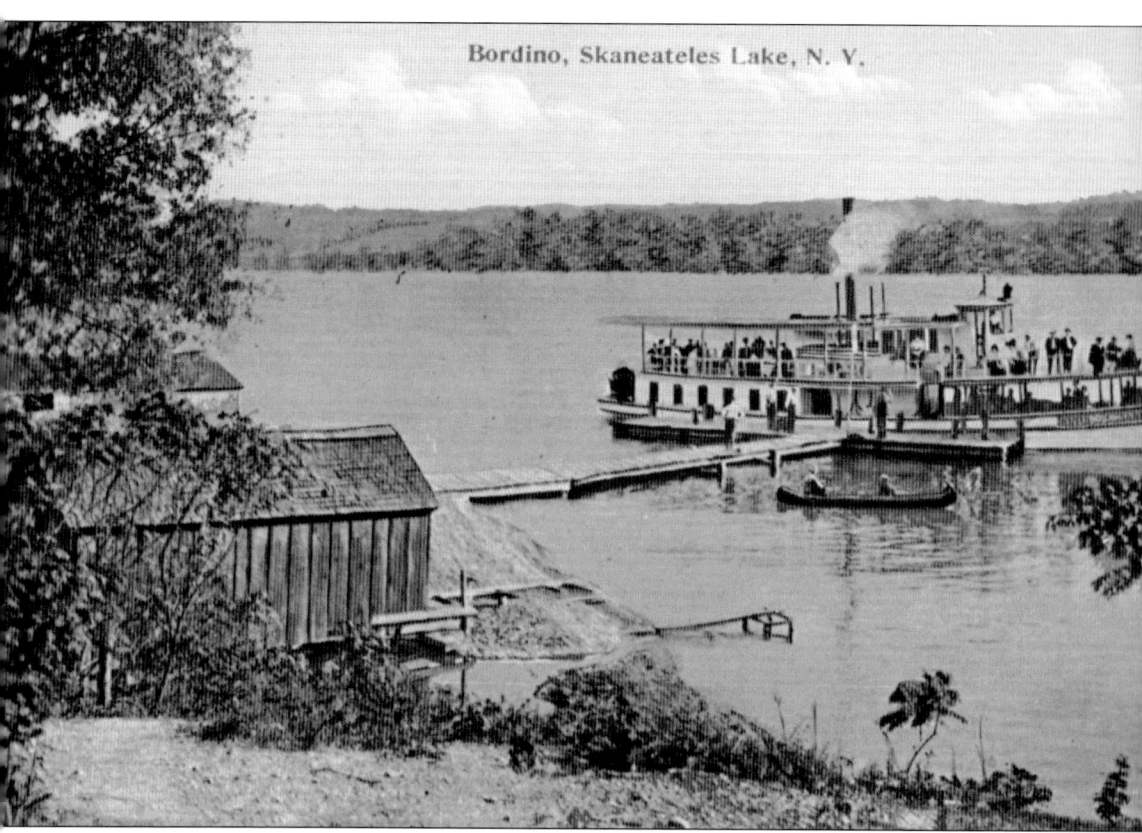

The hamlet of Borodino is located at the intersection of New York State Route 41 (East Lake Road) and New York State Route 174 (Rose Hill Road), which heads east. The first settler came in 1794, followed by others in the early 1800s. The community was first named "Child's Corner" for a local shopkeeper. A prominent local physician, Dr. Benjamin Trumbull, thought the area deserved a better name. It was not unusual to name hamlets and villages for famous battles that were fought around the world. In 1812, the battle of Borodino was fought when Napoleon invaded Russia near the Russian village of Borodino. It was a significant but indecisive battle for the French, very much in the news at the time, and so, the hamlet of Borodino was named.

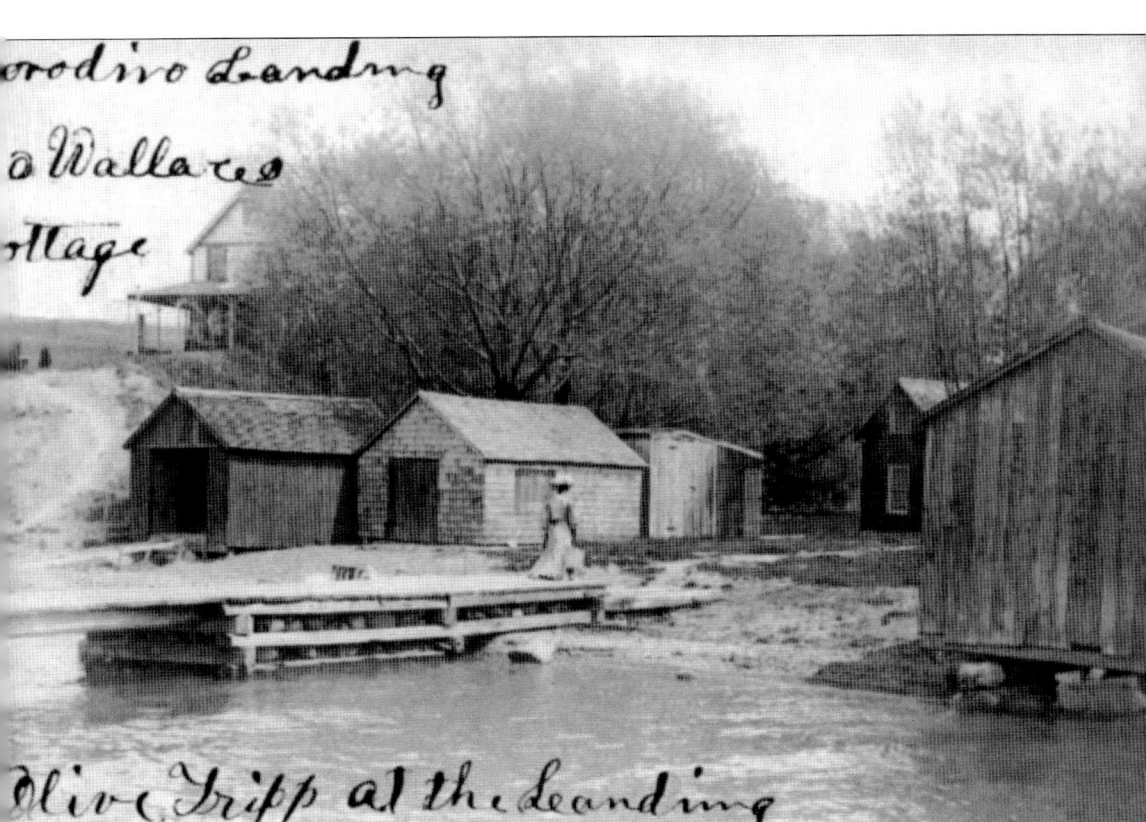

Borodino Landing / a Wallace / llage / Olive Tripp at the Landing

Borodino landing is .75 miles west of the hamlet on the lake. There was a steamboat wharf and boathouses built for residents of the hamlet not living on the water.

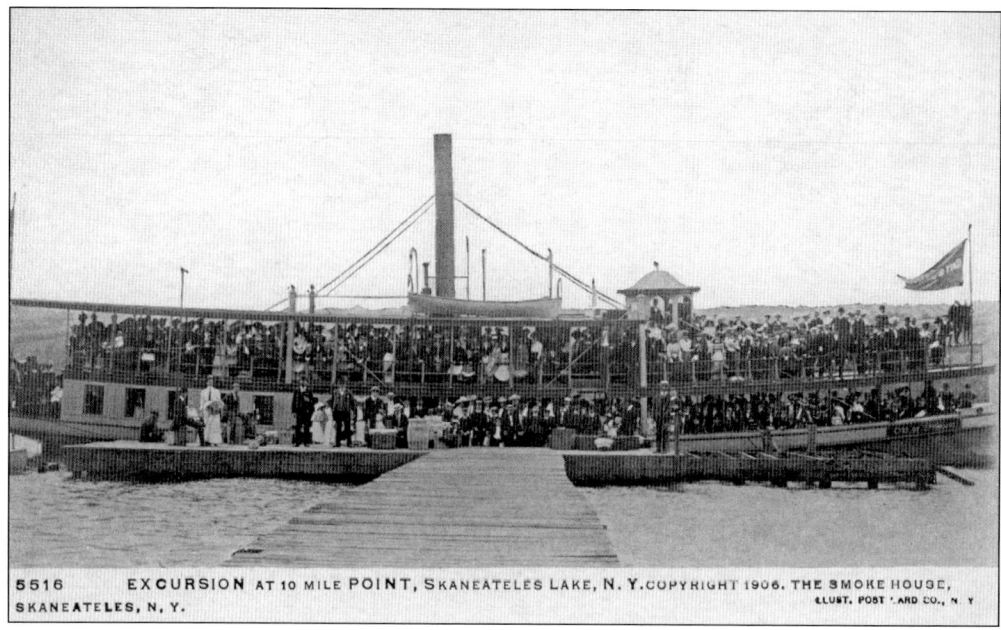

5516 EXCURSION AT 10 MILE POINT, SKANEATELES LAKE, N. Y. COPYRIGHT 1906. THE SMOKE HOUSE, SKANEATELES, N. Y.

Ten Mile Point was a popular destination for lakeside excursions in the late 1800s and early 1900s, as seen in this photograph of the merry group aboard the *City of Syracuse* steamer upon its arrival at the point. The property was owned by the Syracuse & Auburn Electric Railroad and Steamboat Company. A dancing pavilion and a steamboat dock were built for visiting passengers and a place to dry dock steamboats during the winter.

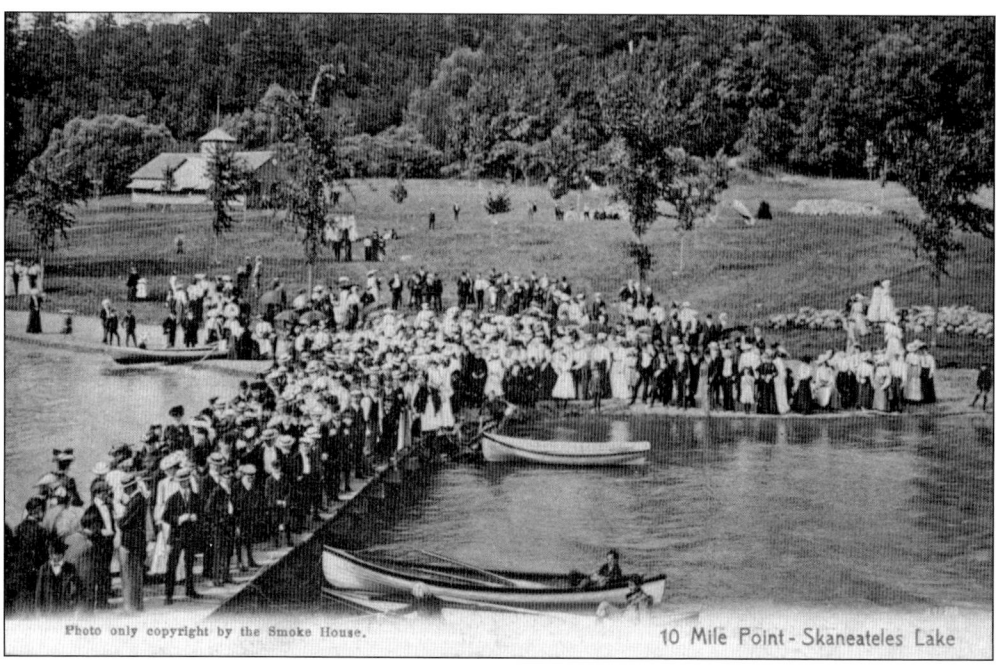

Photo only copyright by the Smoke House.   10 Mile Point - Skaneateles Lake

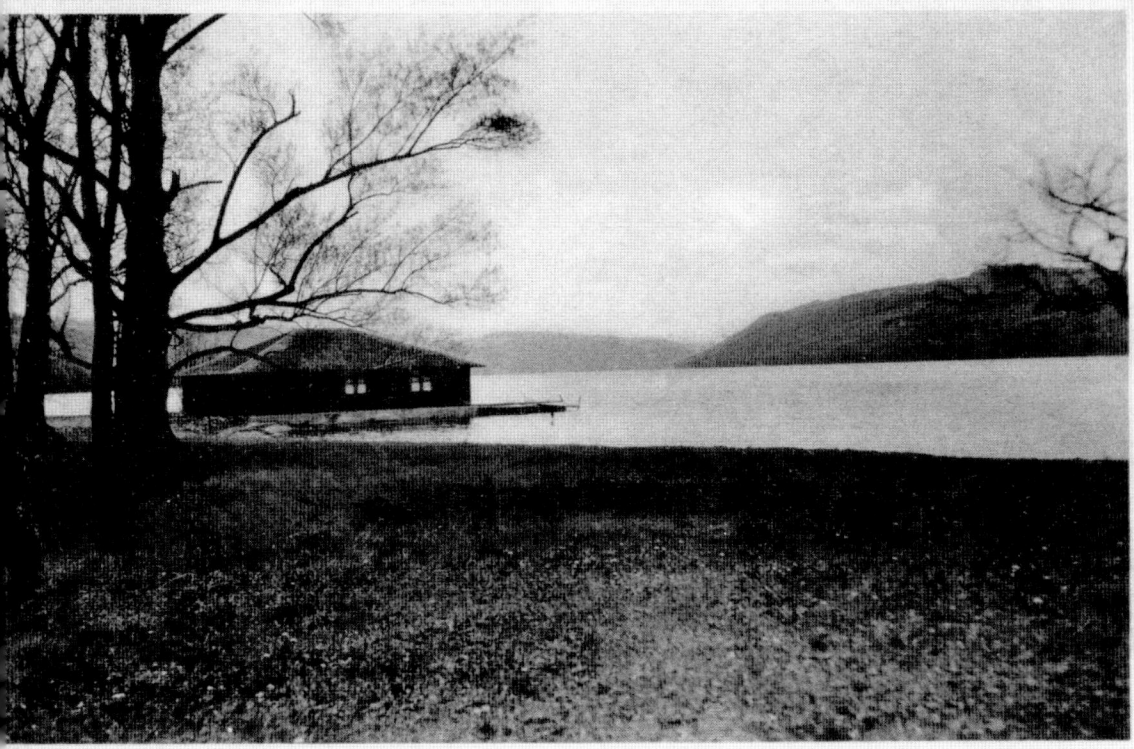
BOAT HOUSE AND LAKE VIEW, LOURDES CAMP, TEN MILE POINT, SKANEATELES LAKE, N. Y.

In 1922, Frederick Harris Nichols bought 50 acres of land on Ten Mile Point from the Auburn & Syracuse Electric Railway. Frederick worked for Nichols Copper in New York City. His wife, Clarinda, was from Syracuse. The acreage accommodated two summer cottages, separate cottages for the Nichols children, a guest lodge, a four-car garage, and a boathouse on the shoreline, seen in the photograph. In 1942, Clarinda was killed in a fire in the cottage, which started from an oil-burning water heater. The family never returned. Having failed to sell the property for $50,000 in 1952, the Nichols family donated it to the Syracuse Catholic Diocese. The family's wish was that the property be used as a summer camp for young people of all denominations. Lourdes Camp was established in the 1960s. The boathouse remains in use today for campers and social events.

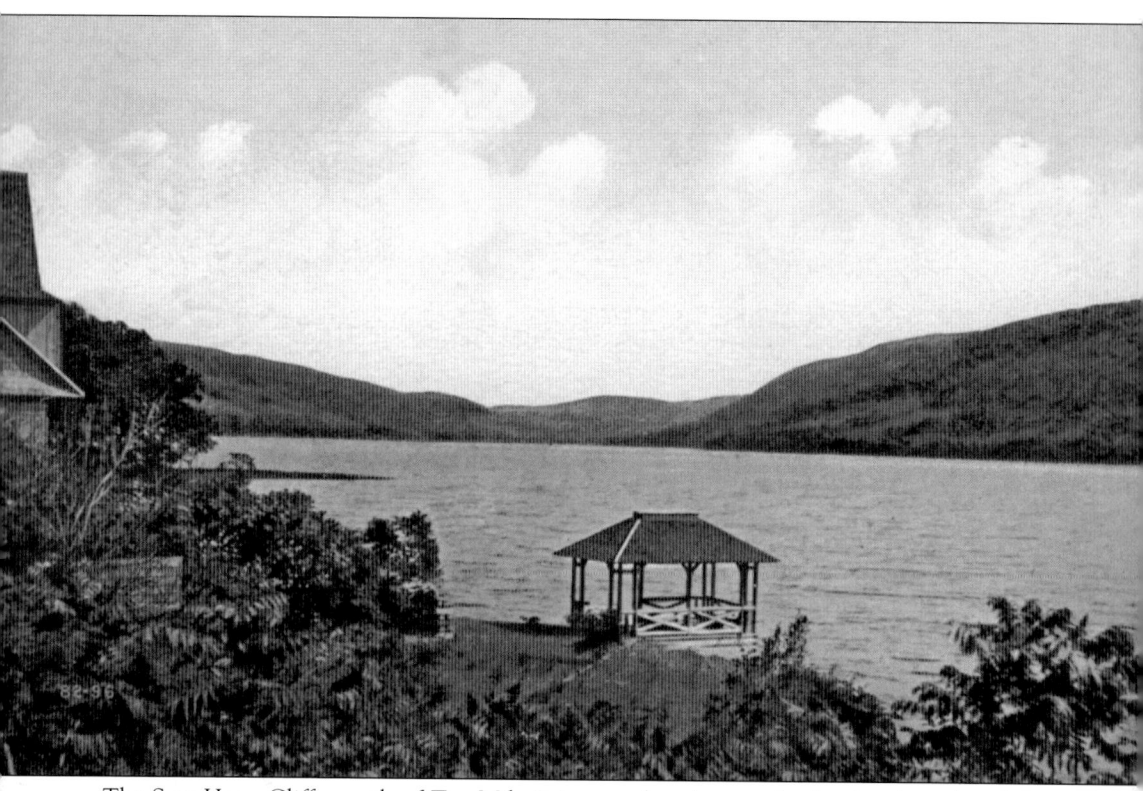

The Stag Horn Cliffs, south of Ten Mile Point, are best known for fossilized coral reefs known as Stag Horn Coral. These reefs were formed 300–500 million years ago when the land area was covered by a shallow sea. Fossilized Stag Horn Coral is found only in two places in the world, Skaneateles and Australia.

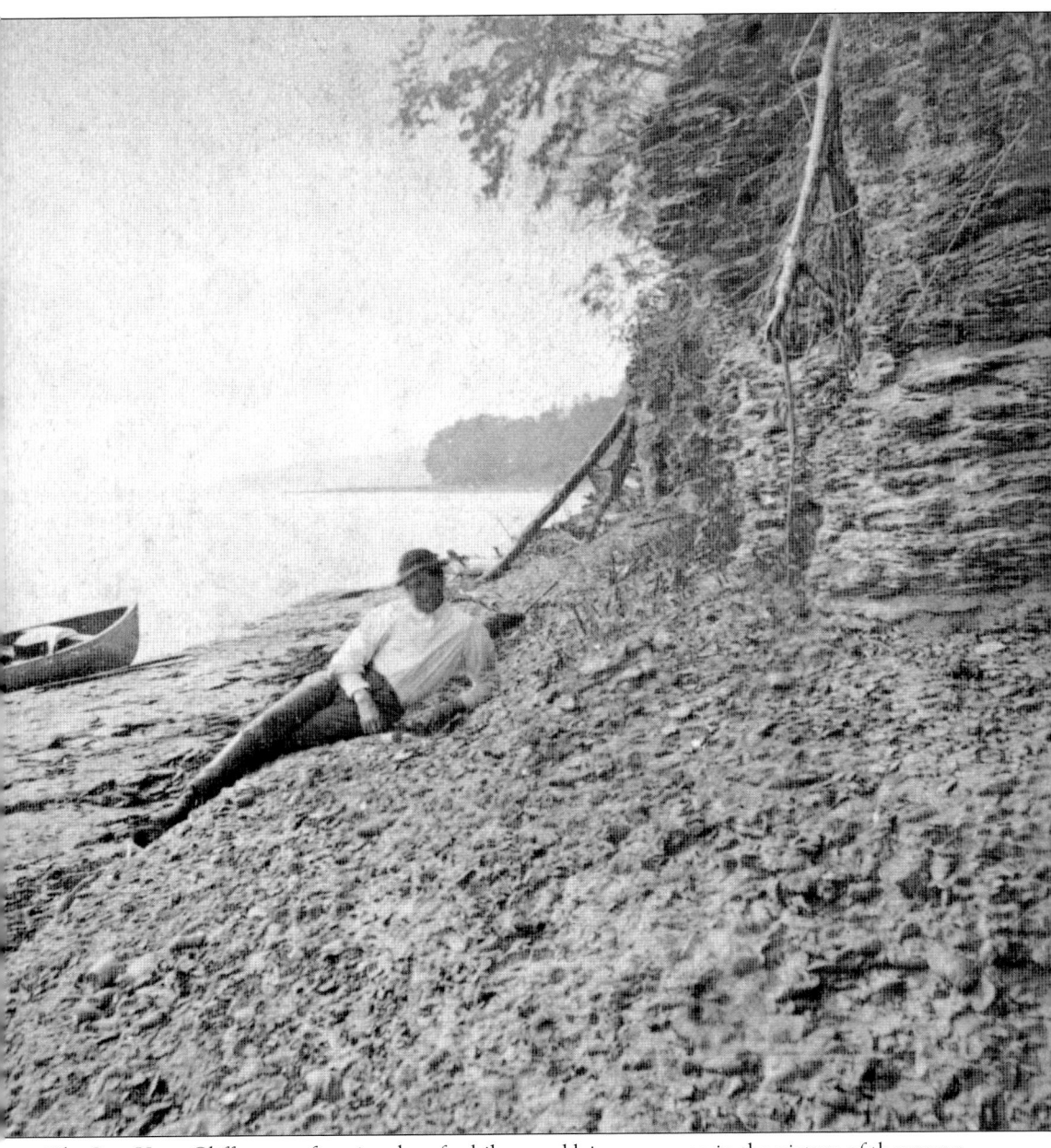

The Stag Horn Cliffs were a favorite place for hikers and leisure, as seen in the picture of the young man relaxing on the beach. Today, these cliffs and fossils are forested and protected as a part of the Cora Kampfe Dickinson Conservation Area.

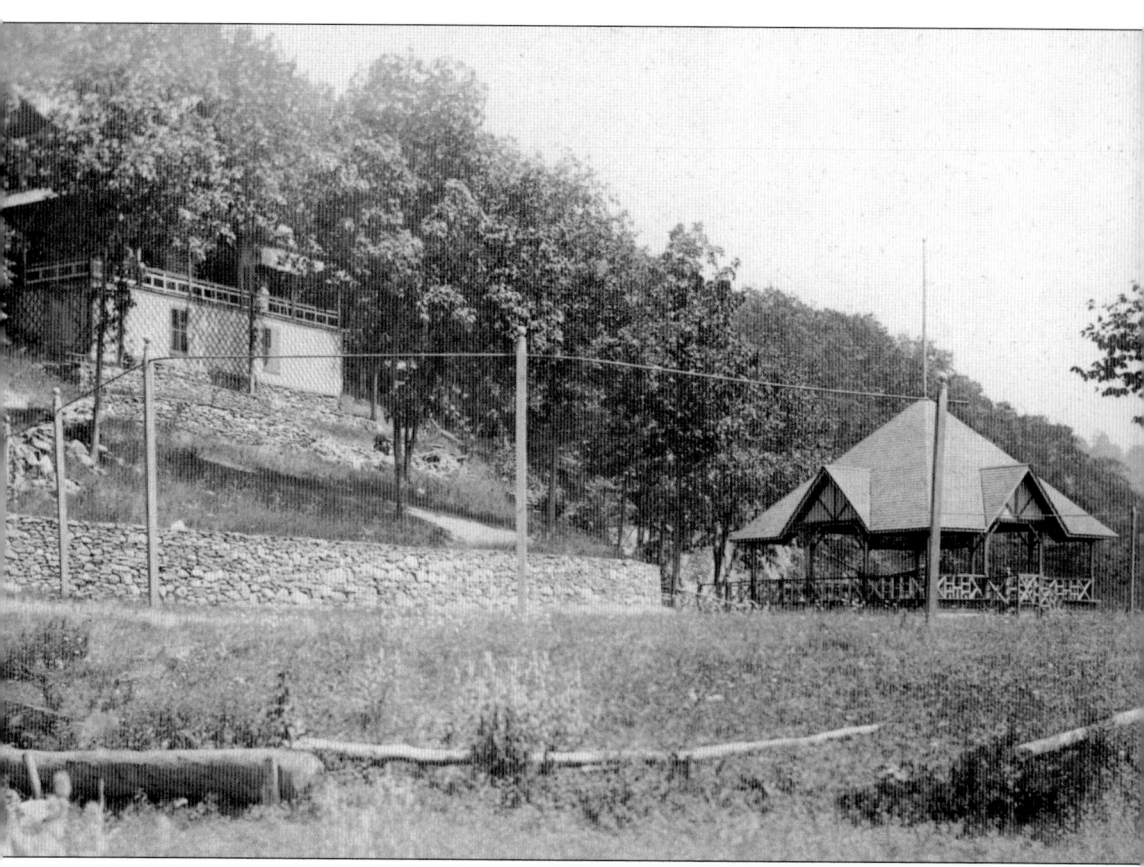

Nestled among the Spafford hills of the Stag Horn Cliffs, the Jenney cottage was the summer place of the Jenney family of Syracuse, New York. The patriarch, Edwin Sherman Jenney, led regiments for the Union army during the Civil War. After returning from the war, he became a leading Syracuse lawyer and the husband of Marie Saul Jenney, who became dean of a Syracuse women's club, providing social and intellectual guidance for generations of women. The Jenneys raised four children, three of whom were successful lawyers and one of whom shaped American social history.

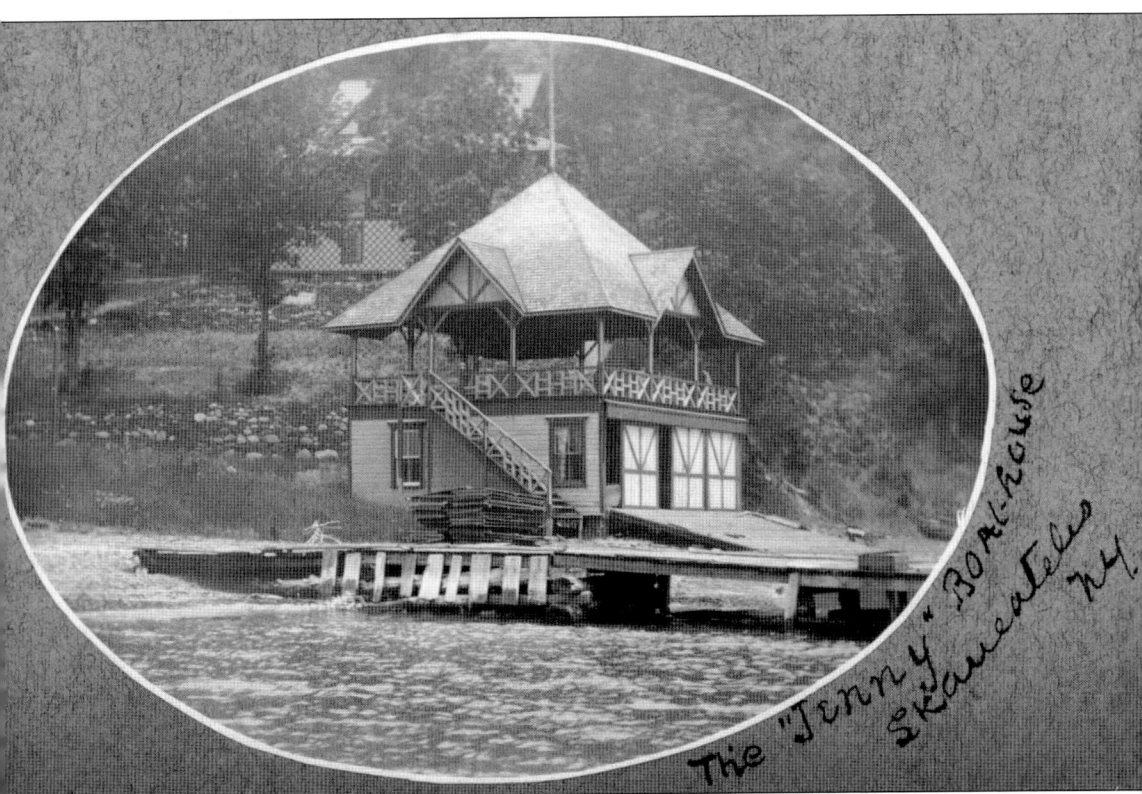

In 1886, Marie Saul Jenney, Edwin's wife, purchased land in the Spafford hills from George Barrow to build a cottage and boathouse (seen in the photograph). In 1904, the cottage was rebuilt following a fire. The extended family was often at the cottage until 1916, when following family illness and death, the cottage became a rental. The grand boathouse no longer exists.

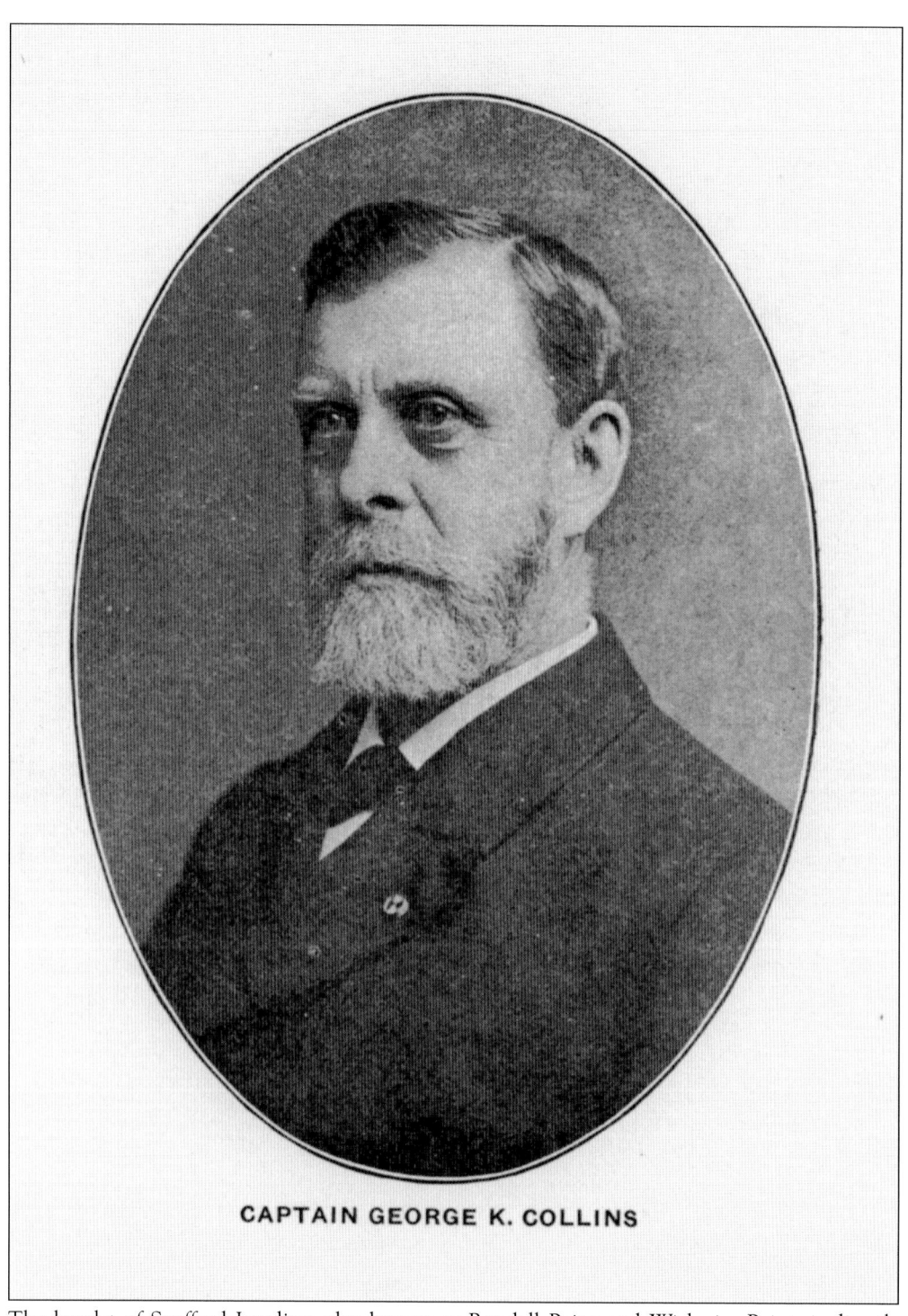

CAPTAIN GEORGE K. COLLINS

The hamlet of Spafford Landing, also known as Randall Point and Wickwire Point, is directly south of the Stag Horn Cliffs. The first private summer cottage was built on the lake by Capt. George C. Collins in 1881. Most people thought this unpretentious building was a foolhardy investment and that summer cottages would never amount to anything.

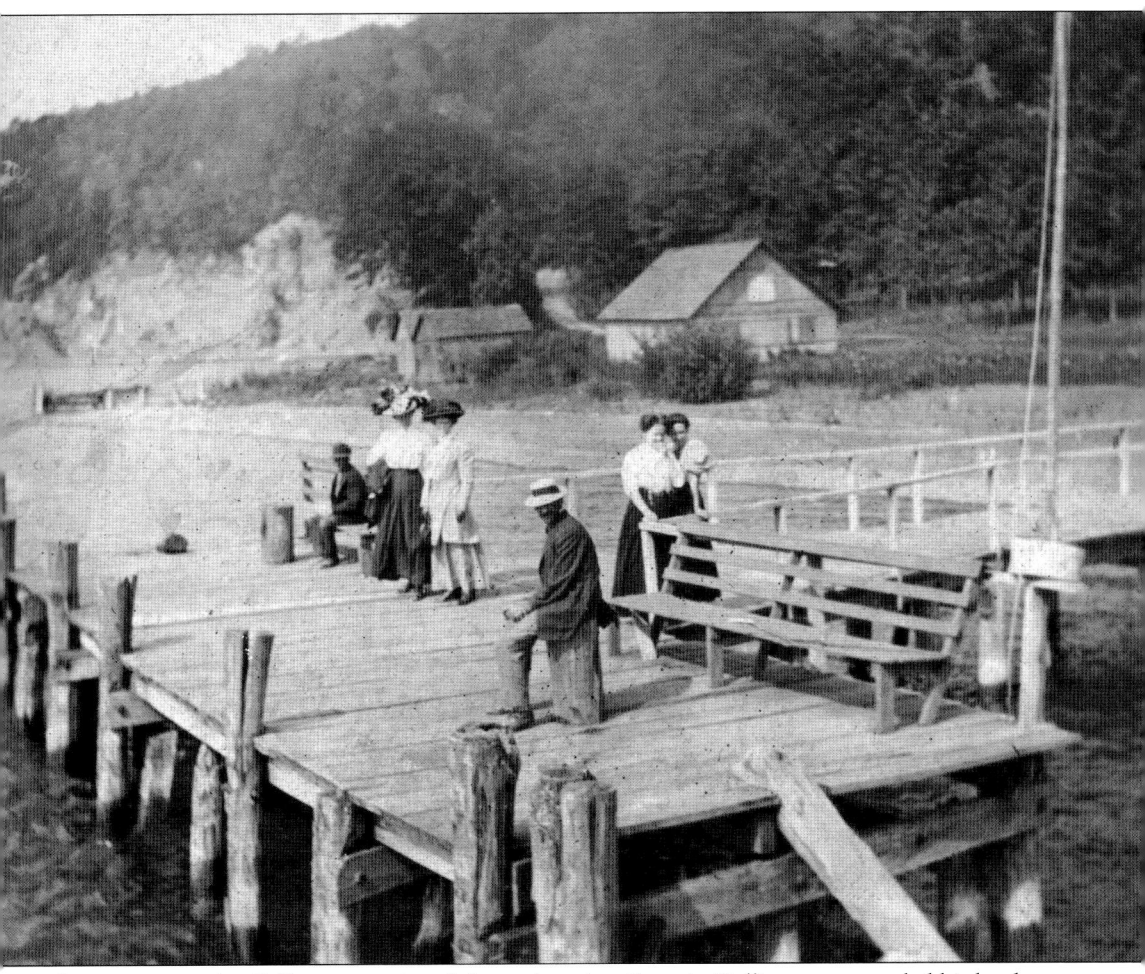
Guests visiting the Collinses so enjoyed themselves that Captain Collins soon parceled his land to make room for more cottages. Many summer cottages followed, and the popularity of the lake as a summer resort was established.

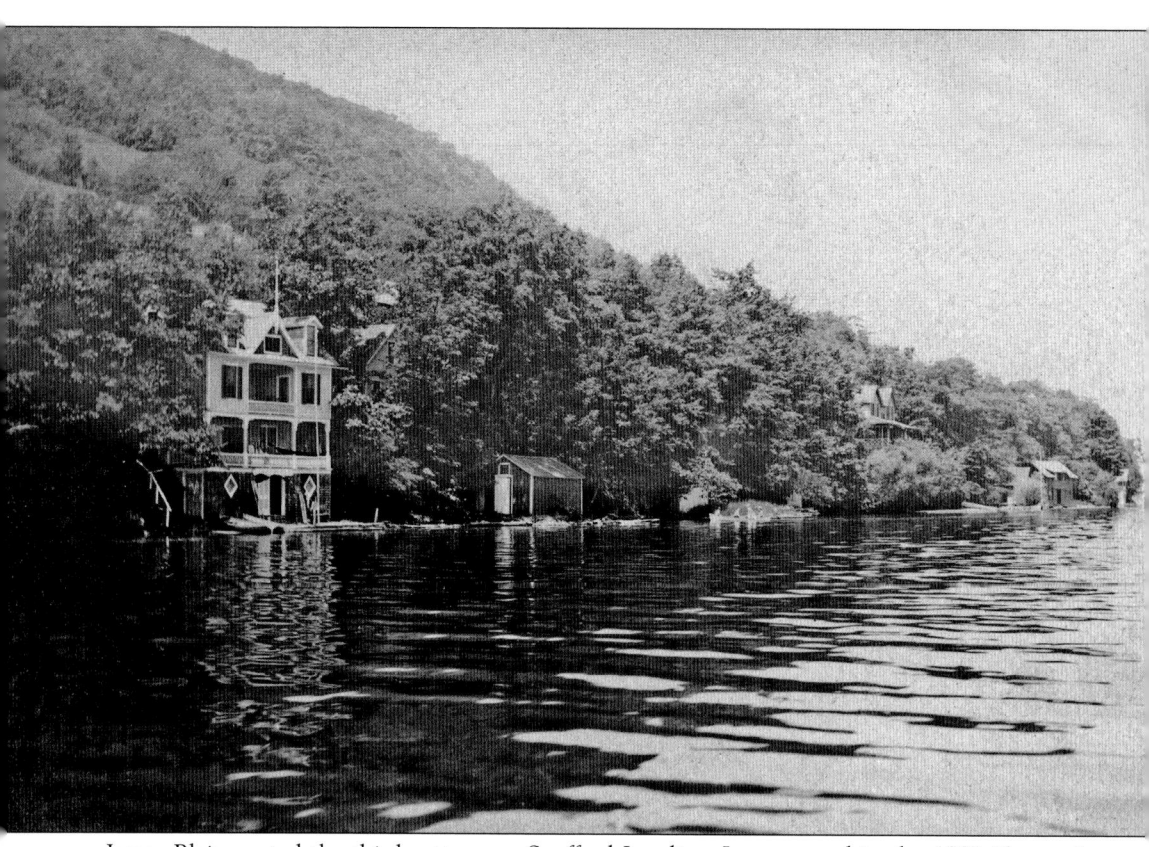

James Blair erected the third cottage on Spafford Landing. It was noted in the 1883 *Skaneateles Democrat* that "James Blair of Syracuse is building a handsome boathouse, similar in design to the one on the premises of Frederick Roosevelt in the village of Skaneateles."

Six

THE SOUTH SHORE

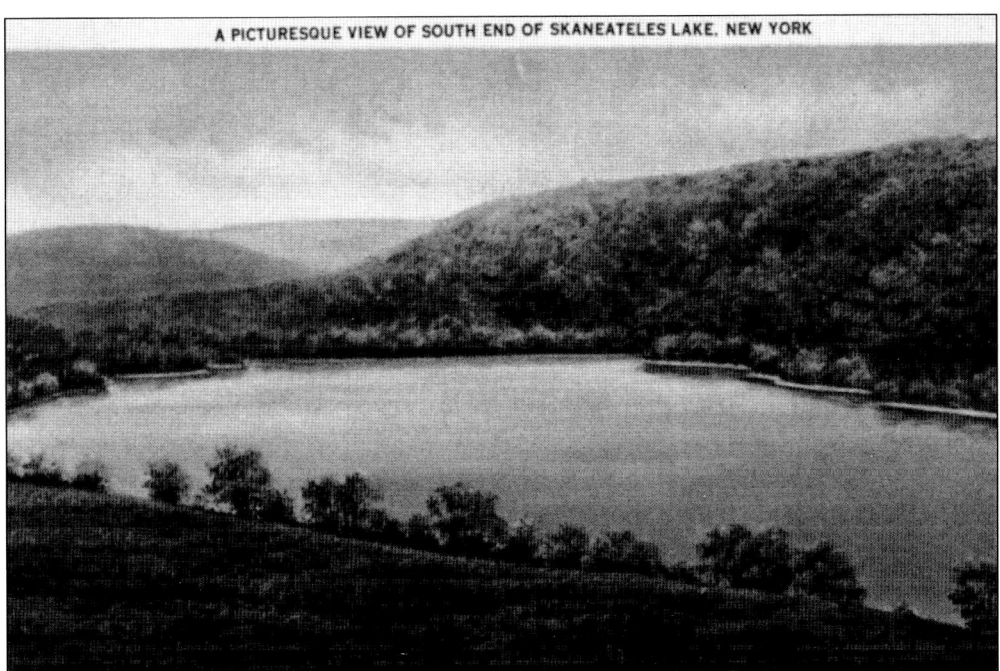

Glen Haven is a small hamlet located at the head of Skaneateles Lake. The eastern portion of the community is known as Fair Haven (formerly Ceylon), located in the town of Scott, Cortland County. The western portion is located directly across the head of the lake in the town of Sempronius, Cayuga County. The two areas are connected by the Glen Haven Road. Collectively, the entire area is known as Glen Haven. The peaceful beauty of this area attracted summer visitors. Hydrotherapy had become popular in the 1840s, and in 1847, the western portion was selected as a site for the Glen Haven Water Cure.

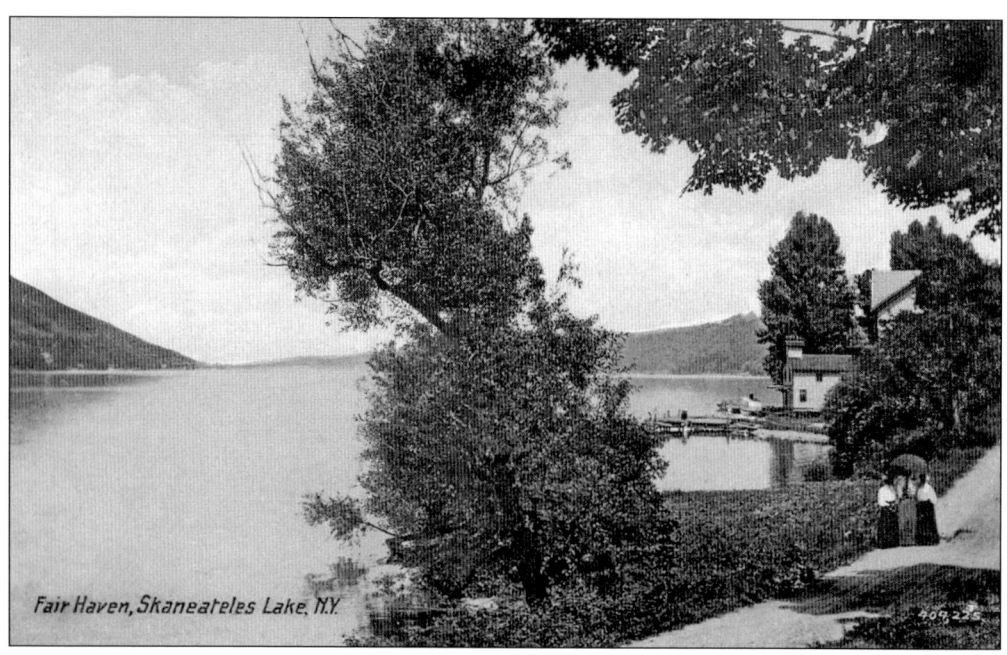

Fair Haven became a community with a sawmill, boat factory, hotel, saloon, hitching barn, general store, and post office on the shoreline. The store and post office in Fair Haven (shown below) had to be moved back when the lake was raised six feet to facilitate its use as a water source for Syracuse in 1894.

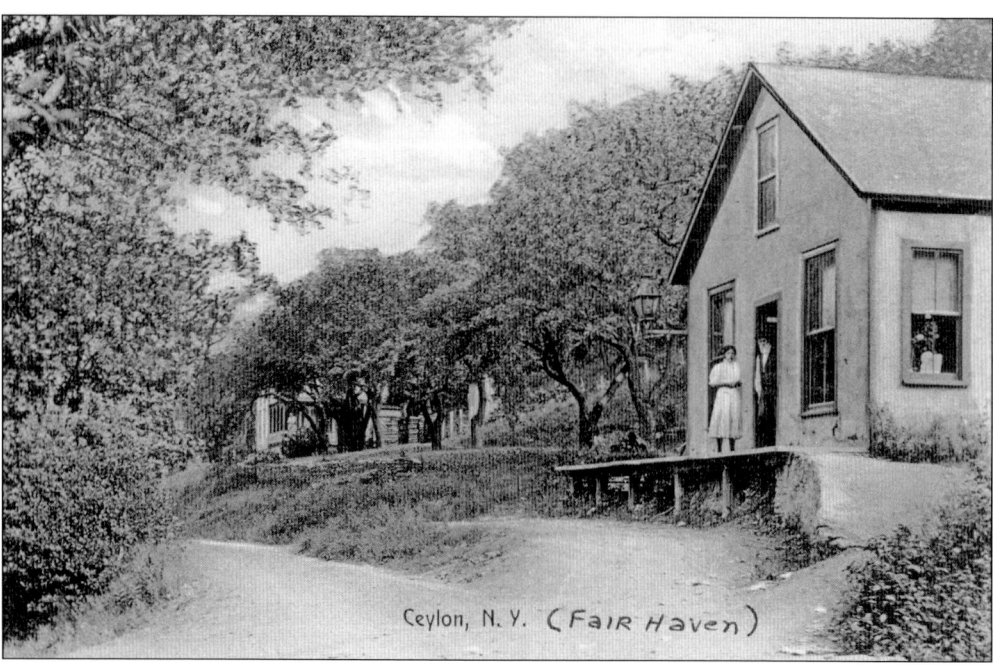

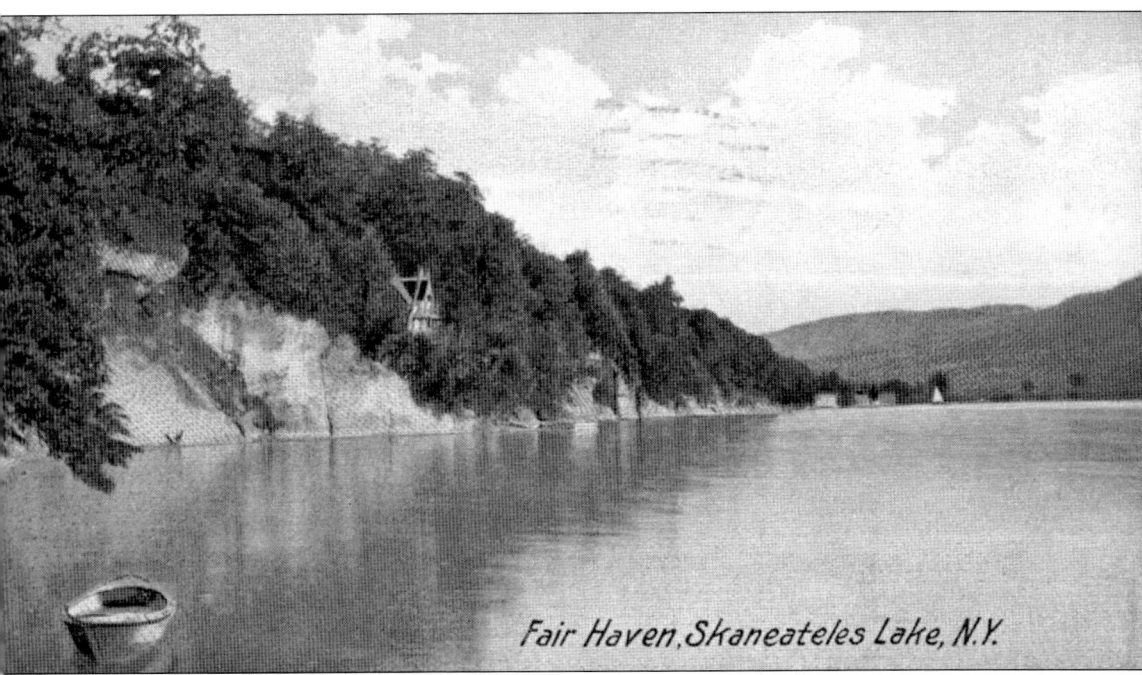

Fair Haven was home to many cottages built for summer leisure. Rockland cottage, constructed in 1884 by steamship builder Samuel Allen, is seen overlooking the lake in this photograph. The cottage had a commanding view of the northwest shore.

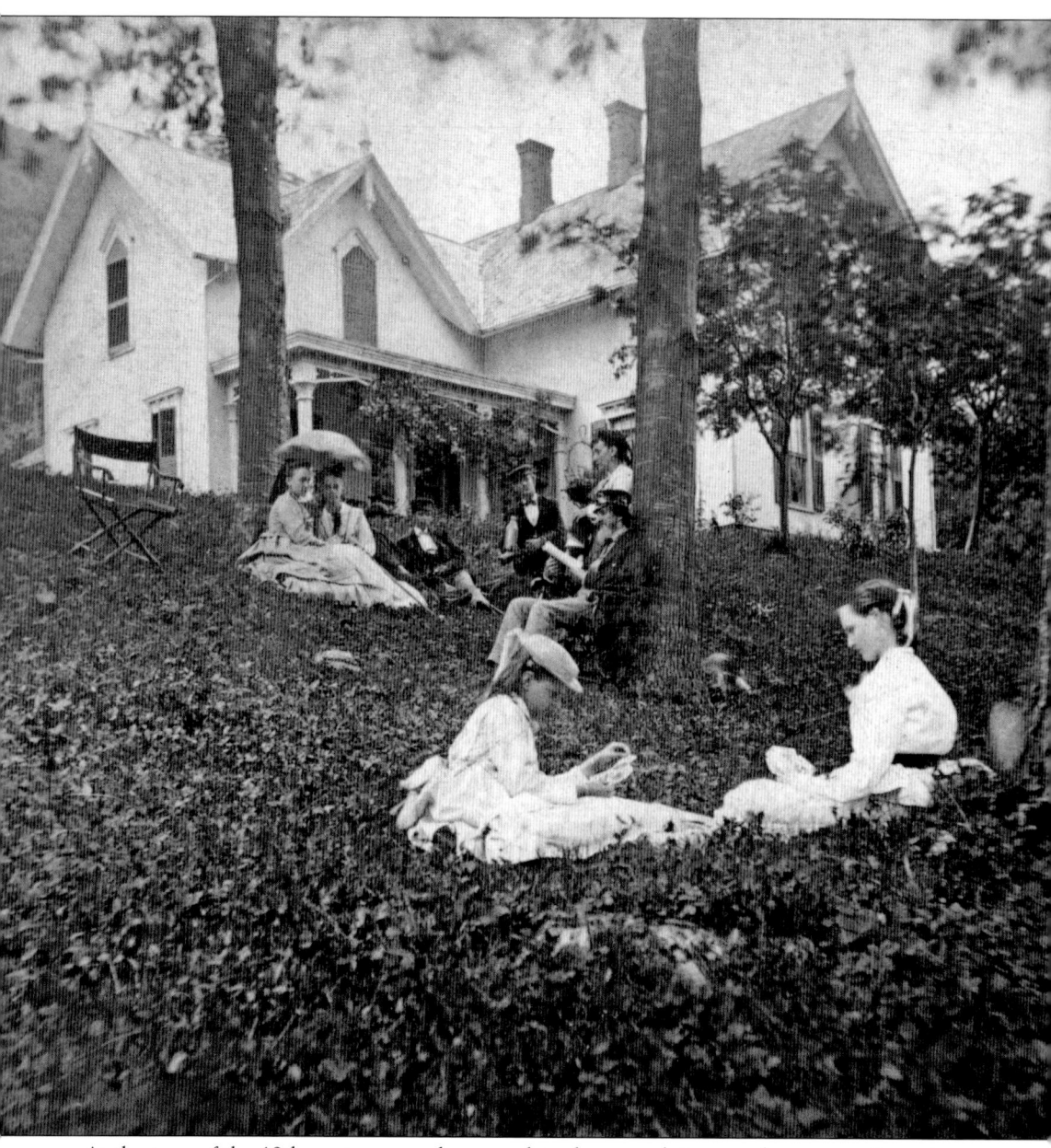

At the turn of the 19th century, people were advised to spend time outdoors, away from the grey atmosphere of cities. The Glen Haven area was becoming a health haven. A trip to the area was a lengthy event requiring much planning. Women stayed for the summer. Men who worked in the city visited on the weekends. Women traveled in long high-collared dresses with suitcases and steamer trunks. The trip began with a trolley ride from Syracuse to the village of Skaneateles. In the village, the walk was a few blocks to the steamboat wharf. Luggage was transported by horse-drawn wagons to the end of the pier and loaded on the steamboat. It was a day-long trip of sixteen miles to the south end of the lake with several stops along the way. Upon disembarkation at the Glen Haven Landing, the luggage was loaded onto horse-drawn wagons, and passengers walked to their destinations. After their exhausting trip, it was time to clean the cottage and then to rest and socialize on the lawn.

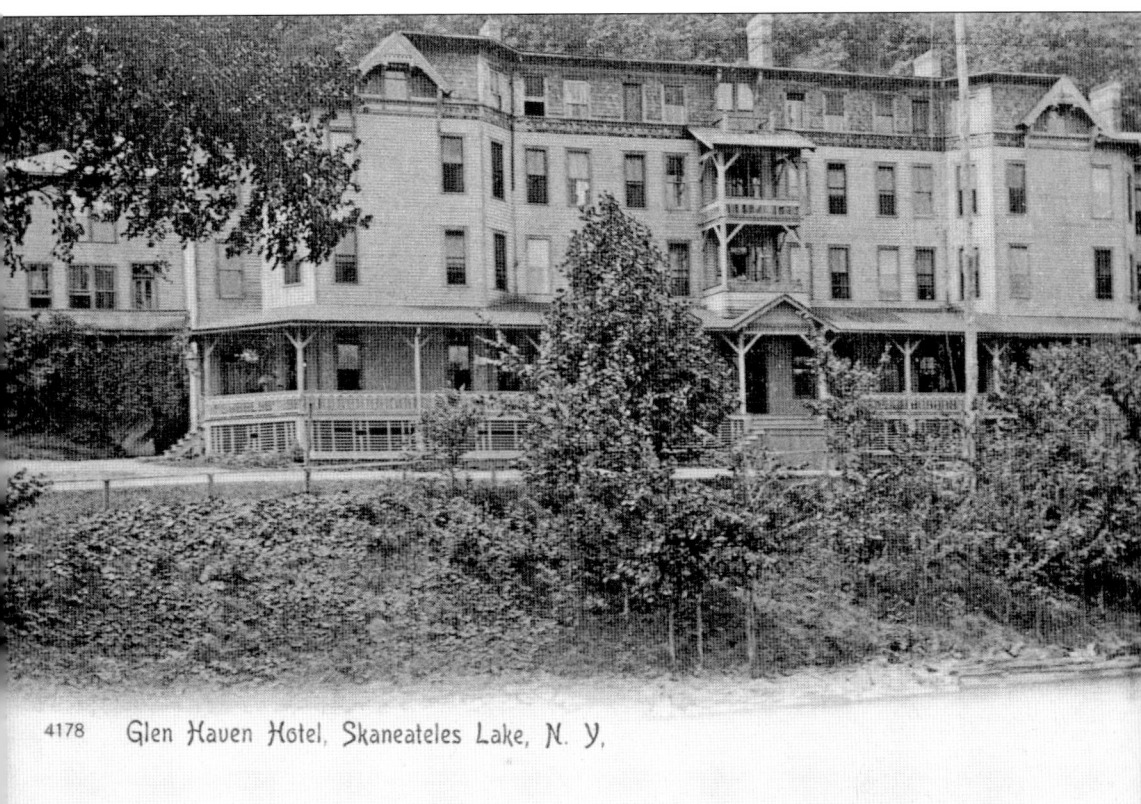

4178 Glen Haven Hotel, Skaneateles Lake, N. Y.

Hydrotherapy, also known as the "water cure," was in vogue in the 1800s for the treatment of many ailments. In 1847, Deacon Hall sold land in Glen Haven to Theidosia Gilbert, Dr. S.O. Gleason, and James C. Jackson. This partnership developed a water cure sanitarium. A hotel was built in 1848, and passengers were transported to the "San" by steamboat. One of the first events at the hotel was the "hygienic festival," held on July 12, 1853. This drew 150 prominent people to enjoy a hydropathic dinner of graham pudding, fish, and dry bread without meat or seasoning. A full day at the sanitarium consisted of wet body wraps, bathing, walking, exercise, and a frugal diet. Smoking and alcohol were not allowed. Swimming in the cold lake was encouraged. Gilbert thought that long skirts worn by women were unhealthy and encouraged wearing pantaloons. The hotel burned in 1853.

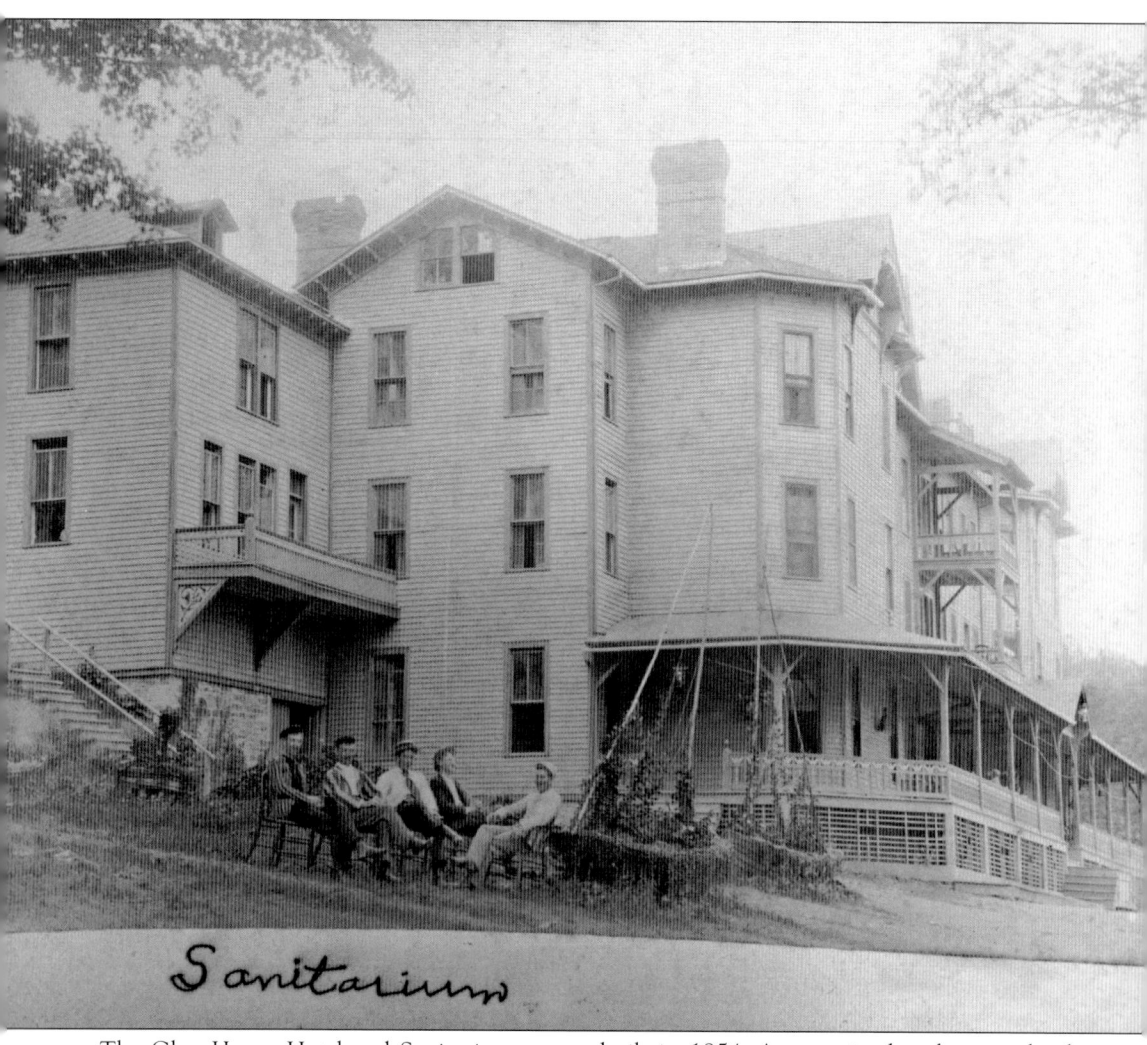

The Glen Haven Hotel and Sanitarium were rebuilt in 1854. As seen in the photograph, the building was very similar in structure to the original, only larger. Eight cottages with balconies and verandas were added. By 1887, the grounds covered 200 acres with orchards and a farm that provided dairy, poultry, and produce for the sanitarium's operation. Guests from all over the United States and Canada came for treatment. Some of the notables were Elizabeth Cady Stanton, Pres. Millard Fillmore, and Emma Abbott, a world-famous opera soprano.

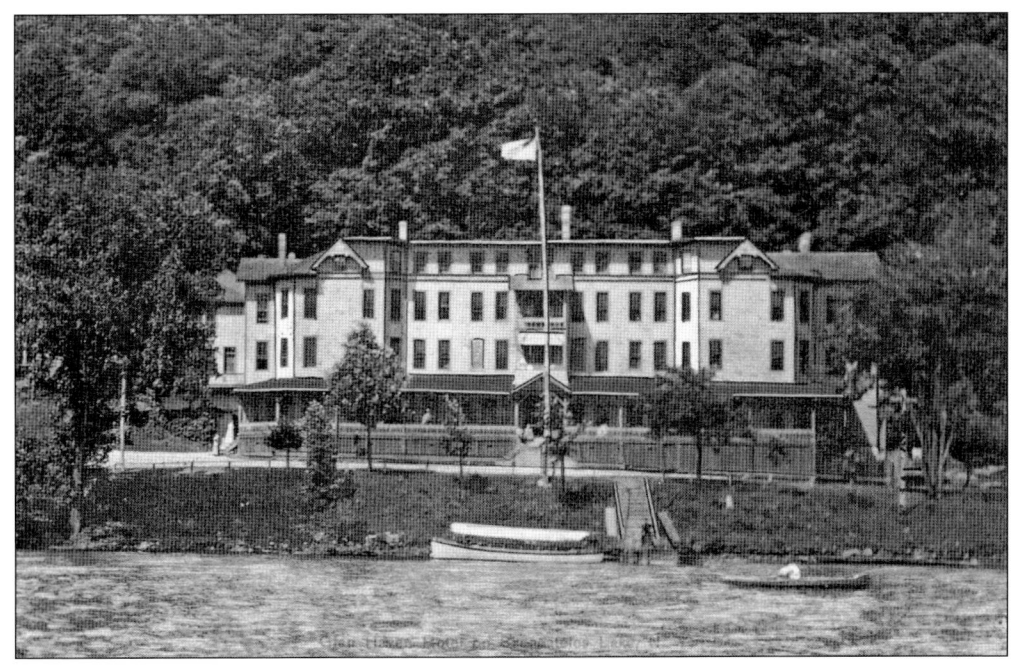

A boat livery provided the Glen Haven hotel guests with boats. Liquor and smoking continued to be banned. However, it was a quick row across the end of the lake to Fair Haven, where a saloon provided liquid refreshments and a cigar.

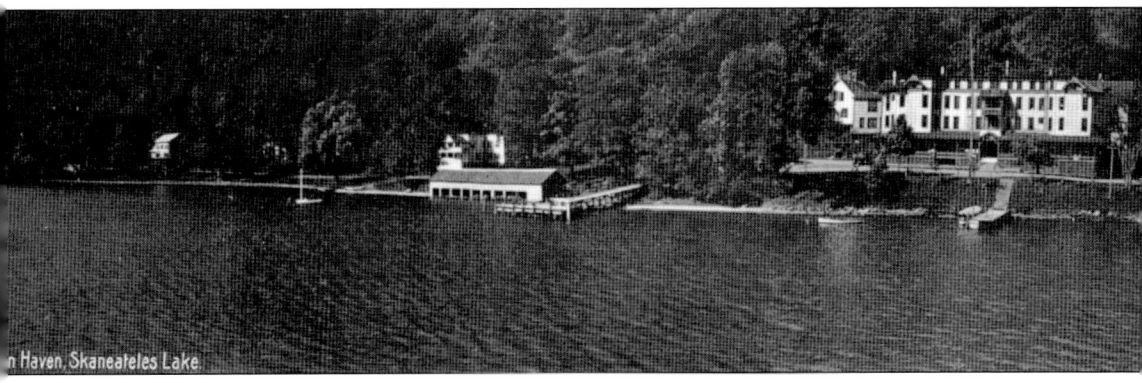

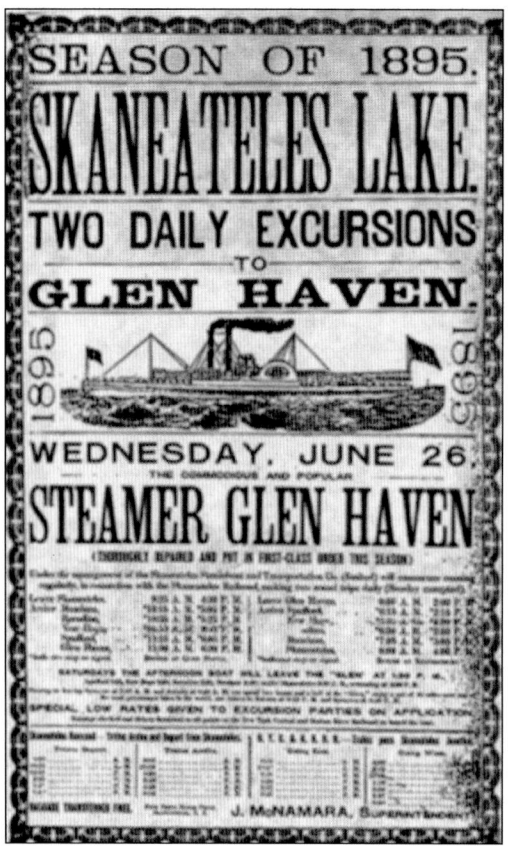

The *Glen Haven* steamboat made daily runs from the Skaneateles wharf to landings on the lake. The steamboat was built by the Syracuse Railroad in 1876. Interest in the Glen Haven Sanitarium started to wane in the 1900s. By that time, the sanitarium was more of a summer home for visitors than a medical facility. Steamboats were losing business to the automobile. In 1911, the property was sold to the City of Syracuse to protect the watershed. The hotel was demolished in 1913. The *Glen Haven* steamboat had become waterlogged. There are two stories regarding the ship's demise. It was reported in a 1929 *Post Standard* article that in 1916, the ship was towed two miles up the west shore and cut into kindling. Others maintain that the steamboat was purposely sunk near Ten Mile Point in the 1920s.

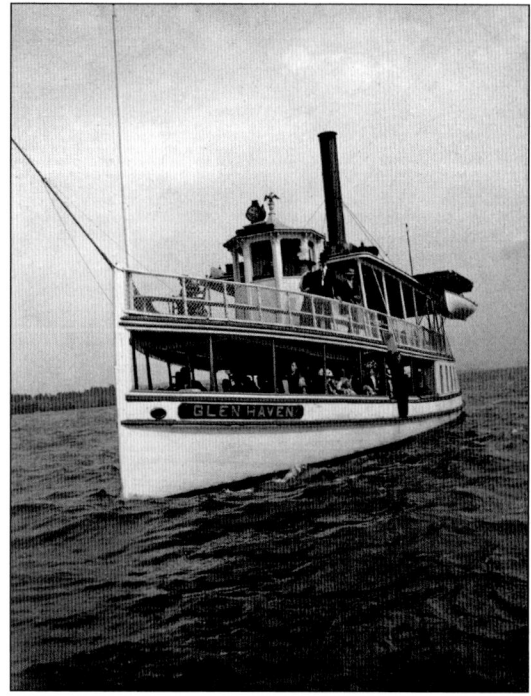

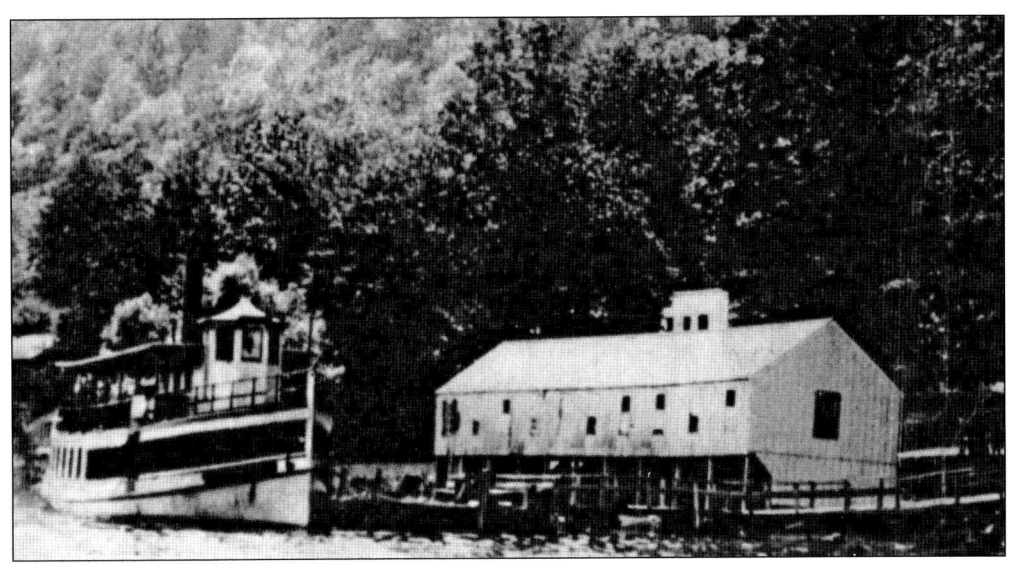

There was a public boathouse at the Glen Haven landing. Dances were held in the boathouse on Saturday evenings. Music was provided by the Lights Fantastic from Homer, New York. The *Glen Haven* steamboat provided transportation.

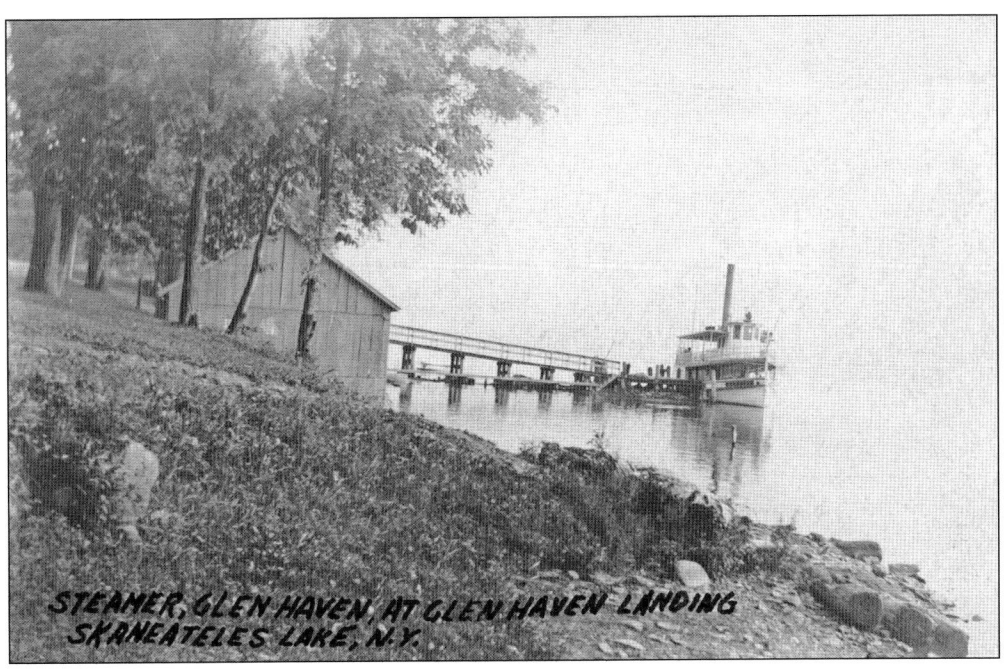

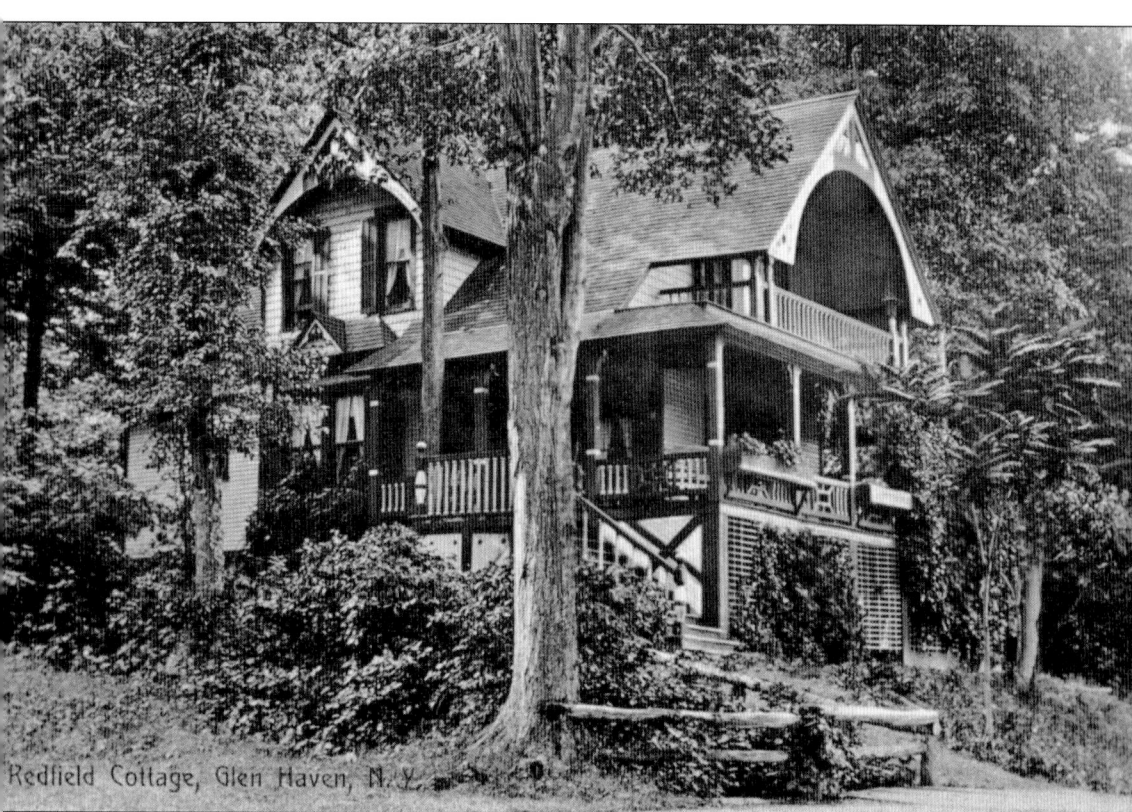

Redfield Cottage, Glen Haven, N.Y.

Although the Glen Haven Hotel was the focus of the western landscape, private cottages were also built. One of the most prominent cottages was situated north of the hotel. The cottage was known as Brookfield and was built in 1886 by Charles T. Redfield for his wife, Fanny, and their son Robert. It was a modern and convenient cottage suitable for year-round use. A Cortland newspaper reported in the summer of 1886 that the location of the cottage was "the choicest that could be selected, its broad piazzas commanding a charming view of the lake." Charles was a retired hardware merchant from Syracuse. In his retirement on Glen Haven, he built and sailed boats of different types. There was also a boathouse on the property. The cottage and outbuildings were torn down as part of the 150 acres purchased by the City of Syracuse in 1911.

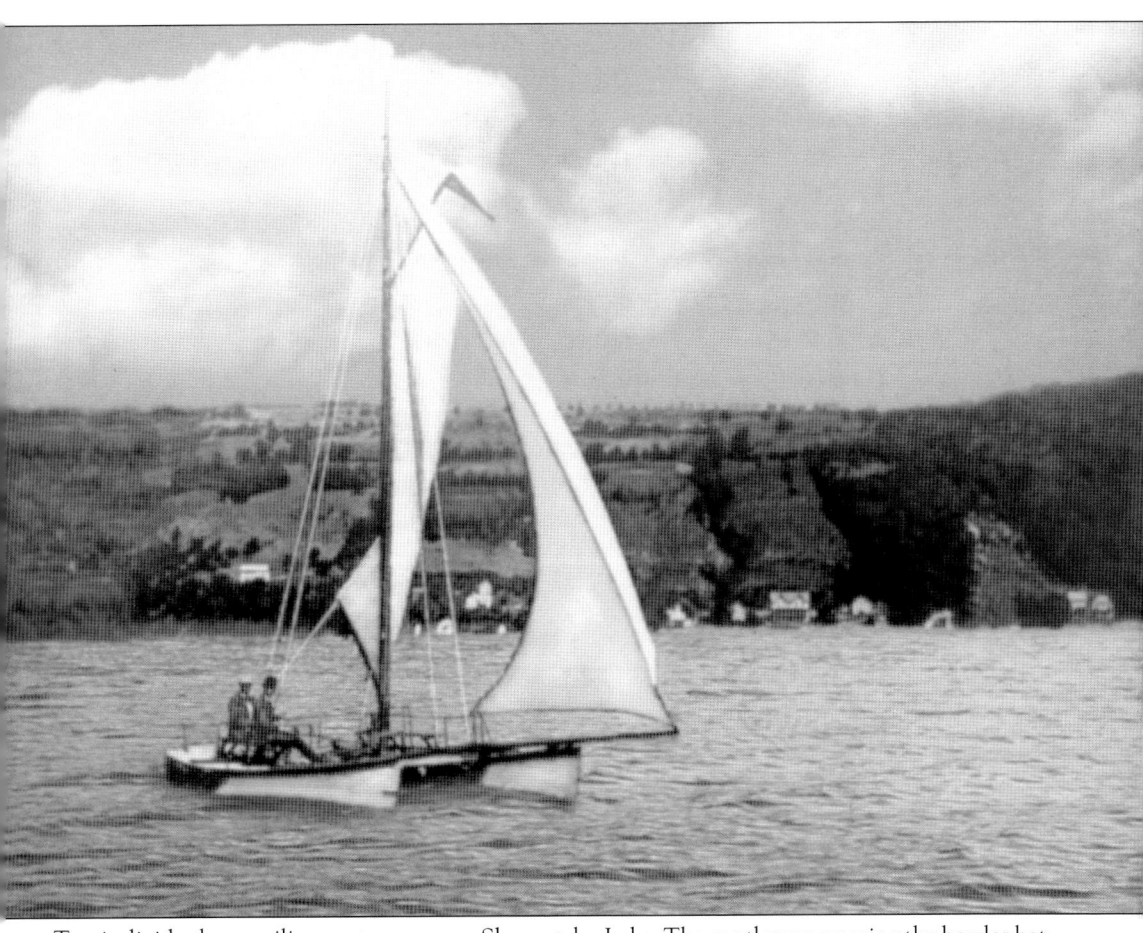

Two individuals are sailing a catamaran on Skaneateles Lake. The gentleman wearing the bowler hat is thought to be Charles Treadwell Redfield (1837–1923). His father, Lewis H. Redfield, published the first newspaper in Onondaga County. The exact date for this photograph is unknown, but it was likely taken in the late 1800s, around the time Charles had a boathouse and cottage built in Glen Haven (1886–1887).

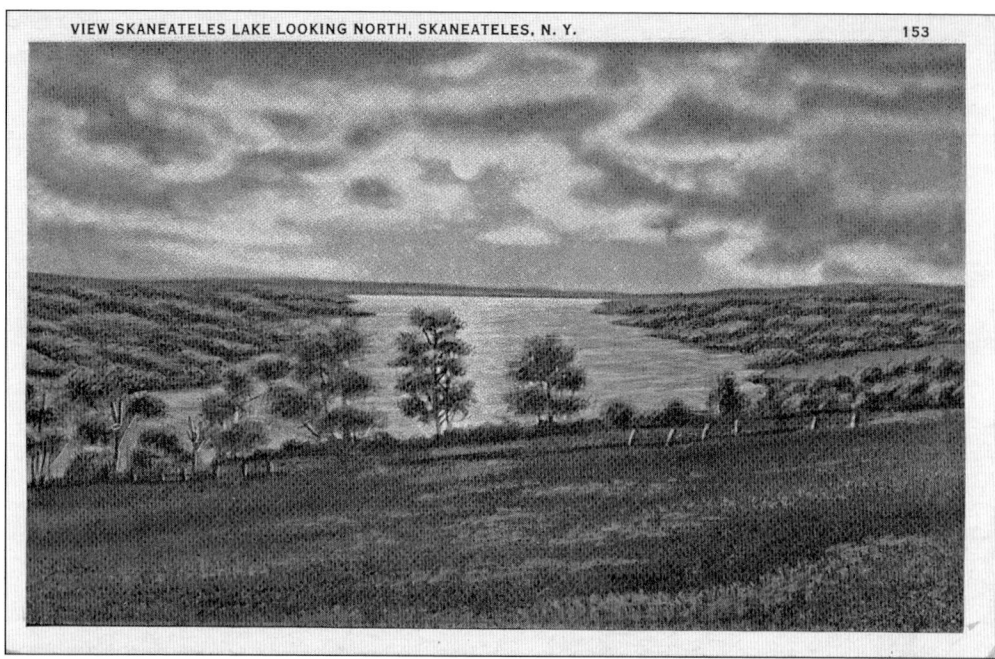

The beauty of the lake flowing northward is undeniable. However, the most important underlying current flowing through these pages is that water is the world's most valuable resource. It is essential for all life on earth, yet it is often taken for granted. Only a small fraction of water available on earth is fresh and available for human use. As demands for water increases, it is the responsibility of industries, governments, and individuals to adopt sustainable practices of water conservation so that future generations may have access to fresh clean water they need to thrive.

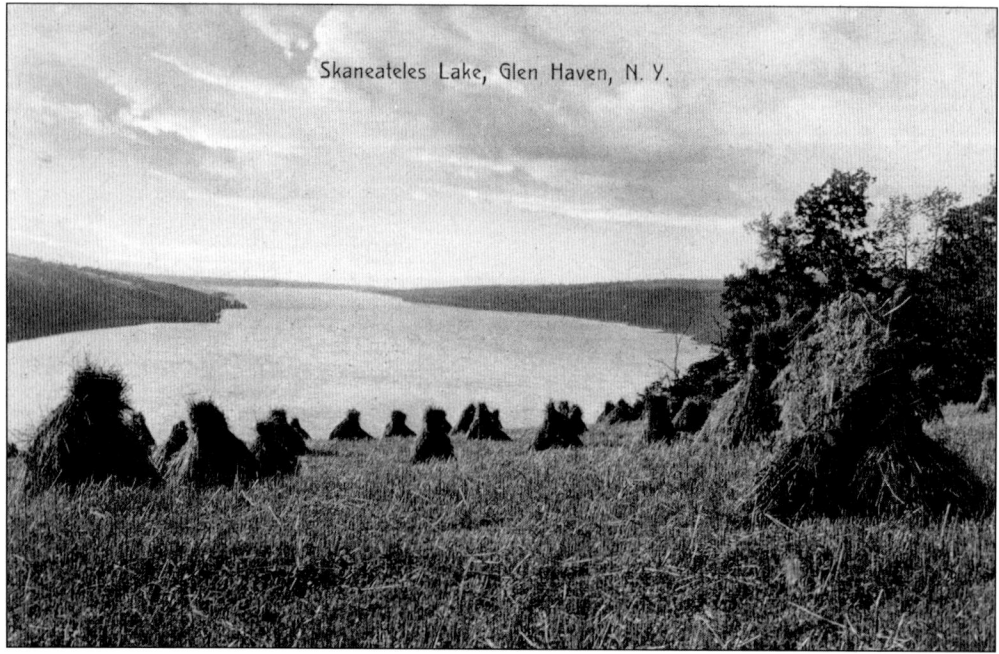

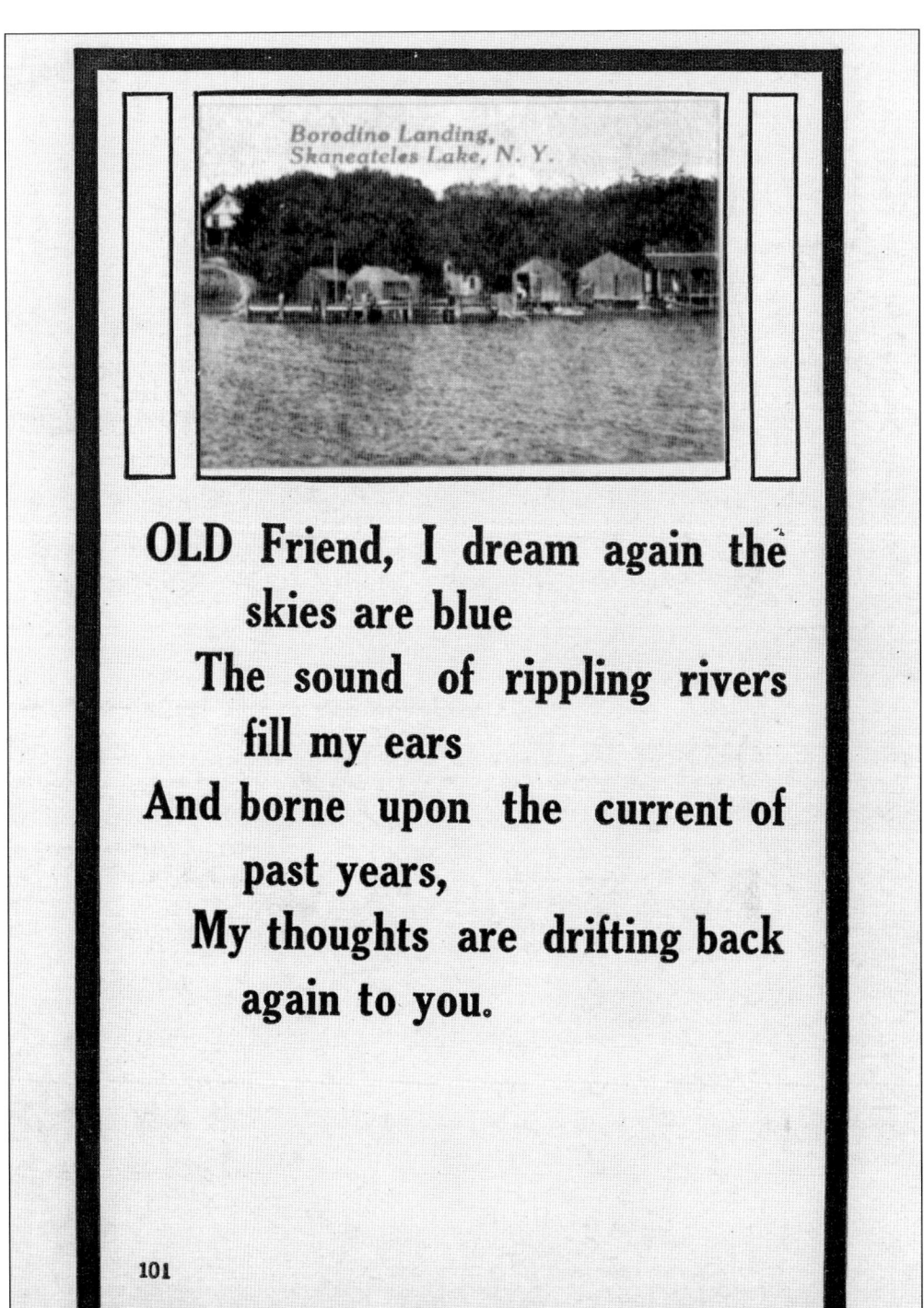

As our journey around Skaneateles Lake ends, we hope that you have enjoyed it and, as this 19th-century postcard suggests, that your dreams will once again be borne upon the current of past years as thoughts drift back again to this beautiful place.

Bibliography

Adams, Spencer L. *The Long House of the Iroquois*. Chicago: The Lakeside Printing Press, R.R. Donnelley and Sons, 1944.
Beauchamp, Rev. William Martin. "Notes of Other Days in Skaneateles." *Annual Volume of the Onondaga Historical Association: 1914*. Syracuse, NY: Dehler Press.
Collins, Capt. George Knapp. *History of the Town of Spafford*. Syracuse, NY: Dehler Press, 1917.
DiBagio, Julie, and Sally Holben. *Skaneateles Through Time*. Charleston, SC: Fonthill Media, 2018.
kihm6.wordpress.com
Leslie, Edmund Norman. *History of Skaneateles and Vicinity, 1781–1881*. Auburn, New York: Charles D. Cornell, 1892.
Robinson, Joan, Drew Haaland, and Sara Waltrous. "ReEcho" Celebrating the First One Hundred Years of the Glen Haven School and Public Library. New York: Glen Haven Historical Society. 2007.
Spain, Barbara Bendall. *Five Mile Point Skaneateles Lake*. United States: n.p., 2012.
—— and Karen Anklin Richards. *Glimpses of the Past*. Moravia, NY: Village Printer, 1987.
Sesquicentennial Committee and Chase Design. *150th Anniversary of the Village of Skaneateles*. Skaneateles, NY: Skaneateles Lakeside Printing, 1983.
Winship, Kihm. *Skaneateles: The Character and Characters of a Lakeside Village*. Collierville, TN: Instant Publisher, 2010.

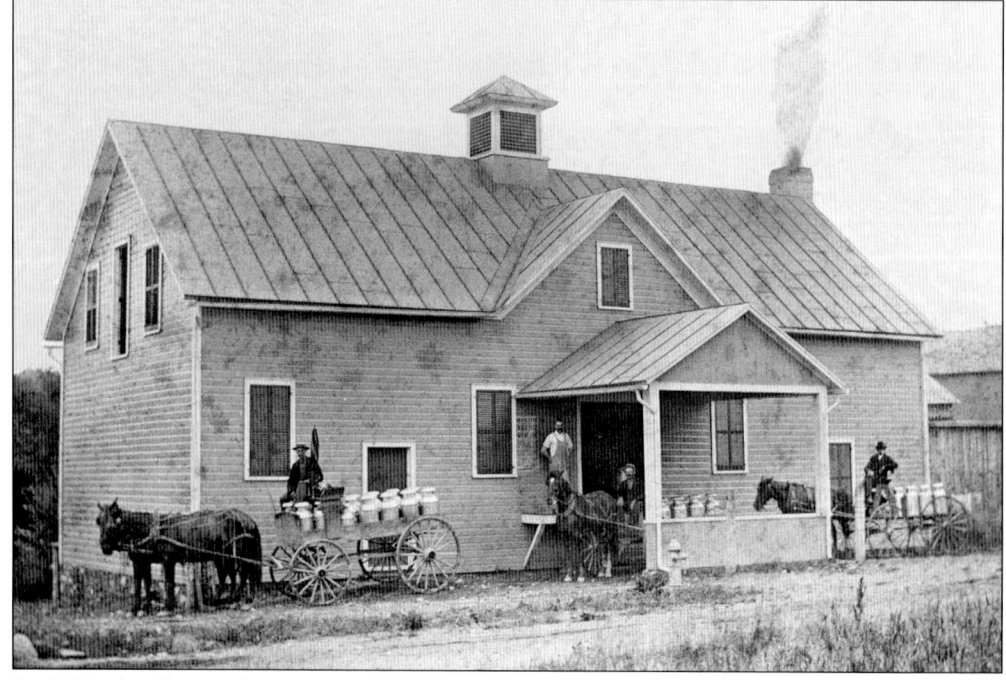

In 1899, the Skaneateles Creamery was a beehive of activity. This provided a market for over 200 farmers to sell milk or buy dairy products. New York City provided a large market for sweet (unsalted) butter.

About the Skaneateles Historical Society

Founded in 1934, the Skaneateles Historical Society today makes its home in a restored creamery where local farmers once brought their dairy products. The Museum, located in the heart of Skaneateles village, features both permanent and changing exhibitions on life since the early 1800s in this unique community. The museum also showcases Skaneateles-made wooden boats, canoes, and riverboats and, in addition, features displays on the steamboat industry along the lake. Within its mission of collecting, preserving, and displaying memorabilia related to Skaneateles history, the society offers programs, lectures, and events year-round. Extensive archives and resources for genealogists and historians are also available. Its motto is "The Past Is Here, Come Join Us."

Geralyn Huba, Executive Director (2019-2024)

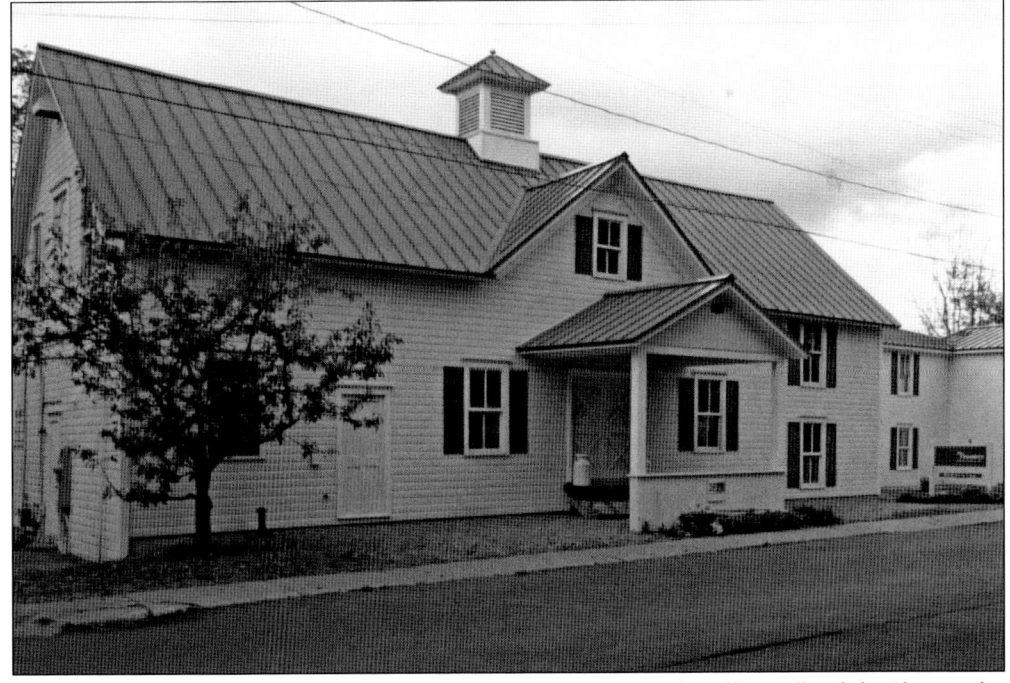

The creamery building fell into disrepair over 100 years. In 1989, the village offered the Skaneateles Historical Society an opportunity to lease the building. The building opened in 1992. A boat wing addition was opened in 2010

Discover Thousands of Local History Books
Featuring Millions of Vintage Images

Arcadia Publishing, the leading local history publisher in the United States, is committed to making history accessible and meaningful through publishing books that celebrate and preserve the heritage of America's people and places.

Find more books like this at
www.arcadiapublishing.com

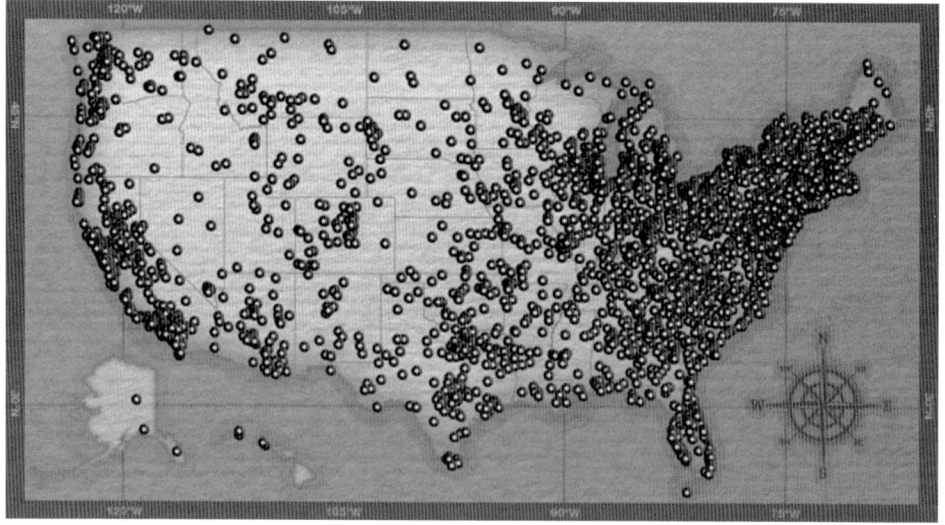

Search for your hometown history, your old stomping grounds, and even your favorite sports team.

Consistent with our mission to preserve history on a local level, this book was printed in South Carolina on American-made paper and manufactured entirely in the United States. Products carrying the accredited Forest Stewardship Council (FSC) label are printed on 100 percent FSC-certified paper.

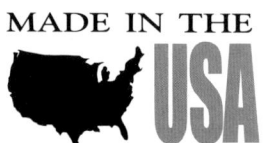